Praise for Cohen's earlier work *The Art of the Leader*—

"A valuable reference for industry and for all leaders. I wish I had read it when I was a staff sergeant about to become an armored division second lieutenant. As a matter of fact, I wish I had been able to study it as I moved up the ranks through general, and especially when I became a 'Fortune 500' corporate officer."

LIEUTENANT GENERAL W.D. JOHNSON, USAF RET.
Corporate Vice President, Baxter International, Inc.
former Chief of Staff, Strategic Air Command and
Director, Defense Nuclear Agency

"The range of sources and examples in *The Art of the Leader* is most impressive. Leadership skills can be taught and developed in those who possess that nascent quality. Dr. Cohen's book not only proves it, but contributes to the process."

JOHN D. ONG, CHAIRMAN OF THE BOARD
The BF Goodrich Company

"A most interesting and illuminating book... *The Art of the Leader* will be particularly useful to anyone striving to strengthen his leadership abilities."

GENERAL ANDREW J. GOODPASTER, USA RET.
Chairman, The Atlantic Council of the United States
former Supreme Allied Commander, Europe and
51st Superintendent, United States Military Academy

"Full of excellent examples and analogies—crisp and clear. Well done!"

"Easy reading, good logic, and a novel approach. It will deservedly attract a wide range of readers."

"Leaders aren't born that way, but they do need to learn to the techniques which Bill Cohen has vividly explained in his book."

THE NEW ART
OF THE LEADER

LEADING WITH
INTEGRITY AND HONOR

WILLIAM A. COHEN, PH.D.,
Major General, USAFR, Ret.

Prentice
Hall Press

Library of Congress Cataloging-in-Publication Data

Cohen, William A.
  The new art of the leader : leading with integrity and honor / William A. Cohen.
    p. cm.
  Rev. ed. of: The art of the leader. c1990.
  Includes bibiliographical references and index.
  ISBN 0-7352-0166-8
    I. Leadership. I. Cohen, William A., Art of the leader. II. Title.
HD57.7.C64 2000
658-4'092—dc21   00-037367

Copyright © 2000 by Prentice Hall

Printed in the United States of America

10 9 8 7 6 5 4 3 2 1

658.4092

ISBN 0-7352-0166-8

PRENTICE HALL PRESS
Paramus, NJ 07652

On the World Wide Web at http://www.phdirect.com

DEDICATION

This book is dedicated to the
United States Military Academy
at
West Point, New York
and to
Wentworth Military Academy
Lexington, Missouri
who teach "the art" and keep the spirit alive

ACKNOWLEDGMENT

I want to acknowledge the help and example of thousands of leaders in and out of uniform who have led ethically, honorably, and humanely for the benefit of others than themselves, sometimes at great sacrifice. In doing their duty, they served as powerful examples for the concepts and techniques in this book.

CONTENTS

INTRODUCTION

I've been a student of leadership for almost fifty years. From West Point to combat to the boardrooms of major corporations, I've seen leaders of all types operate in a wide variety of environments.

I thought I knew a lot about leadership, but one thing continued to puzzle me. There is a high demand for leaders everywhere. And leaders are well rewarded for what they do. Good leaders:

- Advance more quickly in organizations.
- Receive more money and other material rewards.
- Have greater prestige and more job security.
- Have more control over their lives.
- Get greater satisfaction from their jobs.
- Are able to get groups they lead to perform more productively.

Of even greater concern, our country needs more good leaders of every type to lead countless thousands of companies, nonprofit organizations, government departments, clubs, associations, schools, universities, churches, synagogues, and many other groups. If we don't get these leaders, our country will surely fail . . . maybe not in war . . . but just as important, in its ability to advance its society and the interests of its citizenry.

What was the one thing I couldn't figure out? With all these incentives to becoming a leader, why aren't there more good leaders? For a long time, this question stumped me.

Some say that leaders are born as leaders and come into existence in no other way. Thus their scarcity is as a result of Mother Nature. Research proves this wrong. Many leaders who later were acknowledged as great leaders went unrecognized for years.

I saw that many factors some thought important for leadership had little to do with, or was of lesser importance to becoming a good leader. These included education, wealth, years of experience, or even position in an organization.

Maybe you thought that you must be the formal manager of some organization to be a leader. I have seen hundreds of outstanding leaders who weren't formal managers of anything. Yet they and their organizations received significant benefits from their leadership.

If you are a manager or an executive, this fact alone is a compelling reason to become a better leader now . . . and this book will help you to do so. But being a manager doesn't automatically make you a leader.

My inquiries finally yielded a simple answer to my question as to why we don't have more good leaders. The answer was so obvious that I was surprised I had overlooked it for so long. Maybe it was too obvious. The answer was this: A good many people that could become excellent leaders just didn't know how, or they have a mistaken notion about what leadership is. So they never really begin to learn about leadership. They do what they've seen their leaders do before them. And even though they know that these previous leaders are not leading well and are not gaining their and others' support, it is the only model they have to follow.

Academic learning in leadership is rarely much better. In teaching leadership to executives in seminars sponsored by major corporations and to organizations in government and to graduate and undergraduate students in a university setting, I discovered that many have a mistaken notion about leadership. Sadly, some think that leadership is simply manipulation. Others think it to be a theoretical subject like philosophy, and not much good in the "real world." Few understand what they have to do to get others to follow them, not because they are simply the boss and give orders, but because those who follow become wholeheartedly committed to the leader's project of their own accord.

To help others perform ethically and to the maximum level that they are able to accomplish any mission, project, or task is the highest expression of good leadership. And just about anyone can become a competent leader to achieve this lofty goal. The only thing you need to know is what to do and then to do it. As President Eisenhower told his son, "The one quality that can be developed by studious reflections and practice is the leadership of men."[1] Eisenhower said "men," but he was talking about both sexes. Once you know what to do, studious reflections and practice about leadership will help you in leading both men and women.

This may sound overly simplistic. The fact is that many intelligent, well-educated, motivated people who want to be good leaders simply don't know how to do it. And some of the things they think they know about leadership are just plain wrong.

So what happens? They try. But without leadership know-how, it's like a doctor doing brain surgery without being taught how. Maybe you can learn how eventually through experience. Chances are after your first big failure, you won't get a second chance. Without knowledge of how to perform brain surgery, you are bound to make mistakes. Those mistakes will probably cause you to fail.

You can't perform brain surgery without knowing how to do it. And you can't lead successfully without knowing how to lead either.

My professor and mentor Peter Drucker said back in 1955, "Leadership is of utmost importance. Indeed there is no substitute for it."[2] He went on to say that the first systematic book on leadership, written by Xenophon three thousand years ago was still the best book on the subject. Xenophon's book may have been the best back in 1955, but it didn't enable people to learn how to become leaders, because most who read this book were unable to apply Xenophon's observations to their own situation.

But, the fact is that leadership can be learned. As General Sherman, famous or infamous, depending on your point of view, for his "march to the sea" during the Civil War expressed it: "I have read of men born peculiarly endowed by nature to be a general . . . but I have never seen one."

General Maxwell D. Taylor, former paratrooper general during World War II and later Chief of Staff of the Army felt the same way. In a lecture on leadership to the Industrial College of the Armed Forces in the spring of 1977 he said, ". . . there seems no reason to doubt that the leadership qualities . . . are susceptible to being taught and learned."[3]

That's why I wrote this book. There are no "blue-sky" theories to master. The emphasis of the book is on how to do it. The leadership techniques I will show you have proved effective over thousands of years. They will work for you as they did for Julius Caesar, Abraham Lincoln, or George S. Patton.

I have used a lot of examples to illustrate every technique. I have especially used military examples. More than that, I have consciously attempted to apply leadership techniques learned "the hard way" in battle to everyday leadership problems you will run into in the company and elsewhere. I have done this because leadership in battle represents a worst-case scenario. There are few leadership situations as severe or as challenging or with more risk and uncertainty. If you know how to lead others on the battlefield, you can lead others in the office, on the sales force, in the Boy or Girl Scout troop, in the church or synagogue, or anywhere else.

In preparation for writing this book, I went back and relearned everything I thought I knew about leadership. I also investigated almost every new concept and read almost every book. I interviewed many general officers for their ideas. Some of these generals had been my students in my leadership seminars.

In the fall of 1988, I was on active duty as a reserve officer in the Air Force. I was extremely fortunate in being able to attend a top-level leadership course taught at National Defense University in Washington, D.C. Nine four-star generals and admirals helped to teach this incredible course. Here I could see leadership from the perspective of a Chairman of the Joint Chiefs of Staff, a Chief of Naval Operations, or a Commander-in-Chief of an entire geographical area. It added immeasurably to the breadth of my own perspective.

I know that what you will learn from this book works. I can't guarantee that you will become a general, admiral, or company president. But if you act on what you will learn in it, you will become more competent as a leader. And no one can say that you can't become a general, admiral, or company president, either.

From this book and these techniques you will learn

- How to Take Charge in Any Situation

- How to Win a Group's Loyalty and Respect

- How to Build Your Organization Like a Winning Football Team

- How to Double or Triple Your Organization's Productivity

- How to Lead Others at Your Level

- How to Lead Your Boss

- When it is Important *Not* to Lead

- Seven Ways to Get Anyone to Follow You

- How to Use the Seven Influence Strategies

- How to Develop Your Self-Confidence as a Leader

This book is a revised edition. What have I learned new that warrants a new edition of this work? Plenty. One graduate student in business who took my leadership course told me that until the course, she thought leadership was a theoretical subject having to do mainly with some nice words and manipulation. She was wondering how I would stretch what she perceived should be a short lecture out to eleven weeks. She was surprised to hear me say that I was still learning about leadership. She was more surprised that by the end of the course, she understood why I was still a student of the art.

Well, a lot has happened since I wrote the first edition that gives me the opportunity to prove that I am still learning. From Desert Storm to Moghedeshu to Bosnia to the air war over Kosovo, our nation has been in more wars in the last ten years than anyone could have imagined. In the corporate "battlefield," companies have fallen and others have risen. Some leaders have succeeded brilliantly. Others have made some serious blunders that have led to major failures.

In my military career, I progressed through the ranks of lieutenant colonel, colonel, brigadier general, major general, and then on into retirement. As a professor, I have continued to write and do research as well as teach. My eldest son, Barak, whom I mention in the first edition of this book as a cadet at West Point in 1989, graduated. He led troops in Kuwait twice, left the army as a captain, and went into a civilian career.

Moreover, since the first edition of *The Art of the Leader* I learned from Barry Goldwater. He liked *The Art of the Leader* and told me so. But he also told me something that I took for granted in the first edition. "All good leadership is founded on basic honesty," he wrote. "If you don't have that, you're not going to be much of a leader." Senator Goldwater's words, along with Peter Drucker's comment about Xenophon, who was a Greek general writing about leadership in combat, led me to conduct research with more than two hundred combat leaders who went on to successful careers as leaders in civilian life. Sixty-two of these individuals were generals and admirals. I believe that the eight principles this research yielded form the basis of all the leadership techniques and procedures in this book, or of any other book on leadership. They are strategic. All leadership techniques are tactical.

So, I revised the chapter on "the combat model" of leadership extensively. The original priorities for the leader of mission and people first and leader last haven't changed. But this now becomes a subset of the seventh principle or foundation of all leadership: duty before self. Moreover, Senator Goldwater's statement on honesty is confirmed by the research. Although the other principles are in no particular order, integrity was easily ranked number one, and many successful leaders in and out of uniform told me so. Clearly, it is something that no leader should assume. I also revised the chapters on influence extensively to reflect my latest research.

But this introduction is too long already. Turn to Chapter 1 and let's get started in examining the art of the leader.

NOTES

1. Stephen E. Ambrose, *Eisenhower: Vol.1* (New York: Simon and Schuster, 1983).

2. Peter F. Drucker, *The Practice of Management* (New York: Harper and Row, 1955), p.194

3. Maxwell D. Taylor, "Military Leadership: What is it? Can it be taught?" *Distinguished Lecture Series* (Washington, D.C.: National Defense University).

CHAPTER ONE

THE POWER OF LEADERSHIP

L eadership has an extraordinary power. It can make the difference between success and failure in anything you do for yourself or for any group to which you belong. I know this is a strong statement, but in this chapter I will give you examples to prove what I say. Further, I will show you that becoming a first-class leader is a lot easier than you may have thought.

HOW ONE MAN MADE THE DIFFERENCE

As a young Air Force lieutenant I was a member of the 11th Bomb Wing at Altus Air Force Base, Oklahoma. It had been one of the finest B-52 bombing wings in Strategic Air Command. This unit had been the only wing to win the coveted Fairchild Trophy three times for competition in bombing accuracy. It was also one of the few wings never to have failed an organizational readiness inspection (ORI). Aircrews were consistently superior in navigation, bombing, aerial refueling, and other flying techniques.

Unfortunately, over a period of months, the unit had begun to drift. We failed to do some of our training requirements successfully. We made some late takeoffs due to maintenance problems. Our sense of mission disappeared. We even failed an ORI, which was an important test of our flying and combat skills. Once we had ranked as one of the top three combat wings based on a point system maintained on a weekly basis. On the same system, we were now ranked dead last.

On alert with my crew one evening, I received a hurried call from base operations. "There's a new commander on base. His name is Colonel Kyes. Stay out of his way."

We couldn't stay out of his way, because Colonel Kyes visited us that night. He canceled all leaves of absence. All "free time" of any sort was rescinded until further notice. This included weekends and even crew rest after flight. Colonel Kyes moved commanders and staff he judged lacking to less responsible positions on the spot. He encouraged others to retire. No career or individual was sacred.

Colonel Kyes met with each of the 1,500 officers and airmen reporting to him. He told each where we were going . . . back to the top position in Strategic Air Command . . . and how we were going to get there. He said we would brief every mission flown to him personally before we could fly it. Pilots had to know as much about the target as did their bombardiers and navigators. And bombardiers and navigators had to be able to back up their pilots as well.

If you wanted a transfer out of the unit, Colonel Kyes would get you one. If you stayed in the wing, you were going to work your fanny off. And this was in peacetime!

At first, we hated Kyes. Our wives and girlfriends hated Kyes. Those whose careers he hurt especially hated him, and some left the Air Force.

But then, our hard work began to show results. Our bombs hit on target. We took off exactly at takeoff time. The ground crews and maintenance personnel maintained our aircraft so that they flew better than they had ever flown before. We worked together as a team, and we worked well.

A couple months after Colonel Kyes arrived, we had another surprise ORI. We not only passed, but scored higher than we ever had in the past. We were rank number one.

A strange thing began to happen. We felt pride in ourselves and pride in Colonel Kyes as our commander. Our hate turned to respect. When Colonel Kyes left the 11th Bomb Wing on his promotion to brigadier general, there was a genuine sense of loss. Our respect had by then turned to something approaching love.

Colonel Kyes eventually wore the three stars of a lieutenant general. But for an untimely death, I believe he would have attained the fourth star of a full general.

General Kyes's life taught me some important lessons about leadership and the difference one individual can make in helping an organization to reach its goals. And I have seen that lesson repeated again and again. I have seen it in large organizations and small, in formal organizations and informal ones, in both military and civilian organizations. The lesson is that one individual and his or her leadership makes all the difference between success and failure.

Professor Warren Bennis at the University of Southern California has spent his entire life studying leaders. At a recent conference he told me, "I first learned leadership as a young infantry lieutenant at Ft. Benning, Georgia, in 1945." More recently, Professor Bennis studied ninety of the most successful leaders around the nation. What did he conclude? "If I have learned anything from my research, it is this: The factor that empowers the workforce and ultimately determines which organizations succeed or fail is the leadership of those organizations. When strategies, processes, or cultures change, the key to improvement remains leadership.[1]

THE AMAZING SECRET AS TO WHY SOME OF THE WORLD'S BEST-KNOWN MEN (AND WOMEN) SUCCEEDED AS LEADERS

Leadership has to do with getting things accomplished by acting through others. Regardless of your own abilities, there are many important goals that you cannot attain without the help of others.

Around the turn of the century, a young newsman by the name of Napoleon Hill interviewed steel magnate Andrew Carnegie. Andrew Carnegie was than one of the wealthiest men alive. He convinced Hill to devote twenty years of his life to a study of what made men successful. Carnegie helped Hill by giving him introductions to the mightiest, wealthiest, and best-known men of his day. These included Henry Ford, Theodore Roosevelt, Charles Schwab, George Eastman, John D. Rockefeller, Thomas Edison, Julius Rosenwald, Clarence Darrow, and many others.

Napoleon Hill discovered an amazing fact from his research. No successful individual became successful strictly by himself or by virtue of what he could do by himself. Every single one of the successful individuals that Napoleon Hill had interviewed had become successful through the help of others. These other individuals had a greater talent in some area.

Who were these others? They were bosses, colleagues, and subordinates. Without them, not a single person that Hill had interviewed became successful.

Carnegie himself must have recognized this, because on his tombstone he had engraved a single sentence. "Here lies one who knew how to get around him men who were cleverer than himself."

While an MBA student at the University of Chicago, I found support for Hill's conclusion. A study of hundreds of top executives showed that every one, whether in business, government, or the military, had a sponsor. What is a sponsor? This is someone else who had actually promoted the executive's success at one or more points in his or her career. No one made it to the top of any organization without a sponsor. Why did a senior executive choose to sponsor a particular subordinate? Because that subordinate was one of those individuals who was "clever," and he or she had assisted the more senior executive in accomplishing his objectives.

Naturally, if you are leading in any task, you tend to do much better if you have expertise and experience in the task for which you are responsible. Yet, I also found scores of examples of senior executives whose experience and expertise in a particular role was limited. Yet these individuals became very successful because others who supported them had the necessary expertise and experience or even style of leadership. As General Colin Powell, former Chairman of the Joint Chiefs of Staff noted, "In every successful military organization, and I suspect in all successful enterprises, different styles of leadership have to be present. If the man at the top does not exhibit all these qualities, then those around him have to supplement."[2]

What does this mean? Quite clearly it means that you can reach the most difficult and important goals only with the help of others, both your bosses and those who work for you. Like Colonel Kyes, you can be successful only through exercising good leadership and helping others to reach their goals.

WHY YOU DON'T NEED TO BE A MANAGER TO BE A LEADER

Once I met a young engineer at a major aerospace company. He had become director of a major program although he was barely thirty. I was very much interested in how this came about. Here's the story a vice president told me.

Once a year there was a savings-bond drive in this company. No one wanted the job of getting employees to sign up for additional bond deductions from their paychecks. Since no one wanted the job, they assigned these duties to the most junior engineer. Most did the minimum work possible and made no serious attempt at convincing people to make additional investments.

Somebody must have forgotten to tell this youngster, because he really took charge. He convinced every engineer and manager in his department who was present to buy. But he didn't stop there. He called all over the country to talk to engineers who were at temporary duty elsewhere. He got them all charged up. "Look," he would say, "at the end of this bond drive, they post results, and our organization is competing with others. We can be number one."

Amused, at first the old-timers bought bonds for this reason. Then, almost in spite of themselves they became excited. They became excited solely due to this new engineer. No one had ever appealed to them in this way before. Of course this organization finished in first place by a country mile. That wasn't the end of it. The department head noticed that although savings bonds had very little to do with engineering, the bond drive had helped to increase productivity. People just seemed to feel better about themselves as members of the organization and wanted to perform better. When they actually won, they really felt good!

The president of the company noticed the unusual bond-drive results and asked about them. He remembered this young engineer's name. He knew that if this engineer could accomplish so much with a bond drive, he would accomplish even more as a manager.

Only four months later, an opening occurred. My informant told me that this young man was promoted over twenty other engineers who had more seniority in the company. It shouldn't surprise you that it wasn't too long after I met him that they promoted this young man again. You guessed it. This time they made him a vice president. And you just know that he will be president some day.

Note that this engineer was a strong leader before he held an official position in the organization as a manager. I'll have more to say about this throughout the book.

How You Can Lead *Before* You Are Promoted

You may have heard someone say, "I'll wait till I'm promoted. Then I'll have an opportunity to demonstrate my leadership." That's like the old story about the freezing man and the wood-burning stove. The man looked at the wood-burning stove and spoke these words. "Give me heat and then I will give you wood."

You may laugh because everyone knows that you have to put wood on a fire before a fire will give you heat. The same is true about promotion. If you want to get promoted, you have to be a leader first. Then someone will promote you.

Tom Peters, the coauthor of *In Search for Excellence* and *A Passion for Excellence* and other books, found similar situations in organizations he studied. All excellent companies had strong leaders at every level. Some were managers, and some were not. I want to repeat this. Some were managers, and some were not, but all were strong leaders. So you don't need to wait to be promoted to be a leader.

You don't even have to be in an organization to be a strong leader. You can start your own organization. Jimmy Calano and Jeff Salzman started a company called Career Tracks Seminars almost right out of college. Within a few years, these two young men found themselves at the head of one of the largest seminar companies in the country. They accomplished this by offering a quality product at a lower price than their competition.

Do Calano and Salzman give these seminars themselves? Absolutely not! Those who give the seminars are individuals who have had years and years of experience, many with advanced degrees in their particular fields. Jimmy Calano and Jeff Salzman don't have to be the experts. They are the leaders. Through their leadership, their employees have made them successful.

Good leaders attract others who are happy to help them achieve success. It is easier than you think to become a good leader. You can become a good or superior leader with others wanting to follow and to help you. They will help you achieve your goals because you will help them to achieve theirs.

THE LEADERSHIP MODEL THAT WILL HELP YOU TO LEAD IN ANY SITUATION

I would like to propose a model of leadership. A model is only a theoretical representation of something real. It can have considerable value if the representation is accurate. Why? Because we can apply the model to a wide variety of situations without having to develop a new representation each time. Having found what works once, we can apply the theory effectively again and again.

Now let's talk first about the model of leadership I would like to propose. I want to propose to you what I call the "combat model of leadership." Why do I recommend combat as a model? The most difficult circumstances in which a leader must lead are in combat. There is a great risk. There is considerable uncertainty due to confusion, changing circumstances, and lack of information. There may be considerable hardship due to the environment or to actions of the enemy. And there is a significant penalty for failure or reward for success. Despite this and great risk, successful combat leaders enable others to accomplish significant goals and objectives while maintaining high morale and esprit de corps. Yet, these leaders don't have the old standby motivators such as salary, vacation, and security to fall back on.

Some are uncomfortable with the combat model of leadership. They think that combat leadership is simply running around shouting orders and others mindlessly obeying. Let me assure you, that's not combat leadership at all. If you saw *Saving Private Ryan*, with Tom Hanks playing the part of Captain John Miller, you saw a caring combat leader who was highly respected by his followers. Captain Miller led a company, and later a special task force of Rangers, one of the most elite and disciplined of our fighting units. Yet, even Captain Miller could not always lead by simply giving orders and assuming they would be obeyed. Human beings just don't work like that. Tom Hanks accurately portrayed a good combat leader.

I'll have more to say about the combat model in Chapter 2. But for now, I want you to recognize that combat is probably the most severe environment in which you will ever lead other human beings in accomplishing any goal. If you can apply the combat model of leadership successfully, you can be successful in leading in many other difficult, but less demanding environments.

General John T. Chain, Jr., then commander-in-chief of the Strategic Air Command once said, "Military decisions are made in the fog of war, resulting in a significant degree of uncertainty about the validity of the very information on which the most critical decisions are made. Decisions must be made quickly and with life-and-death results. Coupled simultaneously with the need to deal with this uncertainty is the military leader's task of inspiring confidence in subordinate commanders and cohesiveness in the troops."[3] That's every leader's task in challenging situations outside of military, as well.

General Frederick J. Kroesen also knows something about combat leadership. He fought in World War II, Korea, and Vietnam. During this time, he rose from the rank of private to four-star general as Commander-in-Chief, U.S. Army, Europe, and the Central Army Group of NATO. Since leaving the army, he has worked with corporations and other organizations on a variety of management and defense issues. During a meeting at which I was present, a friend asked General Kroesen about differences between leadership in the military and corporations. Said General Kroesen, "The principles of leadership aren't different. Where you have a successful leader, you have a successful corporation."[4]

What is the combat model? Well, another man who might know something about the combat model of leadership was General George S. Patton. Again and again, General Patton proved his abilities to lead men in combat. He led small groups during his career. He also led large numbers of men, hundreds of thousands. And he frequently did this while overcoming incredible obstacles under severe hardship and risk of death.

During World War I, Patton was a twenty-nine-year-old colonel commanding the first American tanks in combat. The first use of the tank was to protect against the machine gun and artillery while crossing difficult terrain. The tank had one big problem. It was difficult to see out of. So Patton led his tanks by accompanying them on foot!

He was once wounded while doing this. Nothing is without a price, and that was a price he was willing to pay. Patton's leadership brought victory on the battlefield as well as personal fame and fortune.

Patton defined leadership as the art of getting your subordinates to do the impossible. Is such a definition also applicable to civilian pursuits? Let's see.

Some years ago, there was a company called Sierra Engineering Company, located in Sierra Madre, California. This small company of 350 employees made oxygen masks and other life-support equipment for military and civilian flyers.

Sierra's main competitor was Gentex, a company located on the East Coast. Both companies competed heavily for government contracts in a number of areas.

During a particularly bitter competition involving pilot crash helmets, Sierra Engineering Company ran into extreme difficulty. Part of the reason was the higher salaries on the West Coast. Also, all hourly employees received "time and half" for overtime. But the biggest problem was that everyone had a "business-as-usual" attitude. From worker to manager, they did their jobs. If the company was in trouble that was someone else's problem. They were doing the best they possibly could. Or so they thought.

Then the company suddenly ran out of cash. With no cash reserves, it couldn't produce its products. It could not meet payrolls. It had other problems. Seeing no way out, the president of the company committed suicide. The company went into "Chapter 11." Under this chapter of the bankruptcy law, the bank tries to save the company through its own control.

In desperation, the bank sought someone experienced who could lead the company out of its troubles. Where was the unusual person who was willing to work at minimum salary? Where was someone who had the supreme self-confidence that he would be successful under these conditions? After a difficult search they found a young man by the name of Aaron Bloom. Aaron Bloom had been a vice president of engineering who had left the same firm several years earlier.

Bloom took charge of the company. Gathering the less than fifty employees who remained together, he made an announcement. "From eight in the morning until five in the afternoon, we will all perform our regular duties. If you are a secretary, you'll do secretarial work. If you're a manager, you'll manage. If you are a design engineer, you'll design. After five o'clock, everyone from secretaries to myself will help the production line put the product together. You and I will take our orders from the production supervisors. There'll be no pay for this, but there will be sandwiches for supper."

Bloom answered questions and then concluded: "We are going to return Sierra Engineering to its rightful place of saving lives by supplying a good product at a quality price. We are also going to save our jobs. I know we can do this. If I thought we couldn't, I wouldn't be here."

Within two years, Sierra Engineering Company had returned to its former position and even more so. Once again, it was vibrant, with a full complement of employees necessary to fulfill its mission. Once again, the company was profitable. Clearly Sierra Engineering Company was on top due solely to the leadership of one man, Aaron Bloom.

One interesting thing to me was that everyone worked this hard to turn the company around. And remember, they did so without extra compensation.

An even more interesting question is, why didn't they do this before they went into Chapter 11? Had they done so, they would not have run out of money. No one would have been fired. No one would have had to work this hard. Why didn't they do this? Why was it necessary that 300 members of the company had to leave its employ before this happened? And how could it be that fifty people could do more than 350 had done?

I have thought a great deal about this question, and I'll tell you my answer. I don't believe that the 350 employees knew they could make a difference. Further, I don't believe they cared. Aaron Bloom made them see that they could do it and made them care. He had them do the impossible.

So, the combat model isn't the average model of leadership. It means that the leader must not only take full responsibility for the mission and getting it accomplished. Somehow, someway, with the help of those he or she leads, things have to happen regardless of the situation faced. As General Ron Fogleman, former Chief of Staff of the Air Force says, "The leader is the one who gets things done."

LEADERSHIP IS GETTING PEOPLE TO PERFORM TO THEIR MAXIMUM POTENTIAL

Let me propose a definition of leadership to you. With this definition, it doesn't make any difference whether you are leading a company, an organization, a military unit, or just some friends in a club. Leadership is the art of influencing others to their maximum performance to accomplish any task, objective, or project.

Note that my definition of leadership says nothing about management. We saw earlier that leadership and management are not the same. Can you always get people to perform to their maximum potential? I believe that through leadership you can, but to do it, you must first win over the minds of others.

To Lead, You Must First Win Minds

A good deal of leadership in the winning of victories, in everything you do, has to do with your ability to win the minds of the people around you. If you can do this, you'll not only lead successfully, but you'll be successful in achieving your goals and objectives.

I'd like to go over this again. What we've seen is that the power of leadership is considerable. The resources of your organization, top-management actions, actions of adversaries, the abilities of people whom you're responsible for or who are in your organization, or anything else are all secondary. They are secondary to your ability to help people do things that they didn't know they could do or didn't know needed to be done. To do this, you must first win their minds to your way of thinking.

Proof that Leaders Are Made, Not Born

You may have heard that leaders are born with certain characteristics that make them leaders. You are either born with them or you are not. If you don't have these attributes at birth, too bad for you. There is nothing you can do about it.

This is absolute nonsense. Sure, people are born with certain characteristics that give them the potential for being good at certain things. Some are born with advantages for playing basketball, being a great concert pianist, or being a leader. But learning and developing whatever abilities you have is far more important than what abilities you are born with.

Want proof? Researchers have found that you have a better chance of becoming a company president if you are more than six feet tall than if you are less than six feet. This would seem to support the "born-with" theory. Doesn't being tall say something of your chances of becoming a top leader?

The only problem is, there are just too many exceptions. Napoleon Bonaparte was short, so was Gandhi, Truman, and Ulysses S. Grant. Colonel Kyes, who led his wing so successfully that he became a three-star general, was five feet seven inches tall. David Ben Gurion, the first prime minister of the modern State of Israel, was only five feet three inches. His famous general, Moshe Dayan, was five feet eight inches. The first man in my West Point class to make general was five feet ten inches.

General H. Norman Schwarzkopf, who led our forces to victory in Desert Storm, is over six feet tall. But, he says one of the finest commanders he ever knew was South Vietnamese Colonel Ngo Quang Truong. "He did not look like my idea of a military genius," said Schwarzkopf. "He was only five feet seven, in his mid-forties, very skinny, with hunched shoulders and a head that seemed too big for his body. . . . Yet he was revered by his officers and troops. . . ."[5]

The fact is, there are tens of thousands of company presidents and plenty of outstanding military leaders who are less than six feet tall. If you are wondering about me, I'm four inches short of six feet.

THE FAMOUS AIR FORCE GENERAL WHO WAS CONSIDERED A POOR LEADER

Let me tell you about someone who was taller than six feet, but who definitely learned to be a great leader. And I know that he learned leadership because one of those who taught him told me about it.

Hoyt S. Vandenberg became a four-star general and Chief of Staff of the United States Air Force. He was a unique leader. During World War II, when he commanded the 9th Air Force, he frequently visited his squadrons at their bases. On one occasion a gunner from one of the crews had a complete breakdown. "I can't go today," the gunner screamed. "I won't fly today, sir. I can't go today!" he protested to his aircraft commander.

General Vandenberg saw the disturbance. Running up to the gunner, the general placed his hand on his shoulder. "Sergeant, you don't have to go today. This is not your day. This one is mine." With that, General Vandenberg climbed into the airplane and flew the mission as a gunner. You can imagine its effects on the 9th Air Force. It also must have had a positive effect on the gunner, as he stayed and flew the additional missions necessary to complete his tour of duty.

General Vandenberg was not a born leader. How do I know? When I was a cadet at West Point, one of my best friends was my classmate Ted Wells. Ted's father and his grandfather had also graduated from the Academy. Shortly before our graduation, I was sitting with Ted and talking to his grandfather, Major General Robert M. Danford. General Danford had graduated in the class of 1904 and had long since retired from the army.

"Bill," he said, "I understand that you're going into the Air Force."

"Yes, sir," I said, "I am. I want to fly."

"Well," he said, "you know I was Commandant of Cadets under General MacArthur when he was a superintendent of the Military Academy after World War I. Have you heard of General Hoyt Vandenberg?"

"Oh, yes, sir," I said. "He was Chief of Staff of the Air Force ten years ago."

"I'll tell you something I bet you didn't know about General Vandenberg. When I was commandant, General Vandenberg was a plebe going through his first year at the Academy. General Vandenberg was at one point almost discharged from the Academy."

"Why?" I asked.

General Danford smiled. "Because of a lack of leadership ability," he answered.

General Vandenberg developed himself from the time he was a plebe at West Point to the time he graduated. He became a great leader not because he was born a leader, but because he learned and developed into one.

WHY GOOD LEADERSHIP DOESN'T DEPEND ON GOOD DEALS

I've mentioned this before, but I want to mention it again: Good leadership doesn't seem to have much to do with participation in management or Japanese management or good working conditions or superior pay. You don't have to be a "nice guy."

In western Pennsylvania, there's a tool-and-die company called Oberg Industries. The president is Don Oberg. A magazine article in *INC* magazine called him "The Lord of Discipline."

Western Pennsylvania is right in the middle of union country, but Oberg Industries is nonunionized. It's not due to pleasant working conditions. Oberg Industries has a fifty-hour workweek, with a fifteen-minute lunch break for both management and labor.

Here are some other interesting facts. In a recent year, annual sales for most tool-and-die companies were on the average of $2 million a year. At Oberg they were $27 million. And the average sales per employee was 30 percent higher. There was no recession the year that we're talking about. It may be hard to believe, but 1,600 people applied for only thirty job openings that year.

Now, why is this? Are Oberg employees well paid? Of course they are. However, what is far more important than compensation is that Don Oberg, though he is a hard taskmaster, has managed to instill in all his employees the idea that if you work at Oberg, you're the best. Furthermore, everyone knows that the leader at the top is giving 100 percent himself to be the best. And so Oberg continues to outperform similar firms, and people fight to work there.[6] Good leadership doesn't depend on good deals. Let's look again at our combat model of leadership. You've probably heard that many of our outstanding combat organizations are elite units: Green Berets, Rangers, Marines, the Navy's SEALS, airborne units, fighter squadrons, and others.

Members of these units often receive additional compensation. The official name is hazardous-duty pay. If you think that hazardous-duty pay amounts to quite a bundle, you're dead wrong. Not only is it not a lot, but it certainly doesn't make up for the additional risks that individuals in these organizations face.

Furthermore, in some of these organizations promotions are slower than in comparable regular military units. And the members frequently train much longer hours. Why, then, do people volunteer for elite units? I would say that personal pride ranks fairly high up.

HOW I LEARNED WHAT IT MEANS TO BE AN AIR COMMANDO

I was an air commando in the Southeast Asian conflict. I flew as a member of the 609th Air Commando Squadron, flying in A-26s at night and attacking truck convoys in a heavily defended, mountainous area.

For those flying low on night interdiction missions, these mountainous formations, called "Karst," caused many tragedies. The enemy used every weapon they could get their hands on, from small-caliber ZPU machine guns to 37 mm, 57 mm, and 85 mm antiaircraft artillery.

Yet, in the air commandos we flew an old World War II aircraft that the old army air force used for the first time in 1944. This was 1968! The 609th Air Commando Squadron won the Presidential Unit Citation for its gallantry in combat. The price was the highest per-sortie aircraft-loss rate in the Vietnam War.

What made us do this? On our flying suit we wore a special insignia patch that proclaimed us a "Nimrod." This was also our radio call sign. Nimrod, in the Bible, was the first hunter. This patch said that its wearer had over 100 missions in the aircraft, all night strikes. We wore it proudly.

When I returned to the States, my assignment was to Wright-Patterson Air Force Base, at Dayton, Ohio. I had a nonflying job as a program manager in charge of development of aircraft life-support equipment. Once a month I would put on my flying suit and fly to maintain flying skill.

A few months after I returned, I was walking along in my flying suit on my way to the flight line. A car suddenly stopped directly opposite me across the street. The driver, another officer with his wife next to him, called out, "Could you come over a minute, Captain?"

I went over to the car, and the officer introduced himself. He had flown another type of aircraft in another squadron from my base. He wasn't thinking about himself or what he had done, however. Instead, he turned to his wife and pointed to my "Nimrod" patch with respect. "Honey, this is one of the fellows I was telling you about. This is an air commando. He's a Nimrod." You can bet I was pretty proud of having been a "Nimrod."

Once again, leadership does not depend on good deals or pleasant working conditions or compensation. People will readily follow you in very difficult circumstances for other reasons—if you know how to lead.

SEVEN FACTS YOU MUST KNOW BEFORE YOU BEGIN TO LEAD

1. One person can make the difference between success and failure in any organization. You can be that person through becoming a leader.

2. One of the most amazing facts is that most people become successful only through the help of others. You can obtain this help through the practice of leadership.

3. You don't need to be a manager to be a leader. You don't need to wait to be promoted. You can become a leader immediately.

4. If you learn the basic elements of the combat model of leadership, you will be able to lead in just about any other situation. This is because combat presents the most severe leadership challenge in risk, uncertainty, environmental hardship, and the penalty for failure or reward for success.

5. The essence of leadership is simple. It is to motivate people to perform to their maximum potential to achieve goals or objectives that you set.

6. Leaders are made not born. If you want to be a leader, you can learn how in the same way you learned other skills.

7. Good leadership doesn't depend on good deals or pleasant working conditions. Your ability to motivate people to perform to their maximum is independent of these factors.

Leadership has tremendous power to help you accomplish anything that you want the group or organization that you lead to achieve. You can tap this power through learning to apply relatively simple techniques. Let's start out in Chapter 2 by taking a closer look at the combat model and the eight universal laws of leadership.

NOTES

[1] Warren Bennis, *Managing People Is Like Herding Cats* (Provo, Utah: Executive Excellence Publishing, 1999), p. 81.

[2] Colin Powell, *My American Journey* (New York: Random House, 1995), p.185.

[3] "CINCSAC's Views on Professional Military Education," *Air Force Policy Letter for Commanders* (October 1988), p. 2.

[4] This comment was made at a presentation to a group of students of the Industrial College of the Armed Forces at Ft. McNair, Washington, D.C., on October 4, 1988.

[5] H. Norman Schwarzkopf, *It Doesn't Take a Hero* (New York: Bantam Books, 1992).

[6] Donna Fern, "The Lord of Discipline," *INC* (November 1985), pp. 82-85, 88, 95.

CHAPTER TWO

THE COMBAT MODEL: THE EIGHT UNIVERSAL LAWS OF LEADERSHIP

When Peter Drucker recommended General Xenophon's book on combat leadership for modern managers, he implied that general principles of leadership from the worst-case scenario of warfare are extremely important in the practice of all leadership in and out of the military. But Xenophon, writing more than 2,000 years ago, is not explicit. Nor does he explain specific principles of leadership. If general principles could be distilled from leadership in battle, leaders from all organizations could benefit. They could use these principles to increase productivity dramatically and the likelihood of success in any project in which they were engaged.

BARRY GOLDWATER PUTS ME ON THE RIGHT TRACK

After reading the first edition of this book, Barry Goldwater wrote me that all leadership was founded on basic honesty. I agreed. In fact, I wondered whether this had to do with one of these fundamental concepts that was the basis of all leadership and would come from an analysis of leadership in war.

THE COMBAT LEADER RESEARCH PROJECT—FOR BUSINESS LEADERSHIP

I then instituted what I called the Combat Leadership Research Project. I sought the principles of combat leadership that were universal in all leadership situations. The basis of my research was a survey sent to more than 200 former combat leaders and conversations with hundreds more. I especially sought those who had become successful in the corporate world or in other nonmilitary organizations after leaving the armed forces. Among the responses I received in the initial phase, sixty-two were from generals and admirals. I asked these extraordinary leaders what they had learned from leadership in battle. I asked about the tactics they used. I asked about the importance of their leadership style. I asked about the most important actions a leader must take. I asked whether these principles had been adapted to their civilian careers. To get my subjects to focus on what was most important, I asked them to list what they considered to be the three most important principles.

Their responses left no doubt that there were universal principles that successful leaders followed to boost productivity dramatically and achieve extraordinary success in all types of organizations. All good techniques of leadership derived from these basic principles.

The Surprising Results of My Research

Now, with so many respondents giving me three or more principles, I expected an encyclopedic list. The Emperor Napoleon, one of history's preeminent military leaders wrote down 115 maxims on the conduct of war. If one individual could come up with 115 maxims, how many hundreds of different leadership principles would I uncover after analyzing and tabulating the input from such a large number of respondents?

Surprisingly, I discovered that 95 percent of the responses I received boiled down to only eight principles. But these eight principles were not insignificant. Each of these highly successful leaders had followed one or more of these eight principles to help them achieve extraordinary results in their careers, both military and civilian.

More than a few wrote special notes or letters to express their support for my project. It was if they had seen payment in blood for what they had learned. They knew its value, and they didn't want to see it wasted.

In a latter phase of my research, I interviewed other successful senior business leaders and reviewed dozens of corporate situations and the actions taken by these corporations' senior leaders. Some had combat backgrounds. Some did not. Some had developed their own lists of principles of leadership over the years. While their lists sometimes differed from each other, they invariably included the eight responses I had previous developed from my surveys. As I usually do when researching anything, I also looked at history for further confirmation. Seven thousand years of recorded history gave me an abundance of evidence to support these principles.

THE EIGHT UNIVERSAL LAWS OF LEADERSHIP

The strength of the results of my investigation motivated me to rename these principles the universal laws of leadership. I published the results of my research in some detail in my book *The Stuff of Heroes: The Eight Universal Laws of Leadership* (Longstreet Press, 1998). The laws are important because they are the foundation for all the concepts and techniques contain in this book. Here are the eight universal laws of leadership that constitute what I now call "the combat model":

1. Maintain Absolute Integrity

2. Know Your Stuff

3. Declare Your Expectations

4. Show Uncommon Commitment

5. Expect Positive Results

6. Take Care of Your People

7. Put Duty Before Self

8. Get Out in Front

Let's look at each in turn.

MAINTAIN ABSOLUTE INTEGRITY

The eight universal laws of leadership are in no particular order—except for this law having to do with integrity. A significant majority of responses included this law, and many respondents wrote me letters or notes expressing their feelings that without basic trust between leader and followers, the leader would be forever suspect and would probably have difficulty even if he or she applied the other leadership principles properly. Integrity means doing the right thing. Lack of integrity can have terrible consequences for any organization and any endeavor.

General H. Norman Schwarzkopf Tells Us About Honor

At West Point, we were taught from the first day that honor was the most important thing. I did not know General H. Norman Schwarzkopf when I was a cadet. However, General Schwarzkopf was a senior or "First Classman" during my first year. He writes, "The most important lesson drilled into us during those first weeks was the honor code." In his autobiography, *It Doesn't Take a Hero*, General Schwarzkopf goes on to relate the following story about a first classman with whom he had to deal during his first year.

During his plebe year at West Point, there was a parade going on near his barracks. A classmate whose room was on the other side of the building asked if he could watch from Schwarzkopf's window even though this was against the rules. Schwarzkopf said, "It's your neck. If you want to do it, it's fine with me."

After the parade a First Classman burst into his room. This was a cadet who didn't like Schwarzkopf and told him so. If fact he had threatened to drive Schwarzkopf out of West Point if he could.

The cadet stood Schwarzkopf at attention and chewed him out for looking out of the window during the parade. He told Schwarzkopf that he was going to pay a terrible price. Related Schwarzkopf in his book:

" 'Sir, I did not watch the review.'

" 'I saw you standing on that chair! Who do you think you're trying to fool?'

" 'Sir, I did not watch the review.'

" 'You didn't?'

" 'No, sir.'

" 'All right,' he said and walked out the door. That was the end of the matter. Because of the honor code, despite his dislike of me, he accepted my word. And I was not expected to report the guy who had actually watched from my window, because that was a regulatory breach, not an honor violation."[1]

But integrity means even more than telling the truth. It means doing the right thing.

General Colin Powell Explains What Went Wrong in Vietnam

Military experts are clear in that that we never lost a single battle in Vietnam. How, then, could we lose? What we did, we did right. Our troops fought well. But, we did the wrong things. This had little to do with whether this was a "good war" or a "bad war." Those of us who have been in combat know there are no good wars.

There are only wars in which losing is worse than not fighting. The fact is, whether we should have fought in Vietnam or not, we lost the war. At the strategic level, we failed. This failure can be traced directly to an integrity issue. Here's what General Colin Powell has to say:

"Our senior officers knew the war was going badly. Yet, they bowed to groupthink pressure and kept up pretenses, the phony measure of body counts, the comforting illusion of secure hamlets, the inflated progress reports. As a corporate entity, the military failed to talk straight to its political superiors or to itself. The top leadership never went to the Secretary of Defense or the President and said, 'The war is unwinnable the way we are fighting it.' "[2]

Does Telling the Truth Have Any Value in the Real World?

Organizations have succeeded, sometimes against all odds, simply because their leadership maintained absolute integrity. Lands End, Inc., the billion-dollar catalog giant, was in trouble several years ago. Paper prices had doubled and apparel demand collapsed at the same time as there was a significant postal hike. As a result, third-quarter profits were down 60 percent and falling. Advisers told then-CEO, thirty-four-year-old Michael J. Smith, that he should think about laying off employees to improve his bottom line. That should boost stock prices and please stockholders.

To Smith, that was an integrity issue. Laying off employees simply to make himself look good when things got rough was not doing the right thing. So, he did the opposite. He added benefits. What kinds of benefits? He added an adoption assistance service and mental-health referrals. And part-time employees received full health-care benefits. He refused to lay anyone off. "If people feel squeezed, they won't treat the customer as well," explained Smith. Results? The following year first-quarter profits more than tripled to $4.4 million compared to the previous year. Sales rose 2.3 percent. The stock price of Lands' End shares increased 85 percent.[3]

Even absolute integrity cannot ensure a leader's success, give job security, or guarantee a happy ending. Four years later when competitive pressures and other problems caused sales again to decline, Smith was asked to resign.

What the Air Force Chief of Staff Told Cadets at the Air Force Academy

General Ron Fogleman, then Chief of Staff of the Air Force, told cadets at his alma mater, the United States Air Force Academy: "We earn and sustain the respect and trust of the public and of our troops because of the integrity and self-discipline we demonstrate. Officers should strive to develop forthright integrity—officers who do the right thing in their professional and private lives—and have the courage to take responsibility for their choices."[4]

General Fogleman was not like those generals of whom Colin Powell spoke, who failed to speak the truth to their superiors during the Vietnam War. When he felt a subordinate was to be unfairly made a scapegoat by the secretary of defense, General Fogleman chose the only route open to senior officers of the armed forces when they disagree with a superior. He asked to be separated from the Air Force.

But even if a leader loses a fight, by maintaining absolute integrity he or she retains his or her mandate to lead. Others will still follow leaders such as Smith, Roberts, or Fogleman, while leaders who have violated this law are never fully trusted and always flirt with tragedy no matter their abilities or accomplishments.

Confucius Says . . .

As noted by *Fortune* magazine: "You could do worse than heed the I Ching, a Chinese leadership guide used by Confucius: 'Radical changes require adequate authority. A man must have inner strength as well as influential position. What he does must correspond with a higher truth . . . If a revolution is not founded on such inner truth, the results are bad, and it has no success. For in the end, men will support only those undertakings which they feel instinctively to be just.' "[5]

KNOW YOUR STUFF

Those who follow you don't care two straws what you know about office politics and your ability to manage their career on to successfully higher jobs. They want to know whether you know stuff about *this* job. Carleton "Carly" Florina has been called the most powerful businesswoman in America. In the summer of 1999, she was named CEO of Hewlett-Packard, the number-two computer company. At forty-four years old, she became the first female leader of a blue-chip company. "I've seen a lot of highflying people fall flat because they were so focused on the next job," she told *Investors Business Daily.*[6]

I'm always amazed by the belief some people have that they must have instant success, and if they don't get it, it's due to "politics," or because someone didn't like them. They name individuals who are young or relatively young and are very successful, and they intimate that this success was attained with little knowledge or work and mainly through office politics, connections, or just luck.

How Bill Gates Became the Richest Man in America

In just about every case I've investigated, nothing could be further from the truth. Someone said, well, look at Bill Gates. He's the richest man in America. And he didn't even graduate from college. What could he know? True, Bill Gates didn't graduate from college. But, he was working on computer systems and had started a successful computer business when he was in high school. He never stopped learning and getting experience. So, he dropped out of college after his first year to devote full time to his business. In the area of business that was important to him, he knew his stuff.

Did You Think Steven Spielberg Was an Instant Success?

Many say that Steven Spielberg is another "instant success." I don't think Steven Spielberg would agree. Here's a leader that was so into his profession that he made and sold his first movie to a local theater when he was barely into his teens. True, it made him only a few dollars, and probably the only reason people went to see it was because they were personal friends, but he kept studying and learning on his own. By the time he was in his twenties, he had paid his dues and knew his stuff. Then he could "instantly" direct big moneymakers such as *Jaws* and *Close Encounters of the Third Kind*, and later great films such as *Schindler's List* and *Saving Private Ryan*.

DECLARE YOUR EXPECTATIONS

This universal law includes planning, goal setting, and communicating, all of which we will cover in more detail in a later chapter. During World War I, General Douglas MacArthur was a thirty-eight-year-old brigadier general. He had been in combat for some time, but had just assumed command of a new brigade in France. After planning an important attack, he went forward and waited in the trenches with the battalion that was going to lead the way in a major attack. This battalion had never been in combat previously, much less made an attack. He could see that the young battalion commander was nervous.

He called the battalion commander to him. "Major," he said, "when the signal comes to go over the top, if you go first, before your men, your battalion will follow you. Moreover, they will never doubt your leadership or courage in the future."

Now, normally, a battalion commander was not supposed to lead an attack from the front. The military-tactics manuals said that a battalion commander should be following the company in the lead making the attack. That way, he was not as vulnerable and could better control the attack as it unfolded. But MacArthur knew that there was a time when the rules must be violated and that this was one.

"I will not order you to do this," continued MacArthur. "In the front of the battalion, every German gun will be trained on you. It will be very dangerous and require a great deal of courage. However, if you do it, you will earn the Distinguished Service Cross, and I will see that you get it."

He then stepped back and looked the major over for several long moments. He stepped forward again. "I see you are going to do it. So, you will have the Distinguished Service Cross now."

So saying, MacArthur unpinned a Distinguished Service Cross from his own uniform and pinned it on the uniform of the major.

Now, I ask you, what happened when that signal came to go over the top? Well, you know as well as I do. The major, proudly wearing a Distinguished Service Cross, which he had not yet actually earned, charged out in front of his troops. And as MacArthur had forecast, his troops followed behind him. As a result, they were successful in securing their objective.[7]

Note that although MacArthur clearly declared his objectives and what he expected, he gave no direct orders. In fact, he said that he would not. His declaration of expectations was done in a highly innovative and effective way.

What an Air Force Academy Graduate in Industry Discovered

Air Force Academy graduate Joe Wong found that declaring his expectations worked in industry too. After leaving the Air Force, Joe decided to help set his wife up in business before looking for a job in the aerospace industry. Joe and his wife, Tina, started a luxury day spa called Amadeus Spa, Inc.

Says Joe, "What I learned at the Air Force Academy was leadership and how to build an effective team. I used those skills to pass on the big picture to my employees and show them how they fit into the company as a whole. I learned if I could educate them on what it takes to run a successful spa, we could be partners instead of adversaries."

In an industry where typical employee turnover is eight months, Joe's core group of thirty-five employees has been with the company between eight and nine years. The business now has annual revenue of almost $4 million, and Joe became president and never got that job in the aerospace business he had planned on.

On one critical occasion, he and his wife had put in $300,000 worth of tenant improvements. He was evicted and ended up getting sued for his trouble. Instead of keeping the problem to himself, he called a company meeting to explain what was happening, along with his expectations.

"I'll never forget how one of the employees stood up and said, 'It doesn't matter where we are. As long as we're together, we can do anything.' That really meant a lot to me and showed how the team had developed."

Joe had planned for a 10–20 percent loss in revenue during the transition. But because of communicating the situation and declaring his expectations to everyone, they were closed only two days despite the relocation, and revenue actually increased immediately by 30 percent instead of declining.[8]

SHOW UNCOMMON COMMITMENT

If you want to show uncommon commitment, you've got to be willing to take risks. You may have heard the adage, "No guts, no glory." It's like the body builder's adage, "No pain, no gain." Ask yourself, what is the worst that can happen? Accept that, and then press on.

This Small Company Discovered How to Get Big Business from the Government

A small company had tried for years to get into the business of building gas masks for the United States Army. A large multimillion dollar company that was fifty times the size of the smaller company had all of that business. The large company had hundreds of engineers. The smaller company had only five. The large company had done almost all the work on gas masks for the army for the previous thirty-five years. The smaller company had never had even a single gas-mask contract before. The only difference was in the leadership of the two organizations.

The responsible manager in the smaller company absolutely believed that he and his engineers could do the impossible. He was willing to risk his reputation, company resources, and other opportunities to bid a $2 million gas-mask contract. The largest new-product-development contract ever bid previously was $200,000. He convinced his boss, the company president, that he could do this. More important, he convinced his five engineers.

They worked, and they researched, and they did everything they could think of. They made many trips across country to visit their potential customer. They read everything they could find out about the use of gas masks and their development. Finally came the day that they bid on the contract. For thirty days they labored, putting together the best bid proposal they possibly could. Then they sent in their proposal and bid the contract.

After all of this work you probably think the smaller company deserved to win. Maybe, but they did not. Neither did the rival company. Because of budgetary problems, the government agency made the decision to delay procurement for a year. Both companies were to have the chance to restudy the problem and propose anew.

What this did was to raise the ante. Now both companies had to invest additional time and resources into the project. Still only one would win, and the odds were still with the larger company. The research-and-development leader in the smaller company decided to risk again. He asked his engineers to redouble their efforts. And if there was any doubt before, now these engineers really believed they could win.

A year later they bid the contract again, and they won. That single contract led the company into a new business. That new business was worth millions of dollars in sales a year. The result was due to one individual's leadership and his willingness to risk. No guts, no glory.

EXPECT POSITIVE RESULTS

Research has shown that the higher your goals, the higher goals you will achieve. And I have done the research to prove it.

A University Experiment

As a professor, I have my students participate in an exercise in pricing. One group gets this confidential information:

"Your company designs computer systems for business. Yesterday you received an emergency notice from top management. This message told you that you must withdraw and junk one of your older models, the XC-1000 computer, immediately. This is due to the implementation of a government regulation requiring additional features to prevent tampering, which this model does not have.

"Unfortunately, you cannot modify the XC-1000, as it was built to 'last forever.' You can't even use it for parts. By law, you must sell or get rid of all computer systems such as the XC-1000 by the third of April. [This is the second of April.] If not, you cannot offer it to the market at any price, or even give it away.

"Fortunately, you have only one of the XC-1000s left in inventory. In fact, you haven't sold any of this model in over three years.

This morning your assistant contacted the Acme Junk Company. They will pick up your XC-1000 and melt it down so they can sell it for scrap, at no charge to you.

"Before you can make final arrangements, you receive a call from Consolidated Unlimited. Their director of MIS would like to meet with you tomorrow about the possible immediate purchase of an XC-1000. You told him there was one left and that the price was negotiable. You delay your arrangements with Acme and begin preparing for your meeting.

"Do not reveal any of this information to any person not on your team. Complete the answers to the following questions. You will have thirty minutes.

1. For what price do you expect to sell the XC-1000, and why?

2. What is the lowest price you would accept, and why?

3. What is your strategy for your meeting tomorrow?"

I designate another group as buyers. They also receive confidential information. Their information reads as follows:

"Several years ago you became director of MIS of Consolidated Unlimited, a small company manufacturing copper tubing. One of your first actions was to buy an XC-1000 computer. One of this computer's most attractive features was its lack of need of maintenance. In fact, when you bought the computer, it came with a three-year money-back guarantee if the computer didn't perform well in any way. For three years and one month, the computer performed beautifully, but this morning your XC-1000 failed completely.

"One of the first things you did was have your assistant look for a newer replacement model that would perform the same functions. Unfortunately, as your company grew, all functions were built around your XC-1000, so you have very limited options. As a matter of fact, the lowest-price replacement computer if you can't get an XC-1000 is $50,000.

"You made some tentative calls around the country to other firms that you knew bought XC-1000s. You discovered that most companies replaced them long ago. You were also a little concerned about buying a used model, since none were less than three years old, and the guarantee had expired.

"You called the president to apprise him of the problem, but his response was, 'Get another new XC-1000.' You called the manufacturer of the XC-1000 and arranged a meeting with him tomorrow for an immediate purchase of an XC-1000. When you asked him the price, he told you there was one left and the price was negotiable. You began to prepare for your meeting.

"Do not reveal this information to individuals on your team. Complete the answers to the following questions. You will have thirty minutes.

1. What price do you expect to pay for the XC-1000, and why?

2. What is the highest price you would pay, and why?

3. What is your strategy for your meeting tomorrow?"

Note that both sides in this situation have a problem. If the selling group does not sell the computer, they get absolutely nothing for the computer. The scrap dealer gets it gratis. If the buying group does not buy the computer, they must pay $50,000 to get it from some other source. Of course, at any price other than zero or $50,000, both buyer and seller gain. In fact, one or both sides might even benefit additionally if there were other considerations, for example, the desire of the president of the copper-tubing company for an XC-1000.

If we were calculating a fair price, however, we would probably agree that it would be the midpoint between zero and $50,000. That is, $25,000.

But remember, neither side has the information that the other has. Both know only of their own problem, and not the other side's.

THE UNEXPECTED RESULTS
OF THE EXPERIMENT

Now, the interesting thing about this is that the prices vary widely between 0 and $50,000 among different groups of buyers and sellers negotiating on the same day. Yet conditions are the same for all.

As I write this, I received a letter from Professor Steven W. McDaniel of Texas A & M University. He wrote to tell me that in one class the contract prices were $3,000, $10,000, and $2,500. A fourth team, which he noted was hard to believe, actually sold the computer at $55,000. This is even above the $50,000 that they would have to pay if they couldn't purchase it!

From this exercise, students learn there isn't one single price for which a product must sell. Instead there are many prices, any one of which may completely satisfy a customer.

This little exercise also demonstrates something else. From the answers to my questions, I have found there is a direct relationship between the goals they expect and what they actually get. In other words, those teams that expect the best, get the best price. And it doesn't make any difference whether they are buyers or sellers, so long as they believe their price to be achievable.

SOME VIEWS FROM THE TOP

General David C. Jones had an outstanding military career and served as Chief of Staff of the Air Force, and later as Chairman of the Joint Chiefs of Staff. What are his views on leadership? General Jones cites another Air Force Chief of Staff, General Curtis LeMay. General LeMay built the Strategic Air Command into a major deterrent force. "General LeMay set very high standards for his command. Then he insisted that everyone meet those standards. General LeMay said that over half of the Strategic Air Command would be on immediate alert at all times. Others said that this couldn't be done. But they were wrong. Under LeMay's leadership, safety, performance and readiness reached unparalleled levels."[9]

How Expecting Positive Results Helped Turn Around a Publisher

HarperCollins is a major New York book publisher, and the third largest. Three years ago, HarperCollins was in a downward spiral. Profits had plunged 80 percent. HarperCollins's warehouses were full of unsold books. There had been major layoffs and a $270 million charge against earnings. And many in the industry did not wish HarperCollins well. In an effort to cut costs, the company had taken the unprecedented step of arbitrarily canceling 106 book contracts. Many experts thought that HarperCollins would be sold simply to cut losses. Enter new CEO Jane Friedman. In a meeting of key employees, many thought they were attending to be given notice of dismissal. Instead, Friedman gave an upbeat talk, laying out the positive results and high expectations she expected. "I have confidence in the future," she told them. Within a year, operating income tripled. Operating margins, which had sunk to only 1.6 percent, climbed to 7.1 percent. Noted *Business Week*: "Harper is a rare good-news story in an otherwise dreary consumer-book business."[10]

If you have high expectations in your position as leader, you will find the same to be true. Who wins? Who are successful as leaders? It is generally those leaders with the highest expectations and who expect positive results.

MAINTAIN A POSITIVE ATTITUDE

To expect positive results means that you as leader must maintain a positive attitude. Why didn't the British surrender to the Germans after France fell in the early days of World War II? Some say it was due to one man only: Winston Churchill. In the early part of the war, the United States was not in the conflict and England stood alone. It was able to hold out against terrible odds because Winston Churchill had a positive attitude. This positive attitude helped make him determined to prevail.

You Have More Control Than You Think

Now, here is an interesting fact. Scientists have discovered that to a certain extent we can control our moods and maintain a positive attitude and how we feel regardless of the reality of external facts. Famous psychologist and author of *Your Erroneous Zones* and many other books, Dr. Wayne Dyer, has an interesting comment about external facts. He says, "It's not the facts that are important, but what you do with the facts, and how you interpret them."

I said we could actually control how we feel. Let me demonstrate this to you right now. I would like you to read the next few paragraphs and then do what they request.

Wherever you are, I would like you to get as relaxed as you can. Then I would like you to close your eyes and relax even more.

Now, I would like you to imagine that there is a knock on the door. It is a special delivery for you. A distant uncle whom you have never heard of has just died. You are his only living relative, and so he has left you his entire fortune. This amounts to one million dollars after taxes.

There are no conditions. You can do whatever you want to do with the money. You can buy anything you want. Put the money in the bank and live on the interest of $100,000 a year. Buy a yacht or an expensive car. Take a trip around the world. Or, if you wish, you can give the entire amount or some part of it to your favorite charity. Many of the things that you always wanted to do are now possible.

While you continue to relax and with your eyes closed, imagine all the different things you are going to do with that one million dollars. Are you going to take that vacation that you always wanted to take right now? Are you going to give money to that charity that you felt could help so many people? Are you going to buy that new sports car or that wonderful home? Send your children to the best schools? What is it you want to do? Anything that you want will be yours because at least in your fantasy, you have actually received this check for one million dollars tax-free.

Visualize in your mind all the things you will do with your one million dollars. Visualize all the fun and satisfaction you will receive from doing them.

When you open your eyes, I want you to take note of your feelings. You will feel an increased sense of well-being and happiness. Yet in reality nothing has changed. What has happened? What you have just done in this exercise is not only psychological. It is also physiological.

Even Illness Can Sometimes Be Cured by Focusing on the Positive

Norman Cousins demonstrated just how powerful this physiological effect is in his book *Anatomy of an Illness*. Norman Cousins cured himself of a death sentence from a terminal disease. How did he do it? By locking himself up in a hotel room and repeatedly watching his favorite videos of the Three Stooges. They made him laugh. He found that even though he was in pain, by watching several hours of video, he could get a few minutes' sleep.

As his worry left and his pain diminished he got more and more sleep. Slowly, his body began to heal itself. Eventually, the impossible happened. His body cured itself.

Norman Cousins had been the editor of *Saturday Review*. After this experience, Cousins not only continued to write, he began to give lectures regarding his experiences. Because of his vital insights into the use of the mind for healing, the dean of the UCLA Medical School appointed him to the faculty of one of the most prestigious medical schools in the world, even though he was not a medical doctor.

What was Cousins's secret? Several years ago, I was privileged to hear him as he gave the commencement address at my university. "There is an entire apothecary in the body," claimed Cousins. "Your body contains the most powerful drugs in the world to treat any illness. But we can only access these drugs with positive thoughts and good humor." Cousins found that his body was actually a fully stocked drugstore containing everything needed to heal his body. The key is in learning to use the mind to release the necessary drugs. Cousins did the same thing we did in our exercise of the million dollars.

Our Body's Drugs Can Help Us in Leading

The class of drugs we released in our exercise is endorphins. We released endorphins by fooling our subconscious mind into thinking something wonderful and unexpected had happened. That we didn't actually receive one million dollars was unimportant for our subconscious mind. It heard and saw that we had received one million dollars. It knew that this should make us happy, and therefore it released the endorphins to make this happen. This changed our perspective and gave us a more positive attitude. This more positive attitude existed regardless of anything else that might be happening around us at the time.

Scientists have conducted some interesting experiments with endorphins. You've probably heard about placebos. A placebo is a drug that works even though there is no reason for it to work. There may be nothing medically helpful in it, yet the drug works anyway. Previously scientists thought that this had to do with the patient's belief system. If the person believed strongly enough, the drug worked even though there was no reason for it to do so.

Recently, some medical-research scientists suspected that this might have more to do with the release of endorphins. Their subjects were people subjected to frequent headaches. They divided their subjects into three groups. They told all their subjects there was a medicine whose efficacy in curing headaches they wanted to test.

Only one of these groups actually received a medicine. The second group and third group each received placebos—capsules containing ordinary tap water. However, the capsules taken by the third group did contain one other ingredient that blocked the endorphins from entering the bloodstream.

After the experiment the results were tabulated. There wasn't too much difference between the headache relief received by the first and second groups. However, the third group that had their endorphins blocked from entering the bloodstream received a much lower incidence of headache relief. Thus, although positive thoughts or belief may have a psychological basis, there is a strong physiological dimension as well.

Dr. Denis Waitley, the famous psychologist, is a graduate of the U.S. Naval Academy and a former member of the "Blue Angels" aerial acrobatic team, as well the author of many books and tapes including *The Psychology of Winning*. He says: "If your friends ask if you are on drugs because of being so consistently positive, you can answer, 'Yes, endorphins.' To which they may respond, 'I always knew you were high on something.'"

TAKE CARE OF YOUR PEOPLE

There is an old saying in the military that if you take care of your people, they will take care of you. This implies that loyalty is a two-way street. You cannot expect others to support your interests if you ignore theirs. But if you are the leader, taking care of your people is the right thing to do, period.

I have heard criticism of General H. Norman Schwarzkopf, hero of the Gulf War, that he is overly demanding and tough on his officers. Maybe. But nobody, and I mean nobody, has ever said he didn't take care of his troops. In 1991, two of America's foremost investigative reporters, Jack Anderson and Dale Van Atta, together with a team of associates that produce the nationally syndicated column, "Washington Merry-Go-Round," dug deep to get the first in-depth book out on Schwarzkopf. Typical of what they discovered was his enormous efforts on behalf of his soldiers when he was commander of the 24th Infantry Division (Mechanized). That division was later part of Schwarzkopf's army that fought the Iraqis. Some years later, my eldest son commanded a platoon that he took to Kuwait twice, in the same division.

Here's what the two reporters found: "Although Schwarzkopf put his troops at the 24th through hellish training, he was always on the lookout for their well-being. Troops who served under him at Ft. Stewart remembered him as a good soldier's soldier. He always tried to make the quality of life better for them . . ."[11] I also note that almost every one of his senior commanders from Desert Storm and Desert Shield was later promoted, even those of whose performance he was critical.

This Former Marine Captain Says This Is How He Built FedEx

Frederick W. Smith is Chairman of the Board and CEO of FedEx, which he also founded. Smith is also a former captain in the Marine Corps with several tours of combat duty in Vietnam. Listen now to Captain Smith: "The greatest leadership principle I learned in the Marine Corps was the necessity to take care of the troops in a high performance-based organization. The Marine Corps' strong emphasis on this overriding leadership requirement has been of inestimable importance to me in developing FedEx over the years . . . In short , FedEx owes its success to this simple truth."[12]

He Poured His Heart into It . . . and His Employees

Howard Schultz took over as CEO of Starbucks and grew it from a local Seattle coffeehouse with a few stores to a national colossus with more than 1,300 stores, 25,000 employees, and still growing. Says Schultz: "Our first priority was to take of our people, because they were the ones responsible for communicating our passion to our customers. If we did that well, we'd accomplish our second priority, taking care of our customers. And only if we achieved both of those goals would we be able to provide long-term value of our shareholders." And Schultz means what he says. Starbucks provides generous and comprehensive employee-benefits packages that include health care, stock options, training programs, career counseling, and product discounts. And all workers are included, both full and part time. "No one can afford not to provide these benefits," says Schultz.[13]

Successful Leaders Take Care of Their People

If that philosophy sounds unique, you should understand that it's shared by some of America's most successful businessmen. J. W. Marriot, founder of one of the finest and most successful hotel companies in the world, followed a simple philosophy that echoed Schultz's beliefs: "We take care of our people, and they take care of our guests."

PUT DUTY BEFORE SELF

If you are a leader, you have a duty that encompasses accomplishing your mission and taking care of your people. Usually, the mission must come first. Sometimes, you must take care of your people first, or you may never be able to accomplish your mission. Some battle commanders have forgotten that and have squandered the lives of the soldiers, sailors, airmen, or marines entrusted to them, forgetting that without them, the mission would never be accomplished. But whether mission or people are first at any particular time, this duty always comes before the interests of the leader.

That's what General Colin Powell told his senior officers when he took command of the V Corps in Frankfurt, Germany, in 1986: "Accomplish the mission and look after the troops."[14] That got first priority.

This Young Navy Commander Put Duty Before Self

One of the greatest examples I ever heard concerning duty before self is that of a young American submarine commander during

World War II. His name was Howard Gilmore. Gilmore commanded the U.S.S. Growler. The Growler was on patrol in the South Pacific during the early part of the war. On the night of February 7, 1943, the Growler surfaced to recharge its batteries. Unlike modern nuclear-powered submarines that can remain submerged for months, these old diesel submarines had to surface approximately every twenty-four hours to regain power.

Although all precautions were taken, this was always risky, as without modern electronic detection or optical systems, a sub could not be certain what was on the surface, even though a sweep with the periscope under poor light was routine.

The U.S.S. Growler had the great misfortune of surfacing directly abeam of a Japanese gunboat. The gunboat immediately took the Growler under fire and attempted to ram her. By skillful maneuvering, Gilmore managed to avoid the gunboat and to actually ram her in turn. But the Growler had received battle damage. Gilmore ordered everyone else from the bridge into the submarine in preparation to dive.

Before he could get to the hatch himself, Howard Gilmore was hit by gunfire. His wounds were such that he could not move. Without help, he could not drag himself to the hatch to get below. He knew that every second counted and that the gunboat had already radioed for air and surface help to destroy the submarine. His submarine and its crew were in grave danger of being sunk if it did not dive immediately. Before anyone could come to his aid, he gave the final order that sealed his fate, but gave the submarine its greatest chance of escaping: "Take her down."

His crew obeyed. Well trained, they managed to dive, evade the enemy, and limp back to Pearl Harbor for repairs. Gilmore, of course, was lost.

In civilian pursuits, leaders do not need to sacrifice their lives in putting duty before self. But all leaders must embrace this principle of requiring that they put the interests of the mission and their followers before their own.

GET OUT IN FRONT

There is only one real way to lead, and that is to get in front. You've got to lead by pulling and not pushing. Patton said that leadership is like a spaghetti noodle. You can pull it along fairly easily, but there is no way you can push it.

Admiral McDonald Lays It on the Line

Admiral Wesley L. McDonald retired from his assignment as the Supreme Allied Commander Atlantic, and the Commander in Chief of the U.S. Atlantic Command after having served in the U.S. Navy for more than forty-two years. Speaking on leadership to a select group of senior officers from all services, Admiral McDonald gave his views on leadership: "Set the course—be the guy in front. If you do this, you'll be there when it counts . . . a foot in front every time."[15]

The Israelis Say, "Follow Me"

Did you know that the motto of both the Infantry School of the U.S. Army at Fort Benning, Georgia, and the Israeli Army, are the same. It is: "Follow me."

Both mean what they say. The Israelis have a particularly no-nonsense attitude toward combat leadership and getting out in front.

If you are an officer, you lead by physically being at the head of your troops. Now, this is somewhat contrary to the doctrine taught in the U.S. Army and many other armies around the world. Most armies say that to lead effectively, the commander should be with a forward unit, but not the most forward. If he's leading a patrol, he can be the number-two man, but not the first. Why? Because if he is not at the front, he won't know what is going on. On the other hand, if he is all the way up front, he is more likely to become a casualty. That means a higher casualty rate of the scarce commodity of officer leaders.

The Israelis pay no mind to this, and they tell their officers: "If you are an officer, that's what you get paid for. You have to be in front of your men."

The Israelis have done this in every war that they've been in, and they have been at war with their neighbors since 1948. That they practice what they preach is confirmed by the fact that they have the highest officer casualty rate of any army in the world. Yet they do it anyway because they know that leaders must lead by getting out in front.

Being all the way at the front is not unique to the Israeli Army. During World War I, General Menoher, one of MacArthur's commanders said: "I'm afraid we're going to lose him sometime, for there's no risk of battle that any soldier is called upon to take that he is not liable to look up and see MacArthur at his side. At every advance MacArthur, with just his cap and his riding crop, will go forward with the first line. He is the source of the greatest possible inspiration to the men of his division, who are devoted to him."[16]

No wonder MacArthur was promoted to brigadier general when he was only thirty-eight.

General Grant Got Out in Front and Took Charge

Part of getting out in front is being willing to take charge. If you want to lead, you've got to take charge. During the Civil War, Ulysses S. Grant planned the first combined land/sea operation at the Battle of Fort Donelson. Before he could implement this operation, the senior Union Army commander ordered him to a conference. While he was away, the operation began.

As almost always happens, the operation did not go as planned. There were a number of mishaps. The Union attack by sea was repulsed. The Confederates attacked Grant's right wing, and it was collapsing. As his right wing disintegrated, Grant arrived on the battlefield.

He stopped to blame no one. What he did was to draw his saber and, galloping backward and forward on horseback along the front line, shouted to his men, "Fill your cartridge cases quick; the enemy is trying to escape and must not be permitted to do so."

And they did. Through Grant's actions, the Union troops rallied and won the battle.[17]

THE EIGHT UNIVERSAL LAWS
OF LEADERSHIP

Here again is the combat model—the eight universal laws of leadership that are just as applicable for leading a church group as are the most daring of combat warriors:

1. *Maintain Absolute Integrity.* This is the foundation of all leadership. If you don't maintain your integrity, you will never be fully trusted by those you lead.

2. *Know Your Stuff.* Followers don't care if you're good at office politics. They want you to be good at what it takes to get the job done.

3. *Declare Your Expectations.* You can't get "there" until you know where "there" is, and you let your followers know, too.

4. *Show Uncommon Commitment.* If you aren't committed, no one else is going to be. If you aren't uncommonly committed, no one else will be, either.

5. *Expect Positive Results.* If you expect to succeed or expect to fail, you're right. So, though it makes sense to be ready for the worst, expect the best.

6. *Take Care of Your People.* If you take care of your people, they will take care of you. However, the reverse is also true.

7. *Put Duty Before Self.* If you are a leader, your mission and your people must come before you, or you are not the leader.

8. *Get Out in Front.* Get out where you can see and be seen. That way, not only will you know what's going on, but those who follow will know you are committed.

Review these eight universal laws of leadership every morning. Tell yourself that you are going to look for opportunities to implement them.

At the end of the day, review your actions. Note where you succeeded and where you did not. In those instances where you fell short, replay the events in your mind and this time apply the concepts correctly. See the new outcome as a result of applying these concepts.

If you do this, in a short time you will be implementing the combat model without even thinking about it. The success you will achieve will be dramatic. So don't delay. Start thinking about ways in which you can apply these concepts today.

NOTES

1. H. Norman Schwarzkopf, *It Doesn't Take a Hero* (New York: Bantam Books, 1992), p. 70.

2. Colin Powell, *My American Journey* (New York: Random House, 1995), p. 149.

3. Susan Chandler, "Lands' End Looks for Terra Firma," *BusinessWeek* (July 8, 1996), pp. 128, 131.

4. Ronald Fogleman, "The Bedrock of Integrity," presented at the U.S. Air Force Academy Commandant's Leadership Series, November 8, 1995.

5. Stratford Sherman, "How Tomorrow's Best Leaders Are Learning Their Stuff," *Fortune* (November 27, 1995), p. 92

6. Joseph Menn, "First Woman Named to Lead Blue-Chip Firm," *Los Angeles Times* (July 20, 1999), pp. A-1, A-18.

7. Douglas MacArthur, *Reminiscences* (New York: McGraw-Hill Book Co., 1964), p.70.

8. Karen E. Klein, "Spa's Staff Discovers the Beauty of Loyalty," *Los Angeles Times* (July 14, 1999), p. c7.

9. From a presentation to the Industrial College of the Armed Forces, Ft. McNair, Washington, D.C., October 18, 1988.

10. Larry Light, "The Fall and Rise of HarperCollins," *BusinessWeek* (June 14, 1999), pp. 74, 78.

11. Jack Anderson and Dale Van Atta, *Stormin' Norman: An American Hero* (New York: Kensington Publishing Corp., 1991), p. 77.

12. Frederick W. Smith, quoted in Rod Walsh and Dan Carrison, *Semper Fi* (New York: AMACOM, 1999), p. 140.

13. Matt Rothman, "Into the Black," *INC.* (January 1993), p. 59.

14. Colin Powell, op. cit., p. 319.

15. From a presentation to students of the Industrial College of the Armed Forces, Ft. McNair, Washington, D.C., October 25, 1988.

16. Douglas MacArthur, op. cit., p. 70.

17. *The Armed Forces Officer* (Washington, D.C.: The Department of Defense, 1950), p. 85.

CHAPTER THREE

HOW TO ATTRACT FOLLOWSHIP

No one follows anyone else without being motivated to do so. Look at any situation where men or women follow a leader and you will discover reasons for their doing so. Luck or unusual circumstances may play a part. But mostly it is because of definite actions that the leader takes. In this chapter you will learn four actions that you must take to motivate others to follow you.

THE MOST POWERFUL MOTIVATOR OF HUMAN BEHAVIOR

Everyone wants to feel important, from the youngest child to the eldest grandmother or grandfather. After basic survival, it is one of the most important of human needs. It is frequently the real reason behind both a child's tantrum and an adult's rudeness. A recent television special sought the reason that some children became schoolground bullies. Why do some children insist on dominating and threatening their playmates? Why do some children torment and persecute other children? Sociologists thought that bullies would be less intelligent. They thought that these would be the kids who couldn't do well in class. In most cases, this wasn't true.

What they did discover was that bullies got a sense of importance by lording it over others. As one former bully, now grown up, told television viewers: "The more I was able to make weaker kids do what I wanted, the more important I felt."

But this same motivator can have a tremendously powerful effect. Toward the end of the Civil War, General Robert E. Lee faced a force of 100,000 Union troops with only 30,000 of his own. Just as he was about to be overrun, the Texas Brigade commanded by General John Gregg showed up.

As related by Alf J. Mapp, Jr., in his book *Frock Coats and Epaulets*, "Lee rode up to the front of the brigade, stood in his stirrups, raised his hat from his head and boomed above the martial din, 'Texans always move them.'

"An ear-splitting yell rose from the brigade. One of Gregg's couriers, with tears running down his cheeks, shouted, 'I would charge hell itself for that old man!' "[1]

Making one feel important is more powerful as a motivator than money, promotion, working conditions, or almost anything else. So you know that we do everything possible to make others feel important. Right? Wrong.

We do the opposite. When we meet a surly clerk, we don't think, "This person needs to feel important, and I'm going to make him or her feel that way." Oh no, not us! We think, "How dare this person talk that way to me. I'll show him how really unimportant he is compared with me."

So, we play a game of one-upmanship in rudeness. The results are perfectly predictable. We have what is sometimes referred to in the military as a "pissing contest."

If we have more power than the other person, we will probably get our way. Our subordinate will put up with our tirade, and probably won't argue with us. But at what cost? Analysts term this style of misleadership, "manager disrespect." Professor Jack Mendleson at Bethel College in Mishawaka, Indiana, says, "Preliminary research findings show that manager disrespect has reached an epidemic level in the U.S."[2] So many leaders don't lead. They confront and dominate with manager disrespect.

When you lead with manager disrespect, you may or may not succeed. One thing, however, is certain. The person you are doing this to will not appreciate it. You may not be able to trust that person to follow your lead or your intentions if you aren't around in the future. In fact, if I had to bet some money, I would bet on the opposite. I'm not saying that there aren't times when you must let someone know you are dissatisfied about something done or left undone. But don't belittle that person's importance so that he or she loses his or her self-respect—not if you want to lead and influence people.

A Navy Attack Pilot Skipper Lays It on the Line

Fast-forward ahead a 130 years from the Civil War and Robert E. Lee. We are at war with Iraq and Saddam Hussein's minions. On the aircraft carrier U.S.S. Midway in the Persian Gulf, the attack squadron commander, who is also the lead pilot for the evening's mission, is briefing. The attack pilots have the mission of destroying a munitions dump near Basra, Iraq. But to accomplish this, the enemy's deadly surface-to-air-missiles, or SAMs, must be dealt with. This is the job of the EA-6B Prowler aircraft.

"When the strike package enters the SAM envelope here," he says as he points to a set of overlapping rings connoting the SAM threat, "we will be counting on the Prowlers to eliminate the associated acquisition radars of SAM systems so that we can ingress and egress safely."

Lieutenant Sherman Baldwin, call sign "Ironclaw," is the pilot of a "Prowler." These are aircraft that are especially designed to deal with enemy electronic defenses. "I nodded to the Eagle skipper, acknowledging our responsibility, and realized that if we did not do our job some of these A-6 crews might not come back."

The A-6 leader continued, "Once again, the Prowlers are a go-no-go criteria for the strike. No Prowler means no strike," he emphasized.

Writes Ironclaw, "I swelled with pride on the outside at this comment . . ." Ironclaw was an important and vital part of this mission, even though he would not be dropping the bombs that destroyed the target, and he knew it.[3]

The Woman Who Gave Away Pink Cadillacs

Experienced leaders know that making others feel important is crucial. Mary Kay Ash, the founder and CEO of Mary Kay Cosmetics, built a $1-billion-dollar company starting with a $5,000 investment using this concept. If you aren't involved with cosmetics, you may not know of Mary Kay by name. But you may have heard of the woman who gave out pink Cadillacs to her most successful saleswomen. She's retired today, although her company still maintains the philosophy behind her unusual gifts to her employees.

Some years ago, I was fortunate to be selected by the Direct Selling Association as one of a group of about twenty professors from all over the country to visit Mary Kay and her company. In 1985, we attended one of her annual sales meetings in Dallas, Texas. About 30,000 women attend these meetings each year, and it was a tremendous, motivating, and exciting experience.

To lead several hundred thousand saleswomen successfully, you have to be one heck of leader. Mary Kay fits that category. She feels that making others feel important is so critical to the success of her business that she crafted a special technique to help her do this. What's Mary Kay's secret? Simply this. She imagines that every person she sees has a sign on his or her head. The sign reads: "Make me feel important." Mary Kay does everything she can to obey the sign's request.

How a General Made an Entire Air Force Feel Important

Do you think only women in the cosmetics business need to feel important? Listen to this. Four-star General Bill Creech became the commander of Tactical Air Command in the Air Force in 1978. Tactical Air Command, more familiarly known as TAC, included more than 100,000 "tigers." These were men and women who must be superaggressive in their work and ready to go to war at all times. Tom Peters and Nancy Austin reported what happened to TAC in their book *A Passion for Excellence*.[4]

When General Creech took over TAC, the sortie rate had been falling over a ten-year period at a compound rate of 7.8 percent. A sortie is a flight mission by a single aircraft. So the fact that the number of sorties TAC launched every year was going down was not good. Further, when Creech arrived on the scene it took four hours for a spare part to get from inventory to the aircraft where it was needed.

What was the situation when Creech left TAC in 1984? The sortie rate rose each year of Creech's tenure at a compound annual rate of 11.2 percent. Getting a part from inventory to the aircraft was no longer measured in hours. When Creech left, the average time was only eight minutes!

Now you may think that much of this was due to increased military budgets. Not so. The budget for spare parts actually decreased during this period.

How did Creech do it? Certainly Creech's success as a leader was due to many things he did. But making his people feel important was a major part.

He gave his support troops the importance they deserved, the same as he gave his pilots. He improved their housing, decorated their offices, and rewarded those who did well.

On one inspection tour in the west, he saw a supply sergeant's regulation-air-force chair that had a torn back and only three casters. Instead of the fourth caster, there was a brick. Electrical tape held the torn material in the back together.[5]

"Why don't you get a decent chair," asked Creech. The reply was, "General, there aren't any available for supply sergeants right now."

"Sergeant, let me have your chair. I'll get a new one for you."

General Creech ordered his aide to fly the chair back to his headquarters at Langley Air Force Base, Virginia. He called in his three-star general in charge of logistics.

"General, I have a little present for you. It's a regulation-air-force chair, but its pretty beat up. It's yours until you get our logistic mess straightened out. And, oh yes . . . I need your old chair for a supply sergeant out west."

Supply sergeants were very important to the operations of TAC. By these actions, General Creech made this supply sergeant, and all supply sergeants, feel this importance. General Creech also showed his general in charge of logistics that he was important—and in a very imaginative way.

So rule number one is this: If you want people to follow you, make them feel important.

How to Promote Your Vision

Leaders are not caretakers. They must have some idea as to where they want to go. It doesn't make any difference whether you are the leader of a large Air Force command of thousands of people, a softball team, or a small informal group. If you don't have any idea of where you are going, you can't get there. And neither can anyone else. As the Bible says, "Where there is no vision, the people perish." (Proverbs 29:18).

There is a strange insect called the processionary caterpillar. This insect bears this unusual name because of its unusual method of navigation. A number of processionary caterpillars will attach themselves front to back in a single line. The leader seeks the mulberry leaf, the main food of this caterpillar. Wherever the leader goes, the other processionary caterpillars are sure to follow. And off they go in this way, one continuous line of five or more caterpillars looking for mulberry leaves.

Several years ago a scientist who studies such things conducted an experiment. He took a line of processionary caterpillars and formed them into a circle. What had been the leader was attached to what had been the last caterpillar in the line. Now there was no leader and no follower caterpillars. In the center of the circle of caterpillars he placed a bowl of mulberry leaves. The scientist wanted to know how long they would maintain the circle with no leader and no objective. He knew that eventually they must break the circle to eat the mulberry leaves or starve.

The result of this experiment surprised him. The caterpillars continued in a circle until they were so weak that they couldn't reach the mulberry leaves. Though food was only inches away, they continued to follow the caterpillar in front. They continued to go forward with no objective at all.

Men and women are not processionary caterpillars. If you have no vision of where you want to go, no one will follow you. Instead, your group will follow someone else who does know where he or she wants the group to go.

Professors Warren Bennis and Burt Nanus of the University of Southern California interviewed ninety leaders, including sixty successful CEOs and thirty outstanding leaders from the public sector. All ninety leaders had a well-thought-through vision of where they wanted their organizations to go. Bennis and Nanus termed the concern that these leaders had for their visions "unparalleled." Said Bennis and Nanus in their book, *Leaders . . .:* "Their visions or intentions are compelling and pull people toward them."[6]

Four-star General Andrew J. Goodpaster, a confidant of presidents as well as former Supreme Allied Commander, Europe, puts what he calls: "Be clear about purpose," as his starting point for good leadership.[7]

William G. McGowan, founder and former CEO of the billion-dollar MCI Communications Corporation, was the man who cracked the long-distance monopoly of American Telephone and Telegraph Company. McGowan maintained, "People don't come to MCI for security. They come to be challenged, to be part of something new."[8]

BusinessWeek calls Bill Gates, chairman of Microsoft Corporation, the "Visionary-in-Chief." In an interview with *BusinessWeek* editors, Gates articulated a new vision for Microsoft: "Giving people the power to do what they want, where and when they want, on any device."[9]

People are attracted to a leader's vision and future goals because they recognize that through him or her, they and the organization can become permanently better.

Major General Perry M. Smith, former Commandant of the National War College in Washington, D.C., found, "A leader can permanently affect an organization by establishing a strategic vision and setting long-term goals.[10] Four-star General Edward C. Meyer, former Chief-of-Staff of the Army, a man who helped to permanently change the organization of the Joint Chiefs of Staffs and the youngest ever Army Chief of Staff, says that without vision, organizations will fail.

Vision is clearly pretty important. But having an objective of where you want the organization to go is only half the action you must take. The other half is to ensure that others know what your vision is. By communicating your vision you get a consensus among those you lead.

President John Young of Hewlett-Packard said: "Successful companies have a consensus from top to bottom on a set of overall goals. The most brilliant management strategy will fail if that consensus is missing."[11]

James E. Buerger, publisher of *Travelhost National* magazine, set up his own printing plant by following this principle. He had just forty-five days after ordering a press to raise $100,000, set up his equipment, get trained operators, and find a building to put everything in to. He did it by communicating his goals effectively after setting them. According to Buerger, "A secret goal cannot benefit from the participation and force of others. A well-defined goal, shared with others and sparked with enthusiasm, will draw energy and forces that cannot be measured or suppressed."[12]

If you have a vision and communicate it to others, you will succeed though the odds are against you.

You Can Promote Your Vision Anywhere

Colonel Julian Ewell, commanding the 501st Parachute Infantry Regiment, reached Bastogne, Belgium, on the night of December 18, 1944. Two days earlier, the Germans had begun their Ardennes campaign. This was the Germans' last major offensive of World War II, and history tells us it was a very close thing. Ewell arrived with only one battalion, of less than a thousand men. Higher headquarters couldn't tell him the enemy's situation . . . the friendly situation . . . nothing.

But Ewell had a vision, and he communicated it to his men. "We're going to attack the Germans." They did. In so doing, they stopped the German 27th Panzer Corps of more than 30,000 troops dead in its tracks. It forced Hitler to change his Ardennes plan and may have altered the course of World War II.[13]

Roger Ailes, a communications consultant who has consulted for a number of CEOs and presidential candidates, says that, ". . . the essence of charisma is showing your commitment to an idea or goal."[14] Of course showing commitment to an idea or goal is the same as vision. And behavioral scientists have found a close correlation between communicating vision and being perceived as charismatic.

Martin Luther King, Jr., one of the most charismatic leaders of our time, said, "I have a vision."

If you want others to follow you, you must have a vision too . . . and you must communicate it to others.

Treat Others as You Would Be Treated Yourself and They Will Follow Your Lead

Both the Old and the New Testaments tell us to treat others as we want to be treated ourselves. You may have thought this concept has application only in religion or in the practice of ethical conduct. The truth is it also has a great deal to do with good leadership. Why? Because people do not willingly follow leaders who are unconcerned with how they are treated.

Mary Kay Ash calls this her "Golden Rule System of Management." She not only practices it herself, but recommends it to everyone who leads.

After all, what makes you so special? Do you think you are so much better than others that you are to be treated differently? If you do, better change your way of thinking, or you may never get people to follow you.

Move Over Scrooge, Your Day Is Done

Charles Dickens's famous story *A Christmas Carol* featured Scrooge, who cared little for the personal problems of his employees, specifically one Bob Crachett. By Scrooge calculations, he was paying Crachett, right? Thus ended his responsibilities.

Those days are gone. Many corporate leaders today have discovered that it is good leadership to treat family issues as strategic business issues and to give the welfare of their employees' families major priority. At First Tennessee National Corporation, CEO Ralph Horn did that. Horn dumped the old work rules and let employees figure out which schedules worked best from a family viewpoint. Then, he added a host of new programs to help the families of his employees. He sent his 1,000 managers to three and a half days of training to educate them and get them on board.

Results? Productivity and customer service soared. According to First Tennessee, high retention rates contributed to a 55 percent profit gain in two years.[15]

What We Learned from the Largest Leadership Study Ever Done

During World War II, the U.S. Army recruited sixty-one of the greatest authorities in the field of psychology to prepare and publish a special study. They came from some of the most prestigious universities in the country: Harvard, Yale, Brown, the University of Pennsylvania and many others. When they were done, their research was published under the title of *Psychology for the Fighting Man*.

One of their studies was unique. For the first time in the history of armies, enlisted soldiers were interviewed about what they thought about good leadership. Want to know what these thousands of soldiers thought made good leaders? The number one factor by frequency of response was "competence." The good officer was expected to know his stuff. Did you remember that that was the second of the universal laws of leadership?

Actually, that response was pretty much expected. What was not expected had to do with the next fourteen most frequently cited factors. Listen to this. Of the next fourteen most frequent responses to the question "What makes a good leader?" the second, fourth, sixth, and seventh all had to do with treatment. These were:

- Interest in the welfare of the soldier (second)
- Patience and ability to make things clear (fourth)
- Doesn't boss you around without reason (sixth)
- Tells you when you did a good job (seventh)

The soldiers interviewed gave these responses more frequently than "physical strength" (eighth), "good education" (ninth), or even "guts" (eleventh).[16]

The Armed Forces Officer, a book on leadership written for officers in all of our armed services says: "Though it has been said before, even so, it can be said again: It is a paramount and overriding responsibility of every officer to take care of his men before caring for himself. . . . *It is a cardinal principle!* . . . . If an officer is on a tour with an enlisted man, he takes care that the man is accommodated as to food, shelter, medical treatment or other prime needs, before satisfying his own wants; if that means that the last meal or the last bed is gone, his duty is to get along the hard way."[17]

We had a saying at West Point that a leader should be "hard, but fair." So if you want others to follow you, treat them fairly. Treat them as you would like to be treated yourself, and put the welfare of those you lead before your own welfare.

TAKE RESPONSIBILITY FOR YOUR ACTIONS AND ADMIT YOUR MISTAKES

As a leader, you will be taking the responsibility for attaining an objective. That objective may be one set by a higher organization than the one you are in. It could be an objective set by the followers you lead. Or it could be an objective you set. Who sets the objective is unimportant.

The size of the group isn't important either. It could be a group of hundreds of thousands, or it could be you and one other person. Once you take on the leadership of a group, you and you alone are responsible for reaching the objective.

You can delegate authority to do certain tasks to others you lead. There is no way you can delegate responsibility. It doesn't even make any difference whether those that follow you perform well or perform poorly, or even carry out instructions you have given them.

Of course, you should take responsibility and admit your mistakes. It's the right thing to do. Beyond being the right thing, it is the only thing to do if you want to be a leader. Do this and those you lead will give you their trust and follow you anywhere. Fail to do this and you will not be a leader for very long.

Andrew S. Grove is Chairman and Chief Executive Officer of the Intel Corporation. This company, built largely through the efforts of Grove, is not only a "Fortune 500" company. Intel Corporation is listed in *The 100 Best Companies to Work for in America*. Yet, *Fortune* magazine calls Andy Grove one of the ten toughest bosses in America to work for. What does Grove say about taking responsibility and admitting mistakes? Let's listen to him. "All of us in management (and in teaching, government, even parenting)—men and women, young or old—worry about losing hard-won respect by admitting our mistakes. Yet, in reality, admitting mistakes is a sign of strength, maturity, and fairness."[18]

In war, mistakes are deadly. But even in war, or maybe especially in war, mistakes are inevitable. Admiral Hyman G. Rickover, that extraordinary and uncompromising leader who is known as "the father of the nuclear submarine," said, in testifying before Congress in April 1964: "In war we are always doing something for the first time. It would be a miracle if what we improvised under the stress of war would be perfect."

And General Bruce C. Clarke who rose to lead the Continental Army Command said, "You must be able to underwrite the honest mistakes of your subordinates if you wish to develop their initiative and experience."

A Man Doesn't Get Hired Because He Has Made No Mistakes

In the early days of the Dow Chemical Company, a man approached founder Herbert H. Dow to ask for a job he had heard about. He went over his qualifications in some detail. He had one big selling point that he stressed again and again. This was that he had never, under any circumstances, ever made a mistake at work.

Dow finally interrupted his presentation. "We have three thousand people working here, and on the average, they make three thousand mistakes each and every day. I couldn't insult them by hiring somebody perfect."[19]

Why Did Men Follow Robert E. Lee?

Robert E. Lee is probably the most beloved military leader in U.S. history. Not only to the day of his death, but until years afterward, those who knew him or served under him revered his name. Even his former enemies honored him and flocked to visit him after the Civil War. Here he was, the most notorious defeated enemy general of the Confederacy. And yet company presidents from New York offered him hundreds of thousands of dollars if he would associate with their companies. He turned them all down. Instead he accepted a post as president of a small college in Virginia with only forty students.

Lee had not won the war. He had been forced to surrender his Army of Northern Virginia to General Grant. The best chance that the Confederacy had to win the Civil War was the Battle of Gettysburg in July of 1863. Lee lost that decisive battle.

Sure, Lee had plenty of opportunities for excuses, plenty of bad luck and poor performance by some of his generals on which to blame his loss.

Lee's famous "strong right arm," "Stonewall" Jackson, had been killed at the Battle of Chancellorsville a few months earlier. His brilliant young cavalry leader, Jeb Stuart, went off on his own and didn't appear on the battlefield until the last day. As a result, Lee had very little intelligence about the Union forces he faced. Lieutenant General Ewell, who commanded part of Jackson's old corps, could have won the battle for Lee the first day. All he had to do was to occupy a deserted, but strategically important hill. He failed to do so.

Lee's second in command, General Longstreet, strongly opposed a charge ordered by Lee to be made by one of his divisions commanded by Major General George Pickett. As a result, he failed to give Pickett positive orders. Preparations took longer than they should have. The charge was not coordinated with a diversionary attack as previously planned.

Pickett's troops were fully exposed to the murderous effect of enemy guns and direct fire. Only a few hundred of his troops even managed to reach Union lines. Of the 13,000 Confederates who made the charge, more than 7,000 were left dead or wounded in "no-man's land" between the two lines.

With the battle clearly lost and the remnants of Pickett's men returning to the Confederate lines, it was Lee who went out to meet the survivors.

"It was all my fault and no one else's," he said. "You did your best, but it was I who failed you."

In tears, these battle-weary soldiers shouted: "No! No! You didn't fail, General. It was us."

Robert E. Lee always took responsibility for his actions. And his men loved him for it and fought all the harder. Remember, the Battle of Gettysburg was in early July of 1863. Lee didn't surrender his army at Appomattox Court House until April of 1865 . . . almost two years later.

Why a Squadron Commander Who Was Never There Was Reported for Being Drunk

As a leader, you alone are responsible for everything those who follow you do, or fail to do. Hap Arnold, who was the five-star commanding general of the Army Air Force during World War II, illustrates this in his book *Army Flyer*.[20] A new squadron commander received a message from his group commander.

"You drank too much at the Officer's Club last night. Don't let it happen again."

The problem was, this young officer had never been at the Officer's Club on the night in question. Shrugging it off, he decided to do nothing.

Several days later, he received another message. "You drank too much again. This is your final warning."

Now this new squadron commander was really puzzled, because he hadn't been at the club on that night either. This time, however, he called the deputy group commander to talk it over with him.

The deputy group commander understood the situation perfectly. "Major, you're not responsible for just yourself anymore. You're now responsible for the actions of everyone in your squadron. You personally weren't drinking too much at the Officer's Club. But one of the members of your squadron was. You're responsible!"

Two Unwanted Outcomes That Are Easily Avoided

I know that you may think this a bit strong. How can you be responsible for everything that someone who happens to be in your organization does? In the military, you are responsible because you have a twenty-four-hour-a-day job and have authority over those you lead twenty-four hours a day.

The problem is that many leaders of nonmilitary organizations don't take responsibility for the actions of their charges under any circumstances. You can always find excuses for failing to reach an objective or some other problem. But if you do, this will have two undesirable results.

First, those who follow you will not want you to be their leader. Would you if you were they? After all, the contract is leadership in exchange for responsibility. When you don't take responsibility for the group you lead, you violate this contract.

The second unwanted result will come from whomever you report to. Your boss wants to know that he or she can rely on you. If you aren't responsible for your organization, then who is? Who is it that your boss can rely on?

General Bill Creech, now retired from the Air Force and a consultant for many leading corporations, says that leaders can and must be taught ". . . to accept *personal responsibility* for building common purpose and organizational success."[21] (The italicization of the words personal responsibility is General Creech's.)

You can't delegate responsibility, so don't try. When things go wrong, think of General Lee and say, "It was all my fault and no one else's."

FOUR ACTION STEPS TO GET PEOPLE TO FOLLOW YOU

1. *Make others feel important.* People will follow you when you make them feel important, not when you make you feel important.

2. *Promote your vision.* No one will follow you simply because you decide you want to lead. You have to have a clear idea of where you want to take the group and then you must promote it to your group and convince them that your goal is worthwhile.

3. *Treat others as you would be treated yourself.* This is so basic, why don't we do it more often? After all, would you want to follow someone who treated you poorly? Don't you prefer to follow leaders who have concern for you and your feelings and treat you well? So do those who would follow you.

4. *Take responsibility for your actions and those of your group.* Admit your mistakes. You are responsible for everything the members of your group do or fail to do. So when things go wrong, don't forget to accept this responsibility. If you try to foist this responsibility off on others, you are no longer the leader.

Take the time to digest these four ways to get people to follow you. Then proceed to the next chapter for three additional things you must do.

NOTES

1. Alf J. Mapp, Jr., *Frock Coats and Epaulets* (New York: Hamilton Press, 1987) p. 203.

2. Jack L. Mendleson, "Manager Disrespect," *Business Forum* (Winter/Spring 1998), p. 20.

3. Sherman Baldwin, *Ironclaw* (New York: William Morrow and Company, 1996), pp. 201–202.

4. Tom Peters and Nancy Austin, *A Passion for Excellence* (New York: Random House, 1985), p. 48.

5. Ibid., p. 275.

6. Warren Bennis and Burt Nanus, *Leaders* (New York: Harper & Row, 1985), p. 28.

7. From a presentation to students of the Industrial College of the Armed Forces at Ft. McNair, Washington, D.C., on November 8, 1988.

8. John Wilke, "McGowan: The Man Who Cracked AT&T," BusinessWeek (January 21, 1985), p. 69.

9. Michael Moeller and Kathy Rebello, "Visionary-in-Chief: A Talk with Chairman Bill Gates on the World Beyond Windows," BusinessWeek (May 17, 1999), pp. 114, 116.

10. Perry M. Smith, *Taking Charge* (Washington, D.C.: National Defense University Press, 1986), p. xvii.

11. Jonathan Carr, "Success as a State of Mind," *Financial Times* (February 13, 1984).

12. Charles Garfield, *Peak Performers* (New York: Avon, 1986), pp. 121–122.

13. *The Armed Forces Officer* (Washington, D.C.: U.S. Government Printing Office, 1950), pp. 136–137.

14. Roger Ailes, "The Secret of Charisma," *Success* (July/August 1988), p. 14.

15. Kith H. Hammonds, "Balancing Work and Family," *BusinessWeek* (September 16, 1996), p. 74.

16. Committee of the National Research Council with the collaboration of Science Service, *Psychology for the Fighting Man* (Washington, D.C./New York: Infantry Journal/Penguin Books, 1944), pp. 306–307.

17. *The Armed Forces Officer* (Washington, D.C.: U.S. Government Printing Office, 1950), pp. 28–29.

18. Andrew S. Grove, *One-On-One with Andy Grove* (New York: G. P. Putnam's Sons, 1987), p. 60.

19. Peter Fay, *The Book of Business Anecdotes* (New York: Facts on File, 1988), p. 166.

20. Henry H. Arnold and Ira Eaker, *Army Flyer* (New York: Harper, 1942).

21. Bill Creech, *The Five Pillars of TQM* (New York: Dutton, 1994), p. 301.

CHAPTER FOUR

THREE ADDITIONAL WAYS TO ATTRACT FOLLOWSHIP

In this chapter, we're going to examine three additional ways that will encourage others to follow your lead. The first simply requires a readjustment of the way you do things. You must praise in public and criticize in private. Unfortunately, many leaders fail to do this. As a result, they are resented. In addition, they fail to take full advantage of the opportunity that accomplishment represents. These leaders rarely reach their maximum potential.

Seeing and being seen and using competition as a motivator are two tools you shouldn't be without. Their use will not only help in getting others to follow you, but will aid in your perception as being positively charismatic.

WHY YOU MUST PRAISE IN PUBLIC, CRITICIZE IN PRIVATE

No one likes to be told he or she did something wrong. We all like to think that we do things right, even though we know this is not always true. When we do something really wrong, our feelings are even stronger. Even if no one else is there, the person who criticizes us must be careful. Otherwise, this criticism could cause us to react strongly against the critic.

Sometimes, we must tell someone we lead that he or she did something wrong. When we do this we must think first. When we criticize, this criticism must always be done in a special way. I will show you what I am talking about shortly.

If you really want to make enemies and make your job of leadership difficult, just tell someone that he or she did something wrong in front of others. You will embarrass the person you criticize. Not only will this person not want to follow you, you may never be forgiven. If the others present happen to support the person you criticize, you may make even more enemies. So don't do it!

On the other hand, everyone likes praise. When we receive praise, we'd like everyone to know about it. So the simple secret is, praise in public, criticize in private.

Both of these concepts are crucial. You must let people know how they are doing. You want them to know what they did that was wrong so they won't do it again. But recognizing when someone does something right is equally important. You want them to know what they did that was right so they will do it again.

Kenneth Blanchard and Spencer Johnson, coauthors of *The One Minute Manager* feel that the second element of this concept is so important that they gave it a special name. They call it "catching someone doing something right."[1]

How to Minimize Negative Reactions to Criticism

Okay, so you are going to criticize only in private. How can you do it to minimize the chance of a negative reaction? It's easy. Just say something good about the person at the same time.

Mary Kay goes one better. She recommends saying two good things about the person you are criticizing, before and after. She calls this her "sandwich technique."

How does it work? Let's say that you must criticize someone you lead because he is twenty minutes late in getting to work every morning.

First, you find two things that this person does well. Let's say that this person writes very good reports and is always on time in providing them to you.

Since the purpose of the meeting is to criticize, you talk to him in private. You start with something he does right.

"Joe, you are doing a great job with your reports. They are always accurate and well organized. The advice you give us is a tremendous help in our marketing effort.

Now you put the meat in your sandwich. That's the criticism: "Joe, we also need your advice every morning. Your coming to work twenty minutes late every morning is hurting us. Sometimes I or others need you because a customer on the East Coast calls us. We have to make the decision without your advice, and we don't always guess right. We need you here on time every morning. That's what I expect from now on."

Finally, you complete the sandwich by adding the other thing that Joe does well. "You know because you are always on time with your reports, I rely on your advice in them completely. I couldn't do nearly as well without you, and neither could our organization."

Notice how the criticism is sandwiched between two compliments. That takes the sting out and lets "Joe" keep his self-respect. He knows that you value him and that he is important to the organization. He also knows that you want him at work on time.

Robert E. Lee's Most Difficult Criticism

General Robert E. Lee didn't use the sandwich technique, but he did understand the importance of giving strong praise along with strong criticism.

Remember the Battle of Gettysburg and how Lee's cavalry commander, Jeb Stuart, failed to provide information on the Union forces? Lee could have fired Stuart. Some commanders in the Army of Northern Virginia thought that Jeb Stuart should be court-martialed. But Lee would have lost a great cavalry commander. Still, Lee could not let Stuart's action pass without criticism. Had he done this, Stuart might have repeated it in the future. Major General Jeb Stuart, though only thirty years old was high-strung. If Lee was not careful in his criticism, Stuart might resign from the army anyway. Here's how General Robert E. Lee handled the situation according to famed author, Michael Shaara:

> "You were my eyes. Your mission was to screen this army from the enemy cavalry and to report any movement by the enemy's main body. That mission was not fulfilled."
>
> Stuart stood motionless.
>
> Lee said, "You left this army without word of your movements, or of the movements of the enemy, for several days. We were forced into battle without adequate knowledge of the enemy's position, or strength, without knowledge of the ground. It is only by God's grace that we have escaped disaster."
>
> "General Lee." Stuart was in pain, and the old man felt pity, but this was necessary; it had to be done as a bad tooth has to be pulled, and there was no turning away. Yet even now he felt pity rise, and he wanted to say, it's all right, boy, it's all right; this is only a lesson, just one painful quick moment of learning, over in a moment, hold on, it'll be all right. His voice began to soften. He could not help it.
>
> "It is possible that you misunderstood my orders. It is possible that I did not make myself clear. Yet this must be clear: you with your cavalry are the eyes of the army. Without your cavalry we are blind, and that has happened once but must never happen again."
>
> There was a moment of silence. It was done. Lee wanted to reassure him, but he waited, giving it time to sink in, to take effect, like medicine. Stuart stood breathing audibly. After a moment he reached down and unbuckled his sword, theatrically, and handed it over with high drama in his face. Lee grimaced, annoyed, put his hands behind his back, half turned his face. Stuart was saying that since he no longer held the General's trust, but Lee interrupted him with acid vigor.

"I have told you that there is no time for that. There is a fight tomorrow, and we need you. We need every man, God knows. You must take what I have told you and learn from it, as a man does. There has been a mistake. It will not happen again. I know your quality. You are a good soldier. You are as good a cavalry officer as I have known, and your service to this army has been invaluable. I have learned to rely on your information; all your reports are always accurate. But no report is useful if it does not reach us. And that is what I wanted you to know.

"Now," he lifted a hand. "Let us talk no more of this."[2]

I don't want you to think that only southern generals practiced this important rule of leadership. After the capture of Richmond and the pursuit of Lee's army, General Ulysses S. Grant concluded that one of his subordinates, General George Meade, had made a big mistake. Meade had issued orders that if followed, would have allowed Lee to escape. Grant immediately went in person to explain the situation to Meade, ". . . reaching his headquarters about midnight. I explained to Meade that we did not want to follow the enemy; we wanted to get ahead of him, and that his orders would allow the enemy to escape . . . Meade changed his orders at once."[3]

If you want others to do what you say, praise in public, criticize in private. And combine your criticism with praise.

WHY YOU MUST SEE AND BE SEEN

I don't care whom you are leading. You can't lead from behind a desk. In the four months before the allied invasion of Europe during World War II, General Eisenhower visited twenty-six divisions, twenty-four airfields, five war ships, and numerous military bases, depots, hospitals, and many other military installations. All of his senior subordinates maintained similar visiting schedules. He said, "There is among the mass of individuals who carry the rifles in war, a great amount of ingenuity and initiative. If men can naturally and without restraint talk to their officers, the products of their resourcefulness become available to all."[4] Eisenhower said that this promoted "mutual confidence, a feeling of partnership that is the essence of esprit de corps."[5]

You have to see those you lead yourself and let them see you. Robert W. Galvin, when Chairman of the Board and Chief Executive Officer of Motorola, Inc., said: "I believe we in top management must circulate."[6]

Tom Peters, whom I told you about earlier, believes this because he found seeing and being seen is an action taken by effective leaders in every successful company and organization he visited. As a result, Peters formalized the technique and gave it a name. He calls it MBWA, "management by wandering around."

If it weren't for MBWA, General Creech may never have discovered the supply problems he had when he took over TAC. He certainly could never have communicated his ideas so effectively. When you have a supply sergeant's chair exchanged for the chair of one of your generals, the news gets around.

And maybe that's the idea. When you go out and see and are seen by those you lead, you greatly increase the effectiveness of communications up and down the chain of command. You find out what's right and what's wrong in your organization. You can correct things instantly. You can dramatize your ideas to your followers. That way the word gets around . . . fast.

How General Patton Led by Seeing and Being Seen

As commander of the Third Army, General George S. Patton practiced MBWA. He found that his soldiers didn't always wear their heavy steel helmets. The helmet was an important factor for survival. More important was the implied lack of battlefield discipline, since wear of the helmet was required in combat by army regulations. Other things Patton saw also convinced him that discipline wasn't what it should be. Lack of discipline in combat cost lives and lost battles.

Patton took instant action to correct the situation. He issued orders that any soldier not wearing his steel helmet *and a tie* would be court-martialed.

Combat-dress etiquette dictates that officers be indistinguishable from the soldiers they lead. Otherwise, they could be singled out as targets by the enemy. Patton not only wore a helmet and tie, but fixed his jeep with flying flags. He wore a revolver on one hip and an automatic on the other. No one could mistake Patton on the battlefield, and his visits were legendary. His seeing and being seen helped make him a successful battlefield commander.

Patton said, "The more senior the officer who appears with a very small unit at the front, the better the effect on the troops . . . Corps and Army commanders must make it a point to be physically seen by as many individuals of their command as possible—certainly by all combat soldiers."[7]

While in Israel in 1972, I met another man who believes in seeing and being seen. A General Electric vice president, he was helping the Israelis with their General Electric-built J-79 engines. This man is an American by the name of Gerhardt Neuman.

Neuman was a refugee from Nazi German. During World War II, he was in charge of maintenance for General Claire Chennault's Flying Tigers in China.

Neuman had a problem with engine reliability. The engines of the P-40s that Chennault's flyers flew worked well enough on the ground. In the air it was another story. Sometimes they faltered just when needed during combat against the Japanese.

In other airplanes, a ground crewman could fly in the airplane to investigate the problem. But the P-40 was a fighter with a single seat. There was no space for anyone else. So Neuman's ground crews couldn't find the problem.

But Neuman believed in management by wandering around, or in this case management by flying around. He worked out a means by which he flew sitting in the pilot's lap. This method worked so well that it became the way all test flights were conducted. Soon all of Neuman's maintenance men checked out their aircrafts' engines in this way.

One of Neuman's managers told me that working for Neuman, you always came to work early no matter what job you had or where you worked. The reason was that Neuman always seemed to be on the spot earlier to greet you. It became a game. Neuman's people wanted to be at work early enough to greet him rather than be greeted.

You Must Know Who Your People Really Are

When you go out and see and be seen you not only learn what's going on, you learn who your people really are. A person isn't just a number with certain skills who is paid a certain amount of money and has certain seniority in your organization. A person is a man or woman of flesh and blood. He or she has a wife or husband, girl-friend or boyfriend, children, hopes, dreams, problems, victories, defeats, opportunities. Is it any wonder that leadership is complex—that a person may follow you in one situation and not in another?

To lead successfully, you must see every one of those who would follow you as an individual. For a start, while going out and seeing and being seen, you can learn the names of those you lead. It doesn't really matter how large an organization you lead. They say that Julius Caesar knew the names of thousands of his legionnaires. He called them by name, and they won battles for him.

Surely, if you expect those who follow you to know your name, they will expect no less of you. Learn the names of those you lead because they deserve it. Learn them because it will help you to get to know them. Learn their names because it will make your seeing and being seen even more effective.

My West Point classmate General Fred Franks led the VII Corps during Operation Desert Storm. In his book, *Into the Storm*, written with well-known author Tom Clancy, he says: "You have to know how subordinates communicate, and then you have to know how well they execute in leadership situations. You find that out by visiting their positions and talking to the troops and the small-unit leaders. In time you begin to get an idea of what your leaders are made of, how they issue orders, how they react in leadership situations; and you can determine from that what types of missions you're comfortable giving them in future combat situations."[8]

Douglas D. Danforth, Chairman of the Board at the Westinghouse Corporation, echoes Fred's remarks in the corporate environment: "The better the CEO knows his key people personally, the better he will be able to correctly estimate their strengths."[9]

So if you lead a large organization, you can at least learn the names of those you lead. And if you lead a smaller organization, how fortunate you are! You can learn much more about those who follow you. And the more you know, the more you will see and understand. The better you will know their strengths and weaknesses. The more others will understand what you want and how this fits into the organization's goals and objectives.

What if you are having problems with those you are leading? Isn't it better to stay out of the way for awhile? Shouldn't you avoid the chance of a direct confrontation? Management experts have discovered that even when you expect opposition, face-to-face communications improves the likelihood of understanding. When there are disagreements between you and those you lead, you should see and be seen as you have never done before.[10]

How Pizarro Succeeded by Facing Up to His Problems

In 1531, Francisco Pizarro, the Spanish conqueror, was faced with a general revolt. He and his forces were quartered on La Isla del Gallo (Rooster Island), north of Ecuador, prior to penetrating into the heart of the Inca empire. But many of his troops, even his leading commanders, thought that he had gone too far and had risked too much. They wanted to return to their ships and sail back to Spain.

Pizarro didn't avoid the problem. He sought out the rebels in their own place of meeting. There was a general murmur of disapproval on his arrival. "This doesn't concern you," one shouted. "We don't want to die for your glory," said another.

Pizarro ignored the disrespect and began to speak. "It is true there is great risk in what we do, and no man need be ashamed because he wants to go home. I want to go home myself. But we are under orders of the crown to explore and conquer this land. So I must stay until these tasks are complete. But perhaps you do not. Not every man has the courage to be a conqueror or an explorer. Those who possess such courage win wealth and fame. But not every man needs to win wealth and fame. Let us decide here and now whether you have the courage to win wealth and fame or will return home now."

Pizarro drew his sword and scratched a straight line in the dirt floor between himself and the would-be rebels.

"All those who are men who have the courage to win wealth and fame cross over to my side of the line," he said. "The others may return to the ships."

To a man, all crossed over, and this was the last time Pizarro's leadership was questioned.

By seeing and being seen, you can

- Know what's going on in your organization every day.
- Help those who need help.
- Get help from those who can supply help.
- Discover the real problems.
- Uncover opportunities you didn't know existed.
- Praise and recognize those who deserve it.
- Correct or discipline those who need it.
- Get your word out fast.

- Communicate your vision for the organization.

- Ensure everyone understands your goals and objectives.

Seeing and being seen sounds like a pretty simple action to take. It is. But by this simple action you will accomplish all of the above, and others will follow where you lead.

HOW TO USE COMPETITION TO MAKE STRIVING A GAME

Have you participated in a competitive sport? If not, I'm sure you have at least watched one. Competitive sports include everything from golf to football, from boxing to gymnastics. Competitive sports can be rough, fast, slow, require great skill, endurance, or knowledge. They can be played on the ground, above the ground, on ice, in water, or underwater. They can involve balls, rackets, carts, chariots, guns, cars, airplanes, boats, skis, skates, or ships. One ancient sport actually involved vaulting over live bulls.

Whatever the sport or the manner of its playing, all involve competition with one or more other human beings. The competition makes the sport exciting and fun. Competitive sports are not work, they are play. As a result, while work tires us, we can play at competitive sports on and on.

In this fact lies a secret that all of us can use to make the task we want to do fun, rather than work. All you have to do is make striving a game. Not possible with your kind of task, you say? Let me assure you that it's possible with any task.

Let me tell you first that in competition lie the secrets of setting records in everything in life. Records are set not on practice fields, but in real competition such as the Olympics.

At one time, it was thought that competition brought too much pressure to bear in learning. So a change was made. Students no longer received grades. Instead, their only grades were pass or fail.

Educators thought this would improve performance in the classroom and also in real learning. The idea was that instead of "wasting time" competing, students would be learning. What happened? The exact opposite. Not only did students participate to a lesser extent in the classroom, but objective tests proved that students didn't learn as much.

Scientists tell us that there are two types of stress caused by pressure. One kind is the bad kind of pressure. It is overwhelming and causes performance to fall off. Competition, however, is the good kind of pressure. In most cases it causes performance to increase.

How Eddie Rickenbacker Used Competition to Help Shoot Down Planes

Eddie Rickenbacker shot down twenty-six enemy airplanes to become our "Ace of Aces" during World War I. One day, his commander was killed in action. Rickenbacker became commander of the 94th Aero Squadron in France.

Combat losses were heavy. Worse yet, many pilots were being killed in noncombat aircraft crashes due to maintenance problems. The squadron was dependent on equipment provided by the French, as American airplanes weren't available. The pilots felt that they were not getting the best equipment. Morale was extremely low. At this point, Rickenbacker was made squadron commander.

"First I called the pilots together," he said. "I pointed out that our airplanes were the same as other squadrons at the front including the French. I asked them whether they felt that the French were better pilots. When they indicated that they felt that the 94th Aero Squadron had the best pilots at the front, I challenged them to prove it by a competition with the other fighter squadrons. It was simple to keep score. Whichever squadron shot the most planes down was the winner.

"Next I called a meeting of all our ground crews. I noted that without them, the pilots might just as well stay on the ground. I told them about the competition the pilots were in with the other combat squadrons. While they were part of this competition, I challenged them to compete with the other squadron ground crews. This competition was in number of aircraft fit for flight and in accidents due to maintenance.

"I knew from my racing days that competition works . . . that men will work harder when the goal is to beat someone else . . . even if it is a friend."

It goes without saying that under Rickenbacker's leadership the 94th Aero Squadron became the best American squadron in the war. And Rickenbacker used the same technique to build Eastern Airlines from nothing to one of the best-run airlines of his time.

General Bill Creech, the former Air Force commander who was so successful in the turnaround of a major air command, says this about the decentralized team approach he recommends: "Those critics say the team approach, and the comparisons it naturally yields, invariably create *'workplace competition.'* They further assert that this competition effectively rules out cooperation. . . . Those who make such assertions are wrong . . . in TAC, organizational harmony greatly improved. We also found that the new team-oriented comparisons helped rather than hurt overall cooperation and integration."[11] As he prepared to turn over his command, General Creech published a set of fifteen organizational principles. One was "Set up internal competition where feasible."[12] Remember, this is the man who took an organization with tens of millions of dollars in assets and tens of thousands of "workers" and in a time of declining resources caused measured productivity in some vital areas to increase as much as 6,000 percent.

If you want people to follow you, show them the competition and make your task a game. They'll follow your lead and make your organization a winner.

THREE ACTIONS TO TAKE WHENEVER YOU CAN

1. *Praise in public, criticize in private.* If people have earned your praise, let everyone know about it. Encourage others to earn praise also. If you have something to criticize, do it. But do it in private. Don't embarrass people unnecessarily. Frequently, just the fact that you are displeased is embarrassment enough.

2. *Take the time to see and be seen.* You've got to get around to really know what's going on—to fix what's wrong and to capitalize on what's going right. At the same time, you want to be seen. This provides additional opportunities to talk with and motivate every one in your group. And you can be sure that you will gain secondary motivation. "When I was talking with the boss yesterday...," is a phrase that will be repeated frequently.

3. *Use competition to make striving a game.* People love to compete. That's one of the secrets of successful products from professional sports to video games. You can make competition a positive force to reach your objectives.

When you complete this chapter, you will be ready for the influence strategies in the next two chapters. Mastering them will give you new ways for maximizing the potential in a wide variety of situations that require your leadership.

NOTES

1. Kenneth Blanchard and Spencer Johnson, *The One Minute Manager* (New York: William Morrow, 1982).

2. Quoted from Michael Shaara, *The Killer Angels* (New York: Ballantine Books, 1974), pp. 265–266. Used with permission.

3. Ulysses S. Grant, quoted in *Leadership Lessons from General Ulysses S. Grant* (Paramus, NJ: Prentice Hall, 1998), p. 197.

4. Edgar F. Puryear, *19 Stars: A Study in Military Character and Leadership* (Presidio, CA: Presidio Press, 1971), pp. 229–230.

5. Dwight D. Eisenhower, *Crusade in Europe* (New York: Doubleday and Co., Inc., 1948), p. 314.

6. Chester Burger, *The Chief Executive* (Boston: CBI Publishing Co., Inc., 1978), p. 48.

7. George S. Patton, as quoted in Alan Axelrod, *Patton on Leadership* (Paramus, NJ: Prentice Hall, 1999), p. 102.

8. Tom Clancy with Fred Franks, *Into the Storm* (New York: G. P. Putnam's Sons, 1997), p. 189.

9. Jerome M. Rosow, "A View from the Top," *Success* (February 1986), p. 69.

10. James M. Kouzes and Barry Z. Posner, "The Leadership Challenge," *Success* (April 1988), p. 69.

11. Bill Creech, *The Five Pillars of TQM* (New York: Dutton Books, 1994), p. 461.

12. Bill Creech in Tom Peters and Nancy Austin, *A Passion for Excellence* (New York: Random House, 1985), p. 240.

HOW TO LEAD USING DIRECT-INFLUENCE TACTICS

We lead others by influencing them. Sometimes this influence is accidental. When this happens, we may find that we have led others to a goal successfully with no conscious effort. Experienced leaders may also influence others successfully below their own level of consciousness. However, you cannot learn to lead this way, nor can you develop your leadership abilities. Also, even experienced leaders can frequently lead better by consciously planning and applying the tactics they use in influencing others.

LEADING BELOW THE LEVEL OF CONSCIOUSNESS

Leading below the level of consciousness is like driving a car. When we first learn to drive, we must consciously think about every single move that we make. We must think not only about pushing and pulling on buttons, levers, and pedals, but also navigating the vehicle to where we want to go in accordance with good driving practice and the law. In addition, we must think about avoiding collision with people, obstacles, and other vehicles.

Eventually, everything becomes habit and automatic and we don't have to think much about driving at all. We can successfully operate the car while thinking about work, carrying on a conversation with others, listening to the radio, or even learning a language on tape. We may get where we are going and not even remember turning on the ignition.

Once you are an experienced leader, or if you already are, you may not need to think consciously about influencing others. Like driving a car, you are "on automatic."

However, no one should rely on luck or accident for success in leadership. Also, even as an experienced leader (or driver) there are significant numbers of situations in which you cannot operate "on automatic." This is when you must consciously use your skill and apply the influence tactics.

More Reasons You Must Know and Apply the Influence Tactics

Understanding the influence tactics is important for two other reasons. First, leadership is not limited to leading those who formally report to you. Sometimes you must lead colleagues. At other times, you must even lead those to whom you report.

An understanding of the influence tactics is also important because their use must vary according to the situation and whom you want to influence. In some cases, one influence tactic is appropriate, and it will work wonders and enable your success. In a slightly different circumstance, the same influence tactic will result in failure.

A World War I German combat leader described a classic example of the use of different influence tactics in 1917 by a brigade commander.

Describing his three regimental commanders, the brigade commander said that his first regimental colonel wanted to do everything himself and always did well. His second colonel executed every order, but had no initiative. Finally, there was the commander of his third regiment. He opposed everything he was told and always wanted to do the contrary.

A few days later, the brigade came up against a heavily defended position that had to be attacked. The brigade commander issued different orders to each regimental commander.

To his first colonel he said: "My dear Colonel 'A,' I think we will attack. Your regiment will have to carry the burden of the attack. I have, however, selected you for this reason. The second regiment will be your boundary on the left. The third regiment will be your boundary on the right. Attack at 1,200 hours. I don't have to tell you anything more."

To his third colonel, who opposed everything, the brigade commander spoke quite differently. "We have met a very strong enemy. I am afraid we will not be able to attack with the forces at our disposal."

As he knew would happen, his third colonel didn't agree.

"Oh, General, certainly we will attack. Just give my regiment the time of attack and you will see that we will be successful."

"Go, then, we will try it," said the brigade commander, and he gave him the formal order for the attack that he had prepared previously.

As for the commander of his second regiment, he simply sent the attack order with more details than he had given his other commanders.

All three regiments attacked successfully.[1]

In this chapter, you will learn the four direct-influence tactics and how to apply them in practice over a variety of situations and leadership roles. Your proper use of these tactics will equip you with the arsenal to make you a powerful leader. In the next chapter we'll examine the indirect-influence tactics. With these tactics, you don't go after what you want directly, but others are influenced to your lead anyway.

THE FOUR DIRECT-INFLUENCE TACTICS

What are the four direct-influence tactics? Here they are:

1. Direction
2. Persuasion
3. Negotiation
4. Involvement

As we will see, not only are all of these influence tactics usable, but all are needed to properly lead under the many different conditions a leader may encounter.

How To Use the Direct-Influence Tactic Correctly

There are two situations in which simply giving orders with no discussion is your best choice. But first, in order to employ the direct tactic, you must have more power in the situation than do those you intend to lead. If you try to lead your boss this way, not only will you probably fail, but you may damage the relationship permanently.

The first situation in which you may want to use direction is where there is little time for using the other tactics. What you need done needs to be done now, with no time for discussion. In combat, the leader must frequently be authoritarian and rely heavily on direction for influence. There is no time for dilly-dallying when lives are at stake or when a slight delay can cause a major defeat. But as we will see, even in combat the direct-influence tactic shouldn't be used in all cases.

The second situation in which you should use direction is when the action you want done may be good for the organization, but is less desirable for the individual. You need a report typed by tomorrow morning, but your secretary has social plans for tonight. While you can try to use the other influence tactics first, eventually it may come down to using direction.

Unfortunately, the direction tactic is much overused. One reason is probably the popular image of the leader from the movies. The leader runs around barking orders, and everyone else simply falls into line and obeys. That's not leadership, that's Hollywood! As Dwight D. Eisenhower advised: "You do not lead by hitting people over the head—that's assault, not leadership."

In the military they say that the higher in rank an officer goes, the less you see him (or her, nowadays) bark orders. Of course there have been very effective generals, like Patton, who have barked orders. But in my experience, barking orders routinely is the exception, not the rule. And even Patton didn't bark out orders all the time. As one of his subordinates commented, "General Patton always started a briefing with a soft voice. . ."[2]

Many military leaders never lead this way. General A. A. Vandegrift was a Marine's Marine. He commanded at the Battle of Guadalcanal, one of the most famous Marine victories of World War II. It was there that he issued the order that ended with the stirring words: "God favors the bold and strong of heart."

Did General Vandegrift run around day in and day out barking orders? Here's what they said about him. You can judge for yourself.

"He is so polite and so soft spoken that he is continually disappointing the people whom he meets. They find him lacking in the fire-eating traits they like to expect of all marines, and they find it difficult to believe that such a mild-mannered man could really have led and won the bloody fight."[3]

Direction May Be Too Easy

Another reason that the direct-influence tactic is overused is that once you begin using it routinely, it becomes habit. It's so easy. You don't have to think about those you lead at all. You simply issue an order.

General Bernard Rodgers, who spent more than twelve years as a four-star general and senior Army commander, once jokingly said that his biggest shock after retirement was that he got into the backseat of his car, gave the order to go, and waited for the car to pull out. But, the car didn't move because for the first time in twelve years, he no longer had a driver.

Unfortunately, routinely using direction can have unwanted results. You may no longer get input from those you lead. "Fine," say your followers, "if that so and so wants us to do this and everything gets screwed up, it's not our fault." Mistakes you make that others might have caught are allowed to go on uncorrected. Soon, your organization is brought to a standstill. Yet everyone goes about following your orders to the letter. And that's just the trouble.

Erroneous Assumptions Could Cause Failure

When you use the direction tactic, you've got to make sure it's done in the right way. Many just give orders. They assume they are understood. They may not be.

Back in 1941, the nation was tooling up for World War II. Aircraft companies hired engineers as fast as they graduated. Unfortunately, some of the leaders in these organizations had not been given proper training in leadership. One new engineering supervisor in the Boeing Aircraft Company in Seattle was assigned five recently graduated engineers. On their first day of work, he dealt out jobs one after the other in an automatic fashion. He didn't explain them, and he didn't ask if those on the receiving end had any questions.

He handed one engineer a set of master aluminum "blueprints" for the B-17 engine. He told the new engineer, "I want these cleaned so there isn't a spot on them. And I want them finished by this afternoon. Now, go. Do it!"

These "blueprints" masters were aluminum engravings showing how the engine was manufactured and assembled. They were used as masters to print the paper version, which were used on the production line. The aluminum "blueprint" had picked up ink and grease. It was dirty from use. What was wanted was to clean the ink and grease off these valuable masters. They were valued then at about $10,000 each and worth many times that in today's dollars. But the supervisor said that he wanted them cleaned so "there wasn't a spot on them." The raw engineer, not understanding, got some Brillo® pads and with considerable effort polished the metal until it gleamed, scrubbing off the important engravings. He was fired when he presented them proudly to the supervisor at the end of the day. They probably fired the wrong man. When you use direction, be particularly careful not to make assumptions about your orders. They could cause a disaster.

Direction May Not Be in Your Own Best Interests

Another reason that you don't want to use the direction tactic under all conditions across the board is that, even if it works, it might not be in your own best interests. I knew a young lieutenant once that got so much into using the direction tactic that he used it not only in leading his subordinates, but his colleagues and superiors as well. The amazing thing was that for awhile he was successful. He was so bold in giving his direction, and was frequently right, that everyone just did what he wanted. That is, until he was relieved of command and discharged for receiving a bad officer's effectiveness report. What was his offense? The report didn't use these words, but it boiled down to one fact. He used what is a perfectly good influence tactic under inappropriate conditions. You can lead your boss and your associates, but rarely by giving orders.

Never make a habit of using direction as an influence tactic under all conditions. But when time is short, or the action you want done can hurt the person that must perform this action, the direct-influence tactic may be required.

WHEN AND HOW A LEADER MUST USE PERSUASION TO LEAD

Did you think a leader always has a great deal of authority with which to lead? Unfortunately, this frequently isn't true.

My friend and fellow West Point graduate Colonel Jack Gillette commanded fighter squadrons for years. As a squadron commander, Jack had a lot of authority. He commanded his fighter pilots, and they did what he told them to do.

One day Jack was assigned to duties as a program manager overseeing the development and testing of the F-111 airplane. This was back in 1969, when this airplane was new. There were two versions of the F-111. One was the straight-fighter version. Two squadrons of these aircraft participated in the strike against Libya some years ago. The other version, designated the FB-111, was a bomber that was used by Strategic Air Command.

Because of the two versions, Jack had two groups of pilots flying airplanes for his program, one for each version. Each group reported to a different Air Force colonel. But neither of these colonels reported to Jack. The fighter colonel reported to a general in Tactical Air Command. The bomber colonel reported to a general in Strategic Air Command. Jack, in Air Force Systems Command, was in charge of the F-111 test program. He told me that the only people he commanded was one secretary and one sergeant.

As Jack told me, "It's a real test of my leadership. When I want a test flight made, I can't order a single pilot into the air. I have to persuade either the fighter or bomber commander to do that for me."

Jack was successful because he is a superb leader. His dilemma, however, was not unique. It is familiar to tens of thousands of program managers in government and industry across the country. These leaders have authority over their programs, but no authority or limited authority over the people who work on them.

When Does Persuasion Work?

Persuasion can also work well when leading others who have similar or more power in the situation than you have. This is especially true when you have no other way of rewarding or punishing someone.

Let's say you are the leader of a group of volunteers, or must get other leaders at your level to follow you. Maybe you must induce a group of your superiors to follow your lead. In all these situations, consider persuasion as an influence tactic for getting others to follow your lead.

What means can you use to implement the persuasion tactic? One way is to convince through logic. Simply give the person you want to lead good reasons why he or she should do what you want.

What Baron von Steuben Discovered About Leading Americans

Baron Friedrich von Steuben came from Germany to help General Washington during our War of Independence. His contributions in helping Washington to create a disciplined army were significant. His influence can even be found in the way the Army does certain things to this day.

When General von Steuben first encountered American troops, however, he was amazed. "Back home," he wrote to a friend, "I need only say 'do this,' and the soldier does it. Here in America, I must also explain why and give good reason. Only then does the soldier do what I say."

Everyone wants to know why you want him or her to take a certain action. This is true whether or not you have authority over them. My personal feeling is that this is something you owe to those you would like to follow you. And giving reasons why has an important fringe benefit. When the situation changes and you aren't available to give new instructions, this person knows what you are trying to do. He or she can alter his or her actions based on why you wanted the actions taken in the first place. You will find that you and your organization will be much more successful at reaching goals than would otherwise be the case.

Another Way of Using Persuasion to Lead

Another way of utilizing the persuasion tactic is to emphasize your personal need or the worthiness of your cause. Remember the young bond salesmen who became the vice president in Chapter 1?

You can bet that in addition to speaking about competing with other company units he also talked about the advantages of having savings bonds. He might also have said something about his personal need as a new employee with the responsibility for heading up the bond campaign.

Have you ever been approached by a young door-to-door salesperson who emphasized his or her personal need? It may have been a young man or woman working his or her way through college by selling magazines. It could have been a Boy Scout or Girl Scout competing for an award. It might have been a high-school or college student gaining experience in real business. All these are examples of persuasion by emphasizing personal need. They are used because they work.

Persuasion Plays an Important Part in Winning Against Great Odds

One of the most valiant actions in English history was due partially to the use of leadership through the influence tactic of persuasion.

On January 22, 1879, the British force at Rorke's Drift in Natal, Africa was attacked by more than 4,000 Zulu warriors. These warriors were incredibly brave. During an earlier battle against several thousand British soldiers, they had been victorious.

The British force was not large. There were thirty-six men in the hospital with a surgeon, chaplain, and one orderly. There were also eighty-four infantrymen and a company of Natal Kaffirs. By the time the battle started, including the sick, the English had only 140 effective fighters.

There were two lieutenants. Lieutenant John Chard was senior by less than a year over Lieutenant Gonville Bromhead. Lieutenant Bromhead actually had more total service. He had twelve years to Chard's eleven. In addition, Lieutenant Chard was an engineering officer and held no command at Rorke's Drift. Lieutenant Bromhead commanded the infantry company.

Bromhead wanted to use his infantrymen independently. Using the persuasion strategy and good reasons, Chard convinced Bromhead to follow and accept his leadership. These were his senior in rank, that a fort defense represented an engineering problem, and of the need for urgency for one overall commander.

The battle lasted from the late afternoon until the following morning. The Zulus attacked repeatedly without regard to loss. When the battle ended at about seven o'clock in the morning, Chard had only eighty men left. But the fort held, and the Zulus withdrew.

The highest award the British have for heroism is the Victoria Cross. It is at the same level for heroism in battle as the Congressional Medal of Honor in the United States. Eleven Victoria Crosses were awarded as a result of this battle. This was more than had ever been given for a single engagement, and it was won by almost 10 percent of the soldiers who participated in the battle.

Both Chard and Bromhead received the medal, and both were promoted to brevet major.

The influence tactic of persuasion can be pretty important, even in combat.[4]

USING NEGOTIATION AS AN INFLUENCE TACTIC

Another important influence tactic is negotiation. Negotiation means that you influence by conferring with others to arrive at a settlement that you (and those you lead) find acceptable. It may involve compromise or exchanging something that the other person wants or wants done for what you want done.

Negotiation may be required under certain circumstances. Does what you want done offer little or no perceived benefit to the person or persons you want to influence? Do you and those you want to lead have about equal power? Can both sides help or hurt each other almost equally? If these are your conditions, you may need to use the negotiation-influence tactic.

Let's look at an example. In a university, the addition of new courses must be voted upon by all departments. New courses may be perceived as attracting students from one department to another. Thus there may be no reason for a department to vote for another department's proposal for a new course.

If you want to lead in getting the university to offer a new course, part of your leadership may involve using a negotiation tactic. How can you do this? You could offer to support another department's proposal for a new course. Or you could offer something else that the other department wants in exchange for its support for your proposal.

How George Washington Used the Negotiation Tactic in War

Is a negotiation-influence tactic ever a part of military leadership? Most certainly. It is necessary and used frequently when different types of forces such as army, navy, air forces, and marines are employed together. It is also used when forces of more than one nation are employed together in combined operations.

George Washington gave us a successful demonstration of the negotiation tactic in a battle that was important in winning American independence.

During the War of Independence, our French allies had a contingent of the French Army with General Washington under General Jean Rochambeau.

By the summer of 1781, the two allies realized that the British strength was divided into two strongholds: New York and Chesapeake Bay. These British forces were stronger than the allied American-French force. But together, the combined allied force was stronger than either British force if faced separately. If the two British forces could be cut off from each other they could be defeated individually.

The French had a strong fleet in the area of the West Indies under the command of Admiral François de Grasse. However, the hurricane season started in late summer and grew progressively worse in the fall. De Grasse did not want to get involved in a campaign in the north for fear of having his fleet destroyed by storms.

Washington's original plans called for defeating the British in the Chesapeake Bay area and then moving south for an attack on Charleston or the British base at Wilmington. He got de Grasse to support him by the negotiating strategy.

Washington wrote Admiral de Grasse: "If you sail north and can keep command of the sea during my operations against the Chesapeake Bay force, you can return to the West Indies immediately thereafter."

In other words, Washington let de Grasse off the hook for supporting other allied operations that year in return for his immediate services against the British Chesapeake Bay forces.

De Grasse answered Washington that his fleet would be available until mid-October.

On August 30, de Grasse's fleet arrived off Yorktown, Virginia. He also brought reinforcements and siege artillery. More important, he took command of the sea and isolated the British forces under Lord Cornwallis. Six weeks later Cornwallis surrendered.

The Battle of Yorktown is known as the decisive battle of the War of Independence. Based on the battle's results, the British opened peace negotiations the following spring.[5]

How General Eisenhower Used the Negotiation Tactic

Another military leader who was a master at leading through negotiation was General—later President—Dwight D. Eisenhower. During World War II, he commanded more than three million allied troops. Among the commanders of these allied armies were very strong personalities such as Patton and English Field Marshall

Montgomery. These men were experienced combat leaders. Commanding foreign troops is always tricky, because their senior most commanders usually have direct communication with the leaders of their governments.

For example, during World War I, General Pershing, commander of the American Expeditionary Force (AEF), was subordinate to the French Field Marshall Foch. Foch ordered Pershing to split up the American units as replacements for allied combat losses. Pershing refused and insisted that the AEF would fight as a unit, or wouldn't fight. President Wilson backed him up.

That meant that though Eisenhower might have the title of supreme allied commander, he had to be very careful of how he commanded.

To complicate his problem, Eisenhower himself had never been in combat. During World War I, he was such a terrific trainer and organizer that he was put to work as a twenty-three-year old lieutenant colonel getting tank troops ready for battle in France. Though he tried numerous times to get himself shipped to France, he spent the entire war stateside.

Yet Eisenhower led this incredibly large number of different soldiers in the largest invasion ever attempted. He was successful largely through using the negotiation strategy. He influenced by getting support of the leaders of the second-largest country contingent, the English. And he influenced the English by giving them the senior command positions under him.

If you want proof, you need only look at where Eisenhower's senior commanders came from.

Eisenhower's deputy commander was RAF Chief Marshall Sir Arthur Tedder. The overall commander of allied ground forces was British General Sir Bernard L. Montgomery. The invasion armada was under British Admiral Sir Betram Ramsay. Finally, British and American tactical air forces were commanded by RAF Marshall Sir Trafford Leigh-Mallory. There can be no clearer evidence of Eisenhower's use of the negotiation tactic.

How to Use the Involvement-Influence Tactic

If you can get others involved in what you want done, they will adopt your goal as theirs and become committed to its attainment. Because of this, involvement is a powerful influence tactic and usually can be combined fairly easily with one or more of the other tactics.

That's one of the secrets of a major element of Japanese management. The Japanese call this technique *ringi*. What Japanese leaders do is to take extraordinary pains to ensure that leaders and workers at all levels make an input into a proposed action. Until everyone has an opportunity to study and comment on the proposal, the action isn't taken.

Executives from other countries who do business with the Japanese sometimes get extremely frustrated with ringi. Decisions that take days in the United States may take months in Japan.

However, once the decision is made the entire Japanese organization is totally involved and committed to a successful outcome. The Japanese then implement their decision amazingly quickly and effectively.

In comparison, decisions made in American organizations are sometimes taken quickly, but are then very difficult to implement. The reason is that many members of the American organization are neither involved nor committed to the action or goal.

Ownership of Ideas and Leadership

Why is involvement so important? One dimension is ownership. We work and fight much harder for things that are our own. As a corollary to this, ideas from someone else do not become our own instantaneously.

Dr. Chester Karrass has devoted much of his life to the science of negotiation and has written several well-respected books on the subject. If you've flown the airlines in the last twenty years or so, it would be hard to miss his advertisements, or his slogan: "In business, you don't get what you deserve, you get what you negotiate."

Karrass cautions us to allow enough time when introducing new ideas. "Introducing ideas," he says, "is like introducing new friends. It takes time to know and understand people before someone else's friends become our friends as well. Therefore, when you introduce new ideas to someone else, you must give them sufficient time to get to know them before you can expect agreement."

So involving people succeeds as an influence tactic because it gives ownership to those you need. But we must allow sufficient time for this ownership to take place.

Employees See a Connection of Starbuck's Future and Their Own

In his book, *Pour Your Heart into It*, Starbucks' CEO Howard Schultz says, "If I hang my hat on one thing that makes Starbucks stand out above other companies, it would be the introduction of 'bean stock.' With it we turned every employee of Starbucks into a partner." Schultz goes on to say that privately held companies such as Starbucks at the time didn't have employee stock plans. But, continues Schultz, "My goal was to link shareholder value with long-term rewards for our employees. I wanted them to have a chance to share in the benefits of growth, and to make clear the connection between their contributions and the growing value of the company."[6]

Three Important Subsets of the Involvement Tactic

In her research, Pamela Cuming found that there are three subsets to using the involvement strategy to influence. These are[7]

- Sharing
- Enabling
- Cooperating

All three have to do with building on the ideas of others. You do this in such a way that your ideas, contacts, or other resources and those from people you lead are pooled and exchanged. As a result, something greater results that neither you nor those who follow you could come up with as well on your own.

The Importance of Sharing Information

Please note that sharing information with others is the opposite of the way many leaders mistakenly try to lead. These leaders hoard information and refuse to share it with anyone. They seem to think that if they keep information to themselves, they will look smarter than those they want to follow them.

How wrong they are! When you are the leader, it is those who follow you that make you look smart, or not, as the case may be.

If those who follow you make errors and look bad because they are missing information that you could have given them, you will ultimately suffer far more than they. This is because it is you who are responsible for everything your organization does or fails to do, and no one else.

I once saw a leader go to extraordinary lengths in using the involvement tactic and in sharing information with someone he led.

This leader was the manager of research and development for a company developing and manufacturing ear protectors for the hearing protection of industrial workers subjected to high levels of noise. His name was Bob.

A new government specification required increased levels of protection at both high and low levels of sound for one type of ear protector. This company had been unable to provide it despite an extensive research-and-development program. Thousands of dollars had been spent in trying all sorts of materials, to no avail. They all failed the acoustical test required by the government in either the high or low levels of sound at one or more frequencies.

I happened to be in Bob's office when the latest results from tests on several materials were brought in. Once again, all failed the test. However, as Bob pointed out to me, one material passed at all of the frequencies at the lower level. Another passed on all of the frequencies at the higher level. The obvious conclusion was to try the two in combination.

George, the project engineer, had been working so long and hard that he had looked only at the failed results and had not put two and two together.

Bob asked George to come to his office. I thought that Bob would point out the obvious and might even criticize George for failing to do a full analysis. At the least, I fully expected Bob to take the credit for the discovery of what ultimately was found to be the solution to the problem.

Boy, was I surprised.

Bob started by saying that he had been going over the results and was impressed at the thoroughness with which George was conducting the testing.

He looked at the results and said, "George, you know this is exactly how Thomas Edison would solve a problem. He would keep testing things and analyzing the results until he found the solution. I know you will eventually find the solution this way as well.

"Sometimes an analysis and comparison is as valuable as the test itself. I know you haven't had an opportunity to analyze these data yet, so here it is. Let me know if you come up with anything."

George left with the data. I stared at Bob in amazement. He only laughed. I ask him why he had shown George what he had shown me.

"Look, George is a good man. He's been working hard on this project for months. He wanted to get the results to me, even bad results, as soon as he could. So he didn't spend much time analyzing the data. Had he done this, he would have seen the same thing I showed you. Now he has the opportunity. It is only fair that George discover the solution. Besides, how much good to me would George be in the future on this project if his boss got the credit for solving the problem?"

Fifteen minutes later George called Bob enthusiastically with the same solution that Bob had shown me. Further, he had an idea for modifying the materials as they were used in combination to make them perform even better. As I said, the solution Bob had originally shown me was found to work. But George got the credit and continued to do good work as an engineer for Bob. He did such good work that both he and Bob were promoted. Bob eventually became president of that company. Are you surprised? I'm not either.

The Four Basic Influence Tactics that You Can Start Using Now

1. *Direction.* Use this tactic when time is too limited for the other tactics. Remember that you must have more power than those you lead to use direction effectively.

2. *Persuasion.* Use this tactic when your authority is limited and others have similar or more power in the situation than you. In this case, give others a reason to follow you and emphasize your personal need and the worthiness of your goals or objectives.

3. *Negotiation.* Use this tactic when the perceived benefits by those you want to lead are limited, and their power is about equal to yours. Offer something explicitly in exchange for their following you.

4. *Involvement.* This is a powerful motivator. Therefore, use it as a tactic whenever you can. All you need to do is give those you lead some ownership in your ideas, goals, and objectives.

Understanding the four direct-influence tactics will go a long way toward enabling high performance as a leader in a variety of situations. However, there are occasions when somewhat different leadership influence tactics are required. These are the three indirect-influence tactics that you will read about in the next chapter. You will also learn when to use them and when not.

NOTES

1. Adolf von Schell, *Battlefield Leadership* (Quantico, VA: The Marine Corps Association, 1982), p.15.

2. George S. Patton, quoted in *Patton on Leadership* (Paramus, NJ: Prentice Hall, 1999), p. 223.

3. *The Armed Forces Officer* (Washington, D.C.: U.S. Government Printing Office, 1950), p. 83.

4. Byron Farwell, *Queen Victoria's Little Wars* (New York: Harper and Row, 1973).

5. I gave many seminars and workshops as a result of the first edition of this book. On one occasion, I was invited to speak at the United States Navy Station at Yorktown, Virginia. However, in the first edition, the location of the Battle of Yorktown was identified as having occurred at "Yorktown, Pennsylvania." There is a York, Pennsylvania, but I can assure you that the Battle of Yorktown never occurred there. Actually, there were two Battles of Yorktown. The second happened during the Civil War. It transpired at the same place as the first. The Navy and invited notables from the city of Yorktown treated me well despite my mistake. However, they didn't let me forget. They gave me a nice plaque at the completion of my presentation with my name and the date of the presentation inscribed. In addition it had a map of Virginia with a large "X" designating YORKTOWN in large letters.

6. Howard Schultz, *Pour Your Heart Into It* (New York: Hyperion, 1997), excerpted in *Fortune* (September 29, 1997), p. 268.

7. Pamela C. Cumings, *The Power Handbook* (Boston: CBI Publishing, 1981), p. 100.

CHAPTER SIX

THE FOUR INDIRECT-INFLUENCE TACTICS

The four influence tactics you will learn in this chapter are not direct or straightforward regarding your aims, your means, or both. This does not necessarily make them wrong when they benefit those you lead. It does reemphasize that your leadership must be for the benefit of others, not yourself. Indirect tactics are more risky than the four direct tactics because

- They can cause negative feelings.
- They can cause a future lack of credibility.
- If the action they cause turns out to be wrong, you may not be forgiven.

The risk is acceptable when

- They are used for the primary benefit of your mission, task, organization, and those you lead . . . not yourself.
- The situations are dangerous or critical.
- The four direct-influence tactics either can't be used, won't work, or are less effective.

The Four Indirect-Influence Tactics

The four indirect-influence tactics are

- Indirection
- Enlistment
- Redirection
- Repudiation

Let's look at each of them in turn.

Using the Indirect-Influence Tactic

The indirect-influence tactic is used when your authority is limited in the situation and those you want to lead will resist a direct-influence tactic.

I heard a story once about a woman who was poised on the suspension of a bridge, about to commit suicide. A policeman below talked to the woman and tried to persuade her to come down with logic and failed. He tried to order her down. That didn't work either. He tried negotiation and involvement. Nothing. Finally, he called up and said: "Lady, you can jump if you want, but I sure wouldn't want to jump into that dirty water. It's full of sewage and garbage, and smells awful." She immediately hesitated, and then climbed back down, where the police officer was able to use persuasion to get her to safety. That's a good example of use of the redirection tactic.

Children Use the Indirection Tactic Frequently

Do you have children? You know when they begin to be particularly nice, offer to do extra work, or tell you how well you look, watch out! You are about to be led by the indirect-influence tactic.

Your children have no formal power in the family. As parents, the formal power is yours. But you are being led by the informal power of charm.

Do you know where you are being led? You may not know, but you soon will. Chances are your son wants to borrow the car, or your daughter wants to go out on a date in the middle of the week. Or, it may be something else.

My Twelve-Year-Old Son Got a Computer, and It Wasn't Even His Birthday

Nimrod is a biblical name. In the Bible, Nimrod was the first hunter. In Vietnam, my squadron, which hunted trucks at night in North Vietnam and Laos, were called "The Nimrods." So, I gave my son the name, although today he goes by "Nim."

When Nimrod was about twelve, he became very interested in computers. Neither my wife nor I owned one at the time, and they were expensive. Even a used Apple with laughable memory compared with today's systems cost a lot of money. Nimrod talked about computers all the time. He got books and magazines and read about computers. He took a special course on computers given at summer school for older students. He wanted a computer . . . badly.

Nimrod started saving his money. But there isn't lot twelve-year-olds can do to earn money. Even the paper routes of my youth, which was my way to cash, are generally no longer available. So, working every day after school, he started doing odd jobs going door to door. My wife and I calculated that at the rate he was going, it would take years for him to come up with the money. But he kept at it for several months, and continued eating, living, and breathing computers.

"Maybe we should just buy him one," suggested my wife. "No way," said I. "They cost too much money. He'll earn enough eventually." Yeah, right.

One day, I walked into his room to find it spotlessly clean. Moreover, not only was everything in order, but several tables had been set against the wall with nothing on them. A straight-back chair was placed before the center table.

"What's this," I inquired. Big mistake, that question. "It's for my computer," Nimrod answered. I turned around and left the room immediately. That afternoon, my wife and I got a "recycler" newspaper that listed used items for sale. That evening, Nimrod had his computer. Note, he had never asked for one. But, Nimrod had led us where he wanted using the indirection tactic.

If our kids did this all the time, it wouldn't work. Still, it's amazing how often we do allow them to lead us this way even though we may know what's happening. And so, Johnny gets to use the car and Sarah gets to go out Wednesday night even though we intended to encourage her to stay home and study.

When Washington Saved the Country with the Indirection Tactic

After the Revolutionary War, the Continental Army had not yet disbanded and Congress was slow in authorizing back pay. The righting of various other wrongs had been frequently promised by the Continental Congress, but had never been done.

The Continental Army officers knew that George Washington would never go along with seizing power from the civilian authority no matter how just the cause. They asked him anyway. They wanted to march on Congress and give Washington the title of "Dictator." This was wrong, it was treason, and he told them so, only they wouldn't listen. Moreover, he was no longer their official commander and so had no formal power over them.

They had a meeting to organize what amounted to a rebellion. Washington went. He hoped to dissuade them, and they actually let him speak.

Washington spoke to these officers for more than an hour. Remember, these weren't mercenaries or shirkers. Among them were many of the heroes of the revolution. Men such as Alexander Hamilton, John Knox, and "Light Horse" Harry Lee all listened to Washington. Washington talked about why they had fought, what would happen should they rebel, and what Congress was trying to do. It was to no avail. Too many times before they had received promises from Congress only to see these promises broken. These officers were determined to take the law into their own hands!

Finally, Washington reached into his cloak and pulled out a pair of spectacles. No one had ever seen Washington with spectacles before. In the thinking of those days, it was the kind of physical weakness that commanders didn't admit to.

As he slowly put the glasses to his face, he said his final words to his former officers. "Gentlemen, I have grown old in your service, and now I am growing blind."

There wasn't a dry eye in the house. Washington turned and left. At first there was only silence. Then, somebody said, "Oh, what the heck. Maybe George is right. Let's give Congress one more chance." The rebellion, of course, never took place.

Washington's officers didn't know that he had worn spectacles for years. Even his closest aides didn't know that he wore glasses. Washington judged that the loss of his vanity and the risk of his prestige in opposing this treason was a worthwhile price to pay for an America free from a military dictatorship. He used the indirection influence tactic to get what he wanted after direct tactics, such as persuasion, failed.

To use the indirection tactic, those that you want to follow must know what you want. Then, you do something that will influence them to do it without asking for what you want directly.

USING THE ENLISTMENT-INFLUENCE TACTIC

With the enlistment-influence tactic, you just ask. It works in situations where you don't have the power, or may have the power but may not want to use it. Just asking works in more situations than you might think. Not too long ago a social scientist looked at the motivation one person used in getting others to do things. He found that frequently the logic for persuading does not need to be perfect. The person doing the persuading has only to give a reason for wanting the action performed.

During one study, this scientist discovered that many people would allow someone to cut ahead of them in a line to make copies on an office copier only if a reason were given. Did the reason have to be compelling? Hardly. The person had only to say: "May I go ahead of you because I have to make copies?"[1]

I know this sounds crazy, but apparently the key was simply to give a reason, any reason. Just giving the reason was itself sufficiently persuasive. What the reason was wasn't particularly important.

How a Leader Got the "Black Sheep" to Risk Their Lives by Asking

Do you remember seeing the television series *Baa Baa Black Sheep* several years ago? That series was the story of Colonel Gregory "Pappy" Boyington, a unique Marine commander during World War II. Boyington led his fighter squadron, the Black Sheep, against the Japanese. Under Boyington's leadership, the Black Sheep became the highest-scoring squadron in the Pacific in enemy planes shot down. Yet the Black Sheep were all rejects from other combat squadrons, thus their name.

At one point, the Black Sheep had been in combat for a fairly long time. They received word that the following day they would withdraw from combat for rest and relaxation some miles behind the lines.

What do you think happens in a combat squadron when its members know that their last combat mission is over for awhile? Having been in such a squadron myself, I can tell you that if it can, the squadron makes one huge party. The consumption of alcoholic beverages goes up significantly. This is exactly what happened to the Black Sheep.

After several hours of partying, most were sleeping soundly, awaiting their coming departure in the morning. Colonel Boyington himself was about ready to turn in when he got a call from his commander on the main island. It was critical that a mission be sent to strafe a target near Bougainville in the dark before his squadron was flown to a rear area out of the combat zone in the morning.

Pappy Boyington couldn't believe his ears. He didn't know what to do. His entire squadron had just had the biggest party of their lives. They were now no longer disposed to walk, much less fly, on a combat mission. How could he get them to do exactly that? How could any leader get his subordinates to do anything under these circumstances?

Here's what Pappy Boyington did in his own words: "I walked up and down between the cots for some time, trying to think this thing out, occasionally looking at some of the nude bodies that were completely crapped out beneath the mosquito netting. These perspiring and motionless forms were dreaming of anything but a night strafing mission, I was positive. I didn't have the heart to order a flight, or to even ask the members who were assigned to my own flight to go with me.

"As I was thinking, I heard my own voice, not too loudly, and it said: 'Are there any three clowns dumb enough to want to strafe Kahili and Kara with me tonight?' "[2]

One of the Black Sheep looked up, blinked his eyes and said, "I'll go with you, Pappy." Two others mumbled something about "that sounds like fun."

Before you knew it, Colonel Boyington had his flight of Black Sheep. They went out together, and they strafed the two targets. They did combat again, even though a couple of hours earlier they had thought that their combat was over.

Pappy Boyington didn't give any better reason for strafing Kahili and Kara than the researcher did in asking to make copies. And, a night combat mission was certainly a lot more dangerous. Still,

Boyington's Black Sheep followed. Will such enlistment always work? Of course not. But, it can work, and like a doctor who must sometimes try different medicines before he or she finds the right one, the leader must do the same.

WHEN AND HOW TO USE THE INFLUENCE TACTIC OF REDIRECTION

Leaders using redirection don't want to reveal the real reason for the action they want done. They want to redirect those they lead because if they do not do this it will have a negative impact of one kind or another.

Let's say there are two organizations whose offices are located next to each other. The members of these organizations are constantly bickering. The fact that they are located so close to each other allows increased opportunity for hostile contact. So, having their offices moved away from each other physically separates the organizations. Does the memo announcing their move state that they are being relocated due to their bickering? Of course not. The stated reason is probably "efficiency," or "better space utilization."

Redirection is also used when firing senior managers. Senior executives are rarely officially fired. Rather, they are given new assignments. We say that they are "kicked upstairs."

This is a perfectly legitimate tactic with many advantages. We preserve the feelings of the fired executive to the maximum degree we can. We show others that people are important to us. We don't throw people away like old shoes when they fail. Finally, an individual unsuitable for one job can do a superior job at a different time and at a different place.

Remember Colonel Kyes, the wing commander who rebuilt the bomb wing in the Air Force back in Chapter 1? Colonel Kyes fired many people. Later, some were deservedly promoted to important jobs again by none other than Colonel Kyes himself.

Eisenhower's Use of the Redirection Tactic

In February 1943, Eisenhower met his first defeat in Tunisia when Rommel unexpectantly attacked and rolled back his line at the Battle of Kasserine Pass. After the battle, Eisenhower concluded that he had to replace one of his senior commanders, Major General Lloyd R. Fredendall. Fredendall was sent back to the States and replaced by someone whom everyone came to know—a fifty-six-year-old major general by the name of George S. Patton.

What happened to General Fredendall? He was eventually given a training organization in the States. He did such a good job that he was eventually promoted to lieutenant general.

How "Sam" Grant Used the Redirection Tactic

Ulysses S. "Sam" Grant was the man whom Lincoln finally found to beat Robert E. Lee. To beat Lee, Grant also used the tactic of redirection to influence his men.

At his first battle against Lee at the head of the Army of the Potomac, Lee won the day, and Union forces retreated. As they retreated out of the wilderness, the Union columns got only as far as the Chancellorsville House crossroad. There they encountered a squat, bearded general smoking a cigar and sitting on horseback. As the head of each regiment came abreast of him he took out his cigar and pointed to the right fork. That's where they went. They thought they were retreating, but the right fork led right back into battle against Lee's flank.[3]

Redirection can also be used to get the minds of those you lead focused on other things. One scene in the television series *Baa Baa Black Sheep* showed this clearly. One of Pappy Boyington's squadron members came to him with a problem. Thinking about his first combat on the coming day, this pilot was afraid to fight! Instead of consoling him, Boyington said only, "I think I have something that's going to help you."

With that, Boyington hauled off and decked him. Responding out of instinct, the pilot got up and punched Boyington. Before it could go further, Boyington pointed out that in the heat of battle he would forget his fears.

HOW TO USE THE INFLUENCE TACTIC OF REPUDIATION

In using the repudiation tactic, the leader gets someone to do something by disclaiming his or her own ability or power to do it. An analyst goes to his supervisor and asks for help in doing some problems. "Gee, I'd like to help," his supervisor says, "but I haven't worked this type of analysis in quite a long time. How would you approach them? Why don't you start out. Maybe I'll remember a little."

So the analyst begins to work the analysis. Whenever he gets stuck, his leader gets him going again. The supervisor used the repudiation strategy to get the analyst to learn to do the job while doing the job at the same time.

The repudiation tactic can also be used by subordinates to lead their bosses, or by managers to lead other managers. "Boss, I have a problem and I wonder how you would handle it?" The boss is flattered to be asked. Most bosses are more than willing to help out.

Peter Drucker's Example

Peter Drucker once pointed out that the empathy built with the boss in this way is probably more beneficial to the organization than the subordinate's always going off by himself and working out the solution without a consultation. That's not to say that a leader should never work out his or her own problems or that he or she must consult his or her boss about everything. But most executives probably do not consult with their bosses as much as they should.

In one company, Drucker commented on two vice presidents of different operating divisions. While equally competent and with similar backgrounds, each had an entirely different method of operating.

One consulted with the president of the company about his problems fairly often. He used the repudiation influence tactic to lead his boss. The other vice president did everything on his own. He kept the president informed about his decisions, but never talked over a problem with him unless the president requested it.

Both got equally good results. After three years, the president announced his retirement. Which vice president do you think he picked to replace him? Most of us thought it would be the executive who worked out all the problems on his own. However, according to Drucker, it was the one who consulted with him frequently.

The Repudiation Tactic and Boss Sponsorship

I believe that the reason the repudiation tactic can lead to support when used with your boss is that your boss becomes your mentor. Research of top managers both in and out of the military has discovered that no leader reaches the higher levels of the executive suite without a "mentor" or "sponsor." A mentor is someone who has found a subordinate to be someone who the sponsor thinks has special ability. The mentor keeps his eye on his protégé and in various ways helps his or her career along. Outside the military, mentoring has almost become structured in some companies.

General George C. Marshall carried mentoring to an art form. He kept his own list of up-and-coming young officers and their qualifications over a period of thirty years. When World War II came, General Marshall was Chief of Staff of the Army. His knowledge and sponsorship of the young officers he had noticed years earlier led to the elevation and promotion of men such as Eisenhower, Omar Bradley, Patton, and Mark Clark.

However, if you are going to use the repudiation-influence tactic with your boss, you must be extremely careful. You can use repudiation to lead your boss, but do not expect an automatic sponsorship. There is also the question of time and individual preferences. Your boss may prefer that you work out your problems on your own. Finally, if you force the relationship, you're going to get in trouble with your boss as well as with other managers at your level. Nobody likes what has been called variously "teacher's pet," "brownnose," or more kindly, "fair-haired boy."

Many managers use the repudiation tactic to lead other managers at their levels. Instead of competing in an area that the other manager does better, the good leader disclaims her own ability and in doing so gets her colleague to do what she wants.

"Joe, you're the best softball coach the company team ever had much latter than the rest of us. I'm going to recommend that you be named the coach this year again."

WHEN TO USE ONE INFLUENCE TACTIC OVER ANOTHER

One of the most valuable lessons you can learn about using the four direct- and the four indirect-influence tactics is that there is a time and place for all of them. If you have one tactic that you rely on almost all the time, you are almost certain to get into trouble. Stop and think if one of the other tactics might not be more appropriate and might not lead to better results.

Your selection of a particular tactic will depend on

- The individual personality of the person or persons you are leading.

- The frame of mind of the person or persons you are leading.

- Your current frame of mind.

- Your goals or objectives.

- The relative power between you and those you lead.

- The importance of time in the action you want taken.

- The type of commitment you require to complete your desired action.

- Rules, laws, or authority you may have in the situation.

The eight influence tactics can also be used in combination, or one after the other. It is worthwhile to reread how General MacArthur ensured that one of his new battalions was successful in its attack its first time in combat. See how many different influence tactics General MacArthur used in combination.

Certain influence tactics tend to work better than others as the situation changes. A new company or organization is formed. The leader emphasizes attracting qualified people. This requires persuasion tactics. As his organization grows, team building and the exchange of ideas becomes more important. Involvement tactics are more used. Now the organizational units are formed, and the biggest question is how the work should be divided up. This requires negotiation. Once the company is into production, tasks are more routine, but time is critical. This calls for more direction. Throughout, indirection, enlistment, redirection, and repudiation may be used.

THE FOUR INDIRECT TACTICS—WHEN OR WHEN NOT TO USE THEM

Remember that indirect tactics are risky. They should be used only for the benefit of your people or your organization, never of yourself. They are most suitable for situations where the four direct-influence tactics either can't be used, won't work, or are less effective, or to make direct tactics more effective.

• Use indirection when your authority is informal, rather than formal, and direct tactics haven't worked or may arouse resistance.

• Use enlistment when you don't have the power, or it is undesirable to use the power you have in a particular situation.

• Use redirection when you don't want to reveal the real reason for the action you want done.

• Use repudiation when it is important to disclaim your own power or ability to get something done.

One tactic is not the best under all conditions. Any of these tactics may be the best depending on a variety of factors. So in every case the effective leader must consider all of his or her options and all factors in deciding which tactic or combination of tactics to use.

Now you are ready to strengthen your leadership self-confidence for increasingly more difficult leadership tasks. To do this, turn to Chapter 7.

NOTES

1. Robert B. Cialdini, *The Psychology of Influence*, rev. ed. (New York: William Morrow, 1993), p. 4.

2. Gregory Boyington, *Baa Baa Black Sheep* (New York: Bantam Books, 1977), p. 185.

3. *The Armed Forces Officer* (Washington, D.C.: U.S. Government Printing Office, 1950), p. 86.

CHAPTER SEVEN

HOW TO DEVELOP YOUR SELF-CONFIDENCE AS A LEADER

There is an old story told about the Texas Rangers. It happened around the turn of the century. One of the wild gangs that roamed the old West took over a small Texas town. They shot up the bar, threatened the citizens, and drove the sheriff out of town. In desperation, the town's mayor telegraphed the governor, pleading that he send a detachment of Texas Rangers to right the situation. The governor agreed that the problem called for the famous Rangers and promised that a detachment would be on the next day's train.

The mayor himself met the train on which the Rangers were to arrive. Unbelievably, only one Ranger got off the train.

"Where are the rest of the Rangers?" asked the mayor.

"There aren't any," was the answer.

"How can one Ranger handle the gang?" asked the mayor indignantly.

"Well, there's only one gang, ain't there?" replied the Ranger.

This story may not be 100 percent true, but it is based on fact. Less than 100 Rangers protected the entire State of Texas. And no Ranger felt himself outnumbered, though he might be working alone. The Ranger would look the situation over and do what had to be done. He would lead posses, motivate and organize disheartened citizens, and guide lawmen. The situation was almost always dangerous. Yet the Ranger routinely led and directed others in life-and-death situations. From such facts came legends, such as the story I've told you, or the fictional hero that you may have heard of. His creator called him "The Lone Ranger."

WHAT IS THE SECRET THAT EMPOWERS LEADERS?

How is it possible that leaders take charge and assume responsibilities for lives, jobs, and billion-dollar companies? How is it possible that leaders can take responsibility for the future of nations, if not of humankind itself? How is it possible that leaders sometimes lead thousands or even millions of men and women in accomplishing something? Yet they may do all these things seemingly without blinking an eye. Where do they get such tremendous self-confidence?

Self-Confidence Comes from Knowing That You Can Succeed

An old Air Force training manual on leadership says, "No man can have self-confidence if not convinced in his own mind that he is qualified to perform the job he is assigned."[1]

It's a fact. If you know that you can succeed at something, then you will have self-confidence that you can do it. The truth is, it is impossible not to. So the problem is how can you know you will succeed before you actually try something?

General Curtis LeMay built the Strategic Air Command into the mightiest military force ever forged. Later he became Air Force chief of staff. Before World War II, he was a thirty-year-old captain and a B-17 navigator. Officially, he led only himself. Five years later, he was a major general leading thousands. He was not only responsible for their lives and well-being, but for the success of missions crucial to the outcome of the war.

Early in the war, LeMay was sent to Europe as a colonel and group commander. The bombing results before LeMay arrived were terrible. This was due to heavy concentrations of antiaircraft artillery efforts by the Germans.

"You can't fly straight and level for more than fifteen seconds," the "old-timers" told LeMay. "If you do, you'll get shot down."

A bomber needed to be a stable platform to deliver its bombs accurately. The bombardier had to identify his aiming point and accurately determine the winds that would affect the bombs after release. So the plane had to avoid evasive action for a lot longer than fifteen seconds. Otherwise, the bombardier had no real chance to hit his target.

LeMay looked at his losses and at the results. Because results were so poor, his planes had to return to the same targets again and again. The bottom line was that he had high losses as well as poor results due to the repeated missions.

He soon gave new orders. "Every plane will fly straight and level for at least ten minutes prior to 'bombs away.' " The experts gave him warning that his entire force could be destroyed. LeMay listened to the experts, but remained convinced that he was right.

His crews bombed after a ten-minute straight-and-level run from an initial point. The bombs hit accurately on the target. Although losses per mission increased, losses for each target destroyed declined significantly. Eventually, LeMay was promoted to brigadier general.

Two years later, LeMay was sent to the Pacific Theater as a major general to head B-29 operations against Japan.

The B-29 was a remarkable airplane. It was designed as a "Superfortress," with guns bristling from all quadrants. Its four powerful engines were designed to take the plane at an altitude far above the effective range of the antiaircraft guns. The B-29 had a sophisticated pressurization-and-oxygen system and in many other ways was optimized for use as a high-altitude bomber.

The B-29 was an expensive airplane for those days, so much so that General Hap Arnold, commanding general of the army air forces told LeMay that the B-29 should be treated differently from other less-expensive aircraft. Arnold felt that the loss of a single B-29 in combat or by accident should require more than a routine investigation. He told LeMay that he should consider treating the loss of each B-29 in the same way that the navy treated the loss of a capital ship such as a carrier or battleship.

LeMay began his operations. Once again, bombing results were poor. The culprit now wasn't antiaircraft artillery. The B-29 flew well above that. The problem was wind shear. The winds at the altitudes that the B-29 flew were vastly different from the winds at the lower altitudes above the target. Also, the winds acted on the bombs for a much longer time than on bombs dropped at lower-release altitudes. So the bombardiers lost control of where their bombs hit. They might hit anywhere, and they definitely weren't hitting their targets.

LeMay looked at the situation and listened to the recommendations of the crews and his staff. Then he made his decision. He ordered all oxygen and pressurization equipment removed. He ordered the guns removed. Since there were no guns, the gunners wouldn't need to go either. Removing all of this weight allowed more bombs to be carried. Then he proposed that his B-29s bomb, not at 29,000, but at 7,000 feet.

Again, experts told him he was wrong. They told him he would lose his entire fleet of aircraft. They told LeMay that General Arnold would relieve him of command for wasting the lives of his crews and not using the expensive high-altitude and defensive capabilities built into the airplane.

LeMay ordered his crews to bomb at 7,000 feet. The results were devastating . . . to the Japanese. LeMay got far greater results for lower losses than any air campaign in the war.

How did General LeMay summon the courage and self-confidence to make these decisions and take these great risks? Where did such self-confidence come from in an individual who only a few years earlier commanded a single group and only a few years before that commanded nothing?

Without a doubt, in both instances LeMay believed he would succeed before he gave the orders to carry out his instructions. What gave him the idea he would succeed?

How to Know that You Will Succeed Ahead of Time

There is an old saying that nothing succeeds like success—success breeds success, or successful people tend to become more successful. If you have been successful in the past, you have a better chance of being successful in the future.

But how can you become successful until you are successful? It's like the chicken and the egg. Fortunately, you can have a little success before a big success. And a little success counts just as much as a big success as far as our belief system goes. That means if you can win little victories in being successful at something, your psyche will believe that you can accomplish even greater things in the same area. Moreover, you will project this inward feeling outward, and others will begin treating you differently.

Famed bodybuilder and movie star Arnold Schwarzenegger describes how his confidence began to develop while still in high school: "Before long people began looking at me as a special person. Partly this was the result of my own changing attitude about myself. I was growing, getting bigger, gaining confidence. I was given consideration I had never received before . . ."[2]

Many leaders are trained this way. They acquire their self-confidence by leading successively larger organizations with greater responsibilities. At every step their beliefs grow that they can be successful. As we have seen, belief that you will be successful leads to the self-confidence necessary to do the job.

You Don't Need to Be an Expert in Everything

It used to be thought that leaders grow into their jobs because of the technical experience and product knowledge they acquire at each step. However, in this age of technical specialization, it is virtually impossible to be more of an expert in everything than those you lead in most leadership jobs. This means that the technical knowledge is of far less importance than is how you train your belief system.

As a reserve air force officer, I worked for a successful female general officer who commanded important research and development organizations. Yet, her background was not in engineering, but in personnel.

A good example from industry would be John Sculley. He left a successful career as a senior executive with Pepsi-Cola to become the president of Apple Computer. Other than the fact that they are both products, the difference between computers and soft drinks are far greater than their similarities. Yet Sculley was also successful for many years as the leader (CEO) of Apple. Similarly, Carleton Florina, who became the first woman to lead a blue-chip firm when she left Lucent Technologies (communications) to become CEO of Hewlett Packard (computers), also was no computer expert when she arrived at Hewlett Packard.[3]

You May Not Have the Opportunity to Grow into a Leader

Unfortunately, many individuals may not have the opportunity to be trained by leading successfully larger organizations. Some individuals are so valuable to their bosses that they can't be spared for jobs where they would lead organizations. Others are overlooked until later in their careers. Then they had better be ready, whether they led smaller organizations or not.

Want an example? Look at General of the Army Dwight David Eisenhower. By the time he was elected President, Eisenhower already had a lot of experience in leading men and women in very large organizations. However, as we will see, he lacked some experience that many would consider important before he became a general.

In 1940, General Eisenhower was a lieutenant colonel. Despite many requests to be sent overseas during World War I, he spent the entire war training troops in the United States. He never saw combat. Between wars he did valuable work in a variety of staff jobs. He was so valuable, in fact, that he despaired of ever being assigned again to command troops.

With the buildup just prior to the war, he was assigned to the general staff as a colonel in 1941 reporting to the Army Chief of Staff, General George C. Marshall. Marshall promoted him successively to brigadier general and major general. A year later, after Eisenhower completed plans for joint-allied operations in Europe, Marshall sent him to London as the Commanding General, European Theater of Operations. The year after that he commanded the allied invasion of North Africa, and eventually became the Supreme Commander for the allied invasion of Europe. Finally, he wore five stars as a general of the army.

Please note that after years of staff positions and never having been in combat, Eisenhower eventually commanded and led more than three million fighting troops of many different nations. Then later, as president, he went on to lead the most powerful country on earth.

This Man's First-Line Responsibility Was for an Entire Company

Peter Drucker, the famed author, professor, and management consultant, once used a similar case study from his personal experience in a graduate course that I was privileged to attend at Claremont Graduate University in the mid-1970s.

Like Eisenhower, a company executive with legal training had spent his entire career on staff. Then one day, as a senior staff vice president, the board of directors elected him president of the corporation. This was his first real-line job, and like Eisenhower, he was leading thousands.

FOUR WAYS TO BUILD YOUR SELF-CONFIDENCE AND YOUR LEADERSHIP SKILLS

How do leaders get the self-confidence they need to lead? How do leaders like this new company president, General Eisenhower, and hundreds of others acquire the belief in success necessary for the self-confidence to do the job?

I'm going to give you four ways to build your self-confidence and develop your leadership skills. President Eisenhower and thousands of others have used these methods. If you adopt them, you will develop your self-confidence as a leader by numerous smaller successes. Every time you practice them, your belief in your own success will be strengthened. You will become a powerful leader. Like General Eisenhower, you will be ready to assume major leadership responsibilities because you will have the self-confidence to do it.

After returning to troop duty after more than eighteen years on various staff assignments, General Eisenhower wrote: ". . . I have in the few short months I have been allowed to serve with troops, completely reassured myself that I am capable of handling command jobs."[4]

Eisenhower was a lieutenant colonel at the time, but he already had the self-confidence in his own leadership for higher levels of command.

The four ways are

- Become an uncrowned leader.
- Be an unselfish teacher and helper of others.
- Develop expertise.
- Use positive mental imagery.

Take Advantage of the Fact that You Don't Need to Be a Manager to Be a Leader

The first way to develop self-confidence while you develop your leadership skills is to become an uncrowned leader. There are hundreds of opportunities for you to become a leader if that is what you want. I promise you that if you stop to look you will find at least one opportunity, and probably even more, every day. The truth is, people around you are crying for you to help them by seizing the opportunity to lead.

Remember, you don't have to be a manager to be a leader, and as I pointed out in an earlier chapter, the two are not even the same. Being a manager has to do with doing things right. Being a leader has to do with doing the right things. You absolutely do not need to have an official position as a paid manager to be a leader.

Can You Become an Uncrowned Leader?

What is an uncrowned leader? An uncrowned leader means that you will seek out and accept leadership jobs outside your normal responsibilities. You may or may not get paid in dollars for your accomplishments as an uncrowned leader. But the self-confidence you will get from doing uncrowned leadership jobs and the skills you will acquire will more than make up for the money.

How to Become an Uncrowned Leader

The first rule for becoming a successful uncrowned leader is to cheerfully accept responsibility on the job. Even more than accepting leadership responsibility, you must seek leadership responsibility every chance you get.

Remember the young manager in Chapter 1 who was promoted because he did such a great job in leading a bond drive? Well, the bond drive falls into the uncrowned-leader category. You can do the same thing as that young up-and-comer. I don't mean that you necessarily must lead a bond drive. There are lots of other opportunities.

Maybe there is a special report that needs to be done. Perhaps the boss is looking for someone to organize or coach your company's sports program. Does your office want to buy a new computer? Who's going to handle the job of selecting and buying it? Do you have office parties or weekend get-togethers? Entertainment-committee chairpeople are leadership positions also. Every organizing opportunity is another chance to be an uncrowned leader.

And the more you do this, the easier it gets, the more others will look to you as their leader, and the more self-confident you will become in your ability to lead.

How to Find Uncrowned Leadership Jobs

Your uncrowned leadership jobs don't need to be at work. There are cases every day where there are immediate problems that need to be solved and a need for a leader to help others to solve them.

Look around and you will see that everyone is looking at everyone else to lead. No one seems to know what to do. Do you know what to do? Are you at least willing to try? If so, you will be instantly and automatically promoted to uncrowned leader.

The strange thing is that in most cases you will discover that it is not that no one knows what to do. It is that no one wants to do the work or to take the responsibility for doing whatever needs to be done. Under these circumstances, you will be amazed at how ready others are to follow your lead.

You Don't Need to Fight for Uncrowned Leadership

Please don't misunderstand me here. There are also situations in which you find yourself where it seems that everyone wants to lead.

In some of these cases, people want to lead so badly that they will actually fight each other to do so.

You may or not be able to help out here as the group's leader. Whether you can or not, you are unlikely to be asked. When you find yourself in this kind of situation, my advice to you is to sit back and stay out of the fight. If the situation is so critical that some act needs to be done, do it yourself. Help the group as best you can, but don't compete for leadership. No matter how terrific a leader you are, you can't and won't lead in every situation you find yourself in. But that's not important. There are plenty of uncrowned leadership opportunities around.

As marine corps Colonel Al Garsys, my good friend and Industrial College of the Armed Forces classmate, says, "I can lead, and I can follow. An important aspect of leadership is knowing when to do which."

More Uncrowned Leadership Opportunities

Since there are far more uncrowned leadership opportunities than there are leaders, you will find opportunities to lead everywhere. You will find many opportunities where you live. There are neighborhood committees such as the "neighborhood watch" to help your local police guard against crime, there are neighborhood committees to beautify the neighborhood, get out the vote, and many others. There are numerous committees that require leadership positions if you live in an apartment house or condominium.

You will find other opportunities to lead in your church or synagogue, professional organizations, trade associations, political organizations, Boy and Girl scouts, and many others.

Believe me when I tell you that there are many more uncrowned leadership jobs than there are leaders to fill them. Look for unpopular jobs that no one wants to do. Volunteer to do them, and have fun doing them. Your self-confidence will soar as you become more and more successful as a leader.

BE AN UNSELFISH TEACHER
AND A HELPER OF OTHERS

In the first chapter, I explained that we succeed in life only to the extent that we help others succeed in their lives. That's true whether you are a leader of men and women in combat, in the office or boardroom, or even an author of a book on leadership.

If I am successful in helping you to reach your goals in life as a leader, you will make me successful in my goals as an author as well. That's how life works.

So to become a successful leader there is something you must do. You must give up some of your time, some of your resources, and some of your self so that others can succeed.

In doing so, you will develop the self-confidence and success in uncrowned leader jobs without which you cannot move on to bigger leadership jobs in the future.

An Officer and a Gentleman Is First and Foremost a Leader

Did you see the movie *An Officer and a Gentleman?* In it, the hero, played by Richard Gere, does very poorly in naval officer training. He fights and is disrespectful to his superiors. Contrary to regulations, he shines the shoes of his classmates for money. The only thing he does right is the obstacle course. On the obstacle course, he is really good. He is so good that it appears he will set a training record when the class is required to run it officially.

Then he gets into serious trouble when he challenges the noncommissioned officer in charge of his training to a karate fight. He is certain to be eliminated from officer training. However, while his dismissal is pending, his class runs the obstacle course for the record.

One of his classmates is a woman who always has trouble climbing over one of the obstacles. As the hero runs on to set his record, she becomes stuck on this obstacle. It's the hero's moment of decision. What will he do? The only thing he had done well in the entire training program was the obstacle course. Perhaps if he sets a record, he will not be dismissed.

The hero stops and goes back to help his classmate, though he knows this will cost him the record he had hoped to set.

It is this one act of helping someone else that causes those who have authority over him to let him graduate and become "an officer and a gentleman."

This is exactly what I am talking about. If you want to build your self-confidence so that you will be a great leader, teach and help others, even at cost to yourself.

Teachers and Leaders in the U.S. Army

Back in 1932, an article on the U.S. Army appeared in the German journal *Militär Wochenblatt*. The article was written by Captain Adolf von Schell of the German Army. He had attended and lectured at the U.S. Army's Infantry School at Ft. Benning, Georgia.

Captain von Schell stated that the chief role of the American regular officer was, "teacher and counselor." He went on to raise an important question. "But if the American officer is primarily a teacher with his principal training in schools, does sufficient time and opportunity remain to develop him as a leader?"

Von Schell concluded that while everything was done to train American officers as both teachers and leaders, the training of both at the same time was not possible.[5]

Less than ten years later, men such as Marshall, MacArthur, Eisenhower, Patton, and "Hop" Arnold and numerous others proved von Schell wrong.

Many Teachers Became Great Military Leaders

Perhaps it is no accident that many teachers in civilian life have made good military leaders. "Stonewall" Jackson, the hero of the

Confederacy, was a professor at Virginia Military Institute before the Civil War.

In the same war, Colonel Joshua Chamberlain, commander of the 20th Maine, saved the Union line on Little Round Top on the second day of the Battle of Gettysburg. Chamberlain had been a professor of rhetoric at Bowdoin College. He finished the war as a major general.

Robert E. Lee had been superintendent at West Point before the Civil War. Lee turned down offers of considerable sums of money to become the president of a small college.

Of our World War II leaders, almost every one had taught somewhere, whether it was at West Point or Annapolis, a civilian institution, the infantry school, or one of the many military colleges teaching staff or command.

Please don't think my words are too much self-serving when I remind you that your author is also a university professor—and was a navigational and combat flight instructor as well.

Why is experience as teacher of such importance? Because teaching is a more structured way of giving of yourself to help others. In teaching or helping others, you will gain additional success and confidence that will help you as a "paid" or official leader.

WHY YOU SHOULD DEVELOP YOUR EXPERTISE . . . IN SOMETHING

Research has demonstrated conclusively that there is an important source of power that will automatically attract others to you and make you their uncrowned leader. That source of power is expertise.

What is expertise? Expertise is in-depth knowledge or skill about a subject. Expertise can be on any subject: marketing, flying, warfare, management, stock management, record keeping, investments, buying a car, getting a loan, bowling, baseball, and so forth. Expertise can also be on what to eat, how to jog, or even the best way to mow your lawn. Expertise can be about anything human beings do.

Expertise and Its Ability to Make You a Leader

You must understand one important fact about expertise and its ability to make you a leader. Any expertise will cause people to seek you out as a leader. However, the frequency that people make you a leader because of expertise depends on one factor. That factor is how relevant your expertise is to the people around you.

Let's say you have expertise as bowler. Many people will seek you out and make you a leader—if you are in the company of other bowlers. If you want to be an uncrowned leader in a group that has few bowlers, don't depend on bowling expertise. Few will be interested!

To maximize your leadership opportunities through expertise, be sure that your expertise is relevant to the group, that your expertise matches the needs of the people around you.

If you have expert knowledge of how to do something important to the group, there isn't any question but that you'll be sought out as a leader. You will have increased opportunities to lead, and you will gain self-confidence as you do this.

How a Young Lieutenant Became a Major in Three Years—in Peacetime

During my first flying tour of duty in the Air Force, I saw a young lieutenant join our wing. He became an expert navigator. Three years later this young lieutenant was a major, because of his special expertise in navigation, which everyone was interested in.

During World War II, young men barely out of high school became colonels through their expertise at various tasks. Many in their early twenties advanced rapidly because of their ability to fly fighter aircraft and shoot down enemy planes. Robert S. McNamara became President John F. Kennedy's secretary of defense. During World War II, McNamara advanced from the rank of captain to lieutenant colonel in four months due to his expertise in mathematical techniques of analysis.

How George S. Patton Became a General

Certainly one factor that led to Patton's promotion to general just before World War II was his expertise with tanks. During World War I, George Patton had been a full colonel at the age of only twenty-nine. He had led America's first tank unit in combat. However, due to budgetary cutbacks, the army had to cut back on tanks. Patton went back to the horse cavalry and returned to the rank of first lieutenant. By 1940, he had worked his way back up to colonel. Than the army needed someone with tank expertise. Patton was one of the few senior officers who had the expertise that was needed. The army quickly made him a general.

How Expertise Helped Others on Their Way to the Top

Many "fast burners" in industry got to the top rapidly for the same reason. These include Steven Spielberg, CEO of DreamWorks; Bill Gates, CEO and founder of Microsoft; Steven Jobs, who founded Apple; Mary Kay Ash, founder and CEO of Mary Kay Cosmetics; Lee Iacocca, the man who saved Chrysler; Frederick Smith, founder and Chairman of Federal Express; and many others. They all shared a common attribute. They had expertise in a topic that was of some importance to others.

How Ray Kroc Used Expertise to Build McDonalds

Did you think that Ray Kroc, who founded McDonalds, became a millionaire many times over simply because he went into the hamburger business? Not on your life! Many companies made hamburgers before McDonalds. And while McDonalds was growing every year, they were losing money.

No, Ray Kroc didn't invent the hamburger. But Kroc brought a new dimension to the hamburger business because he had developed a special expertise. He not only knew how to make good hamburgers, he knew how to have others make identical high-quality hamburgers at low cost. He used a combination of unique instruction, quality control of methods and franchisees, and techniques such as special measuring cups. Through his methods, even a high-school student could make quality hamburgers. It made no difference whether the McDonalds was located in the north, south, east, or west. The hamburgers were always the same, and they were always good.

If you want people to acknowledge you, even seek you out, as their unofficial leader all you need to do is develop a needed expertise.

Revealed: The Secret About Acquiring Expertise

Now listen. Here's what I find interesting about acquiring expertise. Not only is it interesting, it seems to be a big secret because not too many people seem to know it. You can become an expert in just about anything in only five years or less. There is only one requirement. You must put forth the effort.

Proof that You Can Become an Expert in Anything in Five Years

Want proof? Steven Jobs and Steven Wozniack were college dropouts when they founded Apple Computers and became multi-millionaires. But they had been working on building computers even in high school. The time it took them to become computer experts? About five years.

Dr. Kenneth Cooper has probably made more contributions to health by preventing heart attacks than any man alive. It was Cooper who conducted the research and developed the concept of aerobic training when he was a flight surgeon in the Air Force. His numerous books, lectures, and aerobic center in Dallas, Texas, have helped millions on the way to good health and have prevented millions more from unnecessary, premature death. His efforts got the whole country jogging, walking, cycling, swimming, and doing other healthful activities.

When Cooper first presented his research and proposed that his aerobic training be adopted throughout the Air Force, it did not gain immediate acceptance. Some older, far-more-experienced flight surgeons didn't believe it would work. They couldn't believe that anyone could acquire so much expertise in such a short period of time. You guessed it. When Cooper first developed his theories, he had been working on aerobics for heart exercise for only five years.

Do This Research to Convince Yourself

If you further doubt what I say about how long it takes to become an expert, I challenge you to do a little research. I want you to go to newspapers, magazines, and books and look up the careers of young men and women who are supersuccessful. I recommend that you look for young people because otherwise you may be tempted to fool yourself and count the total years of experience, rather than only the years spent acquiring a particular expertise.

For example, Colonel Harland Sanders was well past sixty when he began to market his secret family recipe that eventually led to the multibillion-dollar Kentucky Fried Chicken franchise.

You could say that he spent his entire life acquiring expertise in the fried chicken business. You would be wrong. He didn't begin to learn anything about fried chicken until he was sixty-two.

I suggest that you look at the careers of supersuccessful people who are young not because older people can't become supersuccessful. They can. Harland Sanders and Ray Kroc are just two examples from thousands. But if you look at younger successes, there will be no doubt regarding how long it took to acquire the needed expertise.

I'm not saying that you will always find success in five years. Sometimes success takes much longer. But we're not talking about success here. We're talking about expertise. If you want to be an expert at flying, karate, dancing, marketing, or business you can do it. You can acquire the expertise you want, and it will take you only five years or less.

Expertise Is Not Automatic

But don't forget. Acquiring the expertise is not automatic. You must put forth the effort required to do it. If you do, like Jobs, Wozniak, Kenneth Cooper, and so many hundreds of others, you will have the expertise, and people will seek you out as their leader.

DEVELOPING SELF-CONFIDENCE THROUGH POSITIVE MENTAL IMAGERY

One of the most important exercises you can do to develop your self-confidence as a leader is to practice positive mental imagery. The effects of positive (and negative) imagery can best be illustrated if I give you an example you can try for yourself.

Imagine a two-by-four plank constructed of hardwood, twenty feet long, placed on the ground. If I put a fifty-dollar bill at one end and told you all you had to do was to walk across the plank to keep it, you would have no trouble. You would stride confidently across and pick up the fifty dollars.

What if I raised the height of the plank to fifteen feet off the ground? You would probably still get to the fifty dollars, but it would be a lot more difficult. You would be much more careful where and how you stepped. Your stride would be much slower and more deliberate. What is the difference? The distance hasn't changed. The width and construction of the board haven't changed in any way.

Nor has the location of the fifty dollars relative to your starting position. Only the height has changed. And that shouldn't really make any difference. Or should it?

Now let's raise the height of that plank to three hundred feet between two skyscrapers. Are you still ready to go for the fifty dollars? Or would you insist on at least a thousand dollars or more to walk across the twenty-foot plank? Even then you might decide not to try it. If you did, I bet you would be mighty careful. Yet nothing has changed except the height. The plank, distance, width, and location of the money haven't changed a whit.

The real difference, of course, is the difference in mental image that the difference in height creates. When the plank is on the floor, our mental images focuses on the fifty dollars. As the height increases, however, we focus not on the fifty dollars, but on falling and the consequences of the fall.

Positive or Negative Mental Imagery Can Have Crucial Effects

Karl Wallenda was probably the greatest tightrope walker who ever lived. He walked across great distances, high in the air, and he did so without a net. Further, Karl Wallenda didn't stop his breathtaking walks as he grew older. He did the same fabulous stunts in his seventies as he had done as a young man in his twenties.

Than, in 1978, while performing a tightrope walk between two buildings in San Juan, Puerto Rico, he fell to his death.

Several weeks later, his wife was interviewed on television regarding Wallenda's last walk. "It was very strange," she said. "For months prior to his performance, he thought about nothing else. But for the first time, he didn't see himself succeeding. He saw himself falling."

Wallenda's wife went on to say that he even checked the installation and construction of the wire himself. "This," she said, "was something Karl had never done previously."

There seems little doubt that Karl Wallenda's negative mental imagery contributed to his falling.

Positive Images Can Significantly Improve Your Self-Confidence

Just as negative images can hurt your self-confidence as a leader, positive images can help your self-confidence considerably.

One of the leading researchers in the area of imagery is Dr. Charles Garfield. Dr. Garfield is a unique individual. He has not one, but two doctorates: in mathematics and psychology. I first read of Dr. Garfield's work in the pages of *The Wall Street Journal* in 1981. The article spoke about Dr. Garfield's research regarding what he called a kind of "mental rehearsal." Garfield found that more effective executives frequently practiced mental rehearsal. Less-effective executives did not.

In his book *Peak Performers*, Garfield describes how Soviet-bloc performance experts in Milan, Italy, confirmed his theories.

Garfield is an amateur weightlifter. However, hadn't worked out in several months. When he had, his best lift had been 280 pounds, although previously when he had worked out regularly, he had done more.

The Soviets asked him what was the absolute maximum he thought he could lift right at that moment. He responded that he might be able to make 300 pounds in an exercise known as the bench press. In this exercise, you are flat on your back. You take a barbell off two uprights. Next you lower the weight to your chest. Than you return the weight to the starting position.

With extreme effort, he just managed to make that amount. As Garfield himself said, "It was difficult—so difficult that I doubt I could have done it without the mounting excitement in the room."

The Soviets then had Garfield lie back and relax. They put him through a series of mental relaxation exercises. Then they asked him to get up slowly and gently. When he did, they added 65 pounds to the 300-pound weight. Under normal circumstances, it would have been impossible for him to lift this weight.

He began to have negative images. Before they established themselves in his mind, the Soviets began a new mental exercise.

"Firmly, thoroughly, they talked me through a series of mental preparations. In my mind's eye I saw myself approaching the bench. I visualized myself lying down. I visualized myself, with total confidence, lifting the 365 pounds."

Much to Garfield's surprise, he lifted the 365-pound weight. He was also astounded to discover it easier to lift than the lighter weight had been earlier.[6]

You Can Use Mental Rehearsal to Build Your Self-Confidence

I have used mental-rehearsal techniques for many years. I can guarantee that not only will you find them effective, but that they are easy and painless with no aftereffects.

The secret is to first relax as much as you can, then to give yourself positive images. What I do is this. I lie back and get as relaxed as I can. Than I start with my toes and tell myself that my toes are becoming numb. I repeat this suggestion to myself several times.

From my toes, I go to my feet, legs, torso, and so forth. In every case, I repeat the suggestion that the particular part of the body I am focusing on is becoming completely relaxed and numb.

When I am totally relaxed, I go to work on my positive imagery. Let's say that the leadership situation that I want to build self-confidence in has to do with a meeting I am going to run.

In my mind, I will picture everything about that meeting in detail. I will see the table, the lighting, and the decorations. I will see the sights, hear the sounds, smell the smells, and feel every sensation. I will see every individual who is participating in that meeting. I will rehearse every item on the agenda. In my mental imagery, I will rehearse not only what I will say, but the responses from those

I will lead as well. Naturally, in my mental rehearsal, everything will go the way I want it to go. In fact, I will make sure that all of my mental-image rehearsals go perfectly.

After I complete the rehearsal once, I repeat the entire rehearsal again. I do it several times at a sitting. If the situation is particularly important, I may repeat the entire mental imagery process a couple of times a day for several days.

Does it work? Amazingly, I have rarely failed when I used this imagery technique. It is true that reality does not always follow my preplanned script. Sometimes the changes are significant. But the results gained by seeing a favorable outcome over and over has a dramatic effect. I never lack self-confidence in any leadership situation that I have mentally rehearsed.

Walter Anderson, who wrote the book *The Confidence Course* says: "If you act as if you're confident, even though you may not feel sure of yourself, your confidence *will* grow. If you firmly *fix the image in your mind* of the person you'd like to be, you *will* begin to become that person."[7]

FOUR ACTION STEPS TO BUILDING LEADERSHIP SELF-CONFIDENCE

You can develop your leadership self-confidence by taking these four action steps. All have to do with one basic fact. Your self-confidence will increase as you accomplish leadership tasks successfully. So, do smaller and easier tasks first. Take on all you can. Then, progress to more difficult tasks. You will find them to be much easier than you thought.

Here are your four action steps to build leadership self-confidence:

1. *Become an uncrowned leader by seeking out and volunteering to be a leader whenever you can.*

2. *Be an unselfish teacher and helper of others.* Others will come to you for leadership.

3. *Develop your expertise.* Expertise is a source of leadership power.

4. *Use positive mental imagery.* Simulations in the mind are rehearsals for success. They are interpreted by the mind as real experiences. So they will boost your leadership self-confidence just like the actual experience.

NOTES

1. *AFM 35-15 Air Force Leadership* (Washington, D.C.: Department of the Air Force, 1948), p. 30.

2. Arnold Schwarzeneger with Douglas Kent Hall, *Arnold: The Education of a Bodybuilder* (New York: Fireside, 1997), p. 24.

3. Joseph Menn, "First Woman to Lead Blue-Chip Firm," *Los Angeles Times* (July 20, 1999), pp. A-1, A-17.

4. Edgar F. Puryear, Jr., *Nineteen Stars: A Study in Military Character and Leadership,* 2nd ed. (Novato, CA: Presidio Press, 1981), p. 155.

5. Adolf von Schell, *Battle Leadership* (Columbus, GA: The Benning Herald, 1933), pp. 92–94.

6. Charles Garfield, *Peak Performers* (New York: Avon Books, 1986), pp. 72–73.

7. Walter Anderson, *The Confidence Course* (New York: HarperCollins Publishers, 1997), p. 166.

CHAPTER EIGHT

HOW TO BUILD YOUR ORGANIZATION LIKE A WINNING FOOTBALL TEAM

In my seminars on leadership, I always ask this question. Can you think of any organization that has all of these attributes?

- The workers work very hard physically, including weekends, with little complaint.
- The workers receive no money and little material compensation for their services.
- The work is dangerous, and workers are frequently injured on the job.
- The work is strictly voluntary.
- The workers usually have very high morale.
- The organization always has more workers than can be employed.
- The workers are highly motivated to achieve the organization's goals.

Do you think that there's no such organization on the face of the earth? That such an organization can't exist? That such an organization is only in someone's dream?

Before you come to such a conclusion, consider a high-school football team. It has all of the above qualities. Do you say that a successful high-school football star can go on to make megabucks as a professional player? Well, that's true. However, the chances of that happening considering the numbers of high-school players versus the numbers of pro players is very slim indeed. Very few perform "work" on a football team for that reason.

WHAT YOU CAN LEARN FROM A GIRLS' SOCCER TEAM

I have selected football as my example, but you can find similar or even more amazing results in other sports. For years, I have been fascinated with the story of Arthur Resnick, who coached a girls' soccer team in Scarsdale, New York.

In a four-year period, Coach Resnick's team won seventy-five consecutive matches. Of course, it won the regional title every year.

I know what you're thinking. This was one of those schools that trained professional athletes. That every student was a "jock." That the male teams achieved even more dramatic results.

All these statements are 100 percent wrong. This was not a particularly athletic school. Others teams at the same school, both male and female, had only a mediocre record.

Because of his incredible success, others have studied Coach Resnick's techniques. Stories have appeared about him and his team in magazines and newspapers including *BusinessWeek, The Wall Street Journal,* and *Boardroom Reports.*

Why are business and management readers so interested in what the coach of a girls' soccer team did? Because they realize that if they can understand what Coach Resnick used to build his girls' soccer team, they can use the same techniques to build their own organizations.

Is There a Correlation Between Leadership and Athletics?

There is some correlation between leadership on the athletic field and leadership in other things in life. After the First World War, the authorities at West Point decided to review the records of former cadets. They wanted to know whether there was anything in the records of cadets who later became generals that could have predicted their later success. Academically, there were no predictors. There were generals who graduated first in their classes, such as MacArthur. However, there were also generals who graduated last in their classes, such as Custer. There were also generals who had been athletes, and generals who had not. But it was a fact that a West Point graduate had a better chance of becoming a general if he had been an athlete while a cadet. As a result of this research, athletics became required for all cadets.

General Douglas MacArthur's View

MacArthur's view is known to every West Point cadet. It is blazoned in stone on the main athletic building at West Point:

"On the fields of friendly strife are sown the seeds, that on other fields, on other days, will bear the fruits of victory."

Military leadership attempts to replicate athletic leadership on the playing field. Its many successes are demonstrated by elite military units as well as the sometimes incredible accomplishments and victories in combat against great odds by winning military "teams."

If you lead your organization or group like a winning football team, what an organization you can have! What accomplishments aren't possible? What victories can't be won?

In this chapter, we're going to learn to apply the techniques used by every winning coaches as well as many winning battlefield commanders to build an unbeatable team.

WHAT EVERY WINNING ATHLETIC TEAM HAS

If we want to build an organization like a winning athletic team, we must first examine winning teams to see what makes them successful. Successful athletic teams have these characteristics:

- *Cohesion* means sticking together. It means that members put the interests of the group over their own interests.

- *Teamwork* means working together so as to maximize the strengths of individual group members and minimize their weaknesses.

- *High Morale* is an inner feeling of well-being that is independent of external factors.

- *Esprit de Corps* is a French word that has to do with the morale of the organization as a unit.

In this chapter, we'll look only at cohesion and teamwork. In Chapter 9 we'll examine the characteristics of high morale and esprit de corps.

WHAT IS COHESION?

Cohesion is known in the military as a combat-force multiplier. This means that the mere existence of strong cohesion in a unit can multiply the effectiveness of this unit in combat. Through strong cohesion, a smaller and weaker military force can overcome one that is larger and stronger.

Many units that fought in Vietnam lacked cohesion. This was due in part to the military's policy of rotating individuals stateside as they completed one year of combat duty. As a result, there was little unit stability as replacements constantly arrived and veterans departed. American military organizations could have maintained the cohesion of these units by rotating the entire unit and replacing it with a new one. The policy of not doing this contributed to a decrease in unit motivation, disciplinary, and combat performance.[1] This lesson was not lost when the U.S. armed forces confronted Iraq in Operation Desert Shield and then went to war in Operation Desert Storm. For the most part, the individuals who went to Saudi Arabia in their units were the same ones that fought there.

Cohesive Organizations Outperform Others

Cohesive organizations outperform organizations that lack cohesion again and again. Some time ago, a researcher studied cohesion in some detail.

Lt. Colonel Jon W. Blades, an army officer at the National Defense University in Washington, D.C., investigated this aspect of cohesion. Blades discovered that significantly better-than-average performance scores in each of four major training areas occurred when cohesion increased.

According to Blades, cohesion had this effect because good working relationships among the members of the group made more efficient use of group assets. Such assets might include the ability of the group's members, available time, and assigned equipment.

Blades also found that a positive increase in group performance was seen in basic training among training platoons that had high cohesiveness. These highly cohesive platoons almost always performed better in such soldierly skills as rifle marksmanship, physical fitness, drill and ceremonies, and individual-soldier skill tests than did platoons with low cohesiveness.

Why was this? Because in the more cohesive platoons, the more talented soldiers voluntarily spent their free time teaching and coaching those who were less talented. From this, Blades concluded that if members had high ability and high motivation, the more cohesion a group has, the better the group performance will be.[2]

If you have ever seen a so-so athletic team that has played together for awhile beat a group of all-stars that have not, this may be the reason.

An Air Force Fighter Pilot Demonstrates Cohesion

During the 1958 Lebanon crisis, an Air Force fighter pilot who had very limited training on his type of aircraft was ordered to fly from his base in South Carolina to Adana, Turkey.

He ran into bad weather. He considered aborting the flight and turning back. Instead, he pressed on. His inexperience led to difficulty in locating his tanker aircraft. Over the middle of the Atlantic Ocean with only four minutes of fuel left, he was desperate. He thought about ejecting from his aircraft and leaving it to crash. Then, just in time, he found his aerial tanker and took on the necessary fuel.

Some hours later, he landed at Adana. When asked about his experience he said, "In my worst moment, I suddenly realized that staying with my gang meant more than anything in the world."[3]

Others studies of men in combat confirm the feelings of this young airman. Army historian Brigadier General S.L.A. Marshall conducted more than 400 interviews with American infantrymen immediately after combat in both the European and the Pacific theaters of war. Marshall concluded that the main motivation for a soldier to fight is a sense of psychological unity with other members of his immediate combat unit. Said General Marshall:"I hold it to be one of the simplest truths of war that the thing which enables an infantry soldier to keep going with his weapons is the near presence or the presumed presence of a comrade."[4]

Sure, patriotism, religion, and ideology are strong motivators. However, "staying with the gang," a good description of cohesion, is even stronger. That's true in battle, and it's true in your organization as well.

How to Develop Strong Group Cohesion

If you want to develop strong cohesion in your organization, you must develop pride in membership in your organization. To feel pride, your group must feel that they are in the best organization of its type, anywhere. That is, if your organization is a production crew making automobile parts, each member must feel that he or she is in the best production crew making automobile parts in the world. If your group does management consulting, then you want every member to feel that he or she is in the world's best management-consulting group. The same principle applies regardless of what kind of business you are in. Every one of your group members must feel that he or she is in the best organization of its kind.

How to Convince Your Group that They Are the Best

Now, if you are going to convince your group that they are the best, they are actually going to have to be the best in some way. This is not as difficult as it appears. The key is to focus on some element that is important to the group and to concentrate on being best at that.

The obvious are things that can be measured: sales, units produced, awards received, and so forth. These quantitative measurements are sometimes called metrics. However, metrics need not be involved, so long as the group members have a valid reason for believing that they are the best.

One squadron I flew with prided themselves at being best at night attack. Another squadron on the same base felt that they were best at low-level flying. I have seen members of organizations that felt that their organizations were the best of their type for all sorts of reasons. These included

- The hardest workers
- The organization that got the toughest assignments
- The organization that worked the longest hours
- The fastest
- The most courteous
- The most thorough
- The most creative
- The most productive

I have also been in a group that thought itself the best of its type because it was the most fun-loving! This was a section of fifteen officers and government executives at the Industrial College of the Armed Forces selected by accident as being most representative by background. This group played together, went to school together, and had such a good time while learning that their seminar number became famous throughout the college.

As the group's leader, it's up to you to develop this "We're the best" attitude. You can do this right at the start, when you first become associated with your group. Assign tasks that you know those in the group can perform well. As their skill and pride of accomplishment increase, select tasks that are progressively more difficult.

Betsy Burton, who as CEO of Supercuts presided over a major turnaround of this company when it was in trouble, is currently CEO and president of Supertans, a California-based chain of tanning salons. Burton says that leaders must focus on their organizations being *great* and not just *good*. She goes on to say, "Great isn't *what* you do, it's *how* you do it. It is a way of thinking. Great doesn't mean you have to be the *biggest*. It means being the *best*. Great doesn't mean you're perfect. It means bouncing back from ups and downs."[5]

Give Recognition Whenever You Can

Of course, every time a task is completed successfully, make certain that the individuals completing them receive the recognition they deserve. And make certain that your entire organization learns of every victory.

Recognition comes in a variety of forms. Official letters of commendation are one way. However, even short handwritten notes and verbal praise are appreciated.

I'll have more to say about recognition in a later chapter.

Symbols Represent the Real Thing

You can and should encourage organizational mottoes, names, symbols, and slogans. They represent the real thing. That's why hearing our national anthem and seeing the flag waving can bring a lump to our throats and sometimes tears to our eyes. It's not that *The Star Spangled Banner* is such a beautiful tune. Originally, it was a beer-drinking song. Nor do the Stars and Stripes as a piece of art evoke emotion. Without what the flag represents, it is simply a multicolored piece of cloth. But representing what it does, it and other symbols are extremely powerful.

As a leader, you should encourage such icons: mottoes, names, symbols, and slogans whenever you can, because they brand us for what we are—to ourselves and to others. And that's why the phrase "rally 'round the flag" is not meaningless.

Establishing a Group's Worth

Finally, you can improve group cohesion by establishing the worth of the organization and its values.[6] The more good things that you can find and can say about your organization, the better. Everyone likes to be associated with winners and winning organizations. No one wants to be in an organization that is thought of as losing. So, if you can establish your group as a winner based on its past, you are well on your way toward a strong, cohesive unit.

What you can do is this: Investigate and find good things in the history of your organization. What are your organization's traditions? What has your organization accomplished in the past that you can promote? The more you can find to promote, the better.

Note that I keep mentioning promotion. Once you ferret out this information about your organization, you've got to use it. You want everyone in your organization to know what a terrific outfit they are are associated with. Publicize this information in newsletters. Post it on bulletin boards, read the information at staff meetings. Use every technique you can to promote your organization as the best around. Get people excited about their membership in the group. Make them feel that they are better than anyone else . . . the best.

When All Other Airlines Lost Money, This One Made It

Between 1990 and 1994, the airlines industry lost a whopping $12.8 billion. To put this in some perspective, that's more money than the industry had made in the previous sixty years! But one airline made money. In fact, it has been profitable every year since 1973, and its profit margins are the highest in the industry. Yes, I'm talking about Southwest Airlines, which also wins high ratings every year for customer service. How do they do it? Two PhDs, Kevin Freiberg and Jackie Frieberg, consultants to Southwest, got Chairman Herb Kelleher to okay a study and find out. They published their research as a book under the title *Nuts!* The title refers to Southwest's no-frills gourmet that is limited to this particular single food. The two researchers found that Southwest celebrates everything. "Southwest throws a party whenever possible to honor and reward people and to give them opportunities to experience the Southwest culture. Southwest is also fanatical about documenting its celebrations so that employees and friends can relive the memories."[7]

Former CEO and president, Howard Putnam said, "I couldn't understand when I first got there why we didn't have any complaints. The employment group worked with the mentality that we hire people who have fun. When I spoke to new employees I'd tell them, 'You've chosen Southwest Airlines and you're going to work harder than at any other airline. You're going to get paid about 30 percent less, but in the long run, when we make this thing work, with your profit sharing you'll be far ahead of anybody else.'"[8]

I must give you one cautionary note here. Some leaders think that they can promote their organization best by tearing down the reputation of the parent organization. This is a mistake. It will backfire. Not only will your superiors come down on you eventually, but you will hurt the very cohesion you are trying to build. Once again, no one wants to be associated with a losing organization, even if it is the parent organization to their own. So don't do it. Even when things go wrong because of actions of your parent organization, and your organization has done its job, build support for both organizations, not one at the expense of the other.

The Amazing Fact that General Schwarzkopf Discovered About Carrying Out Bad Orders— Adopt Them as Your Own!

When General H. Norman Schwarzkopf, hero of Desert Shield and Desert Storm, was a young officer he saw lots of bad orders come down from above. Much to his amazement, he discovered that the best company commanders were the ones who could carry out a bad order if they had to without ruining their troops' morale.

Said General Schwarzkopf: "All seven company commanders protested, but as soon as it was clear the colonel wasn't going to change his mind, the commanders of the three good companies went back to their units and executed the order as if they'd thought of it themselves. They told the men, 'Okay guys. We've got a new mission and that is to get the barracks in shape for the general! Let's show him who's the best company at Ft. Campbell!'"

He contrasted this with the actions of the poorer company commanders. First they kept trying to change the battle-group commander's mind until finally he threw them out of his office. Finally, they returned to their companies and told their men, "The general is coming and battle group says we gotta paint the damn building even though it doesn't need it."[9]

Of course, it isn't wrong to try and change your boss's views. In fact, it is your duty to do this. But once you have made your arguments and they have been rejected, adopt your boss's decision as your own, even if you disagree with it.

If the members of your organization feel that they are in the best organization of its type, which in turn is a part of the best organization of its type, you will build a bonding force that is stronger than superglue. It is a cohesion that cannot be broken, and it will pay dividends in performance in any environment.

How To Develop Winning Teamwork

If you have watched successful athletic teams performing, you were probably amazed at just how easy they made their accomplishments look. So integrated was the performance that instead of seeing the individual members acting, you saw the team as a single entity in motion.

You may even have been seduced into thinking, "Boy, that's not so hard. I can do that." So, if you participate in the same sport, or coach kids, you may have tried the same play of teamwork you saw performed by experts. Only then did you realize just how difficult it was for a group to do what you saw the well-coordinated team perform.

This type of teamwork occurs in other than athletic events. In the military, such performances happen daily on aircraft, ships, tanks, in missile- and artillery-command centers, and in field-training exercises. The performances are amazing. Not only does every team member seem to know exactly what to do, but also how to modify his or her individual performance to fit in with changes in the environment and minor changes in the performances of other group members. The bottom line is that through teamwork, the overall performance is greater than the sum of the performances of all the individual team members.

Peter Drucker's Phenomenon

Peter Drucker found the same phenomenon in a well-run hospital. Doctors, nurses, X-ray technicians, pharmacologists, pathologists, and other health-care practitioners all worked together to accomplish a single objective. Frequently, he saw several working on the same patient under emergency conditions. Seconds counted. Even a minor slip could prove fatal. Yet, with a minimum amount of conscious command or control by any one individual, this medical team worked together toward a common end and followed a common plan of action under the overall direction of a doctor. The similarity to what you saw on the athletic field would be striking.[10]

Teamwork in all activities is crucial. Years ago, the Air Force did a study of their bomber crews in the Strategic Air Command. Individual performance increases with increased experience flying experience as measured by number of flying hours. These researchers wanted to know how performance was affected by increased flying experience on a specific aircraft. They thought that like flying experience in general, more experience on a particular airplane would cause performance to improve. It did. However, the time a crew spent flying together was a far more accurate predictor of improved performance than was individual flying experience.

What an Israeli Army Study Showed

An interesting study by the Israeli Army again confirmed the importance of teamwork. The Israelis analyzed the combat performance of their soldiers in the Golan Heights in northern Israel. Using peer evaluations, the Israelis found that the quality of combat performance was highly related to teamwork in fighting together and much less on individual fighting qualities, or even commitment to goals of the war effort.[11]

Coach Frank Leahy's Reflection

Famed Notre Dame football coach Frank Leahy was an officer in the United States Navy during World War II. He coached hundreds of football games, the majority of which he won. He also witnessed the battle for Iwo Jima. After reflecting, he said: "The burning desire to emerge the victor we see in our contact sports is the identical spirit that gave the United States Marines victory at Iwo Jima."[12]

How Our Pilots Survived Imprisonment in North Vietnam

How can you develop teamwork in your organization? One important thing you must do to develop teamwork is to focus on a common purpose. This should be the overall objective or contribution you are trying to make.

Our pilots who were shot down and made prisoners during the Vietnam War endured unspeakable hardships, starvation, and torture. At the same time, their captors made them brutally aware of the war's controversy back in the States. Their captors flaunted the fact that at least some Americans thought of them as criminals. Yet they held together, maintaining their faith in their God and their country, in some cases over years. They did this because they focused on a common purpose. This was to survive their imprisonment without betraying their country. Despite everything, they succeeded.

It is instructive to know that these beaten, weakened men exercised teamwork in prison even in the face of hardship and death. Forbidden to communicate in any way, they developed the ability to communicate by tapping on adjacent cell walls. In this way, they passed on the orders of the senior ranking American prisoner and news; they comforted each other and even prayed together.

As new prisoners arrived, they were taught the code as well. In this way, these Americans maintained themselves and practiced a highly developed teamwork. Yet this teamwork was developed at great risk and under the constant surveillance of the enemy. It was developed even though in some cases weeks, months, or even years went by without these men ever being able to see one another.

Without focusing on a common objective, little can be achieved. In the Korean War, Americans were also held as prisoners under inhuman conditions. Brave men performed heroically here also, but the record is far less bright. Hundreds of Americans died during their imprisonment. Medical testimony after the war indicated that in many cases these deaths were unnecessary since the men were neither stricken by disease nor malnourished to the point of death.[13]

What happened was that our men gradually lost their will to live. Experts tell us that their will to live would probably have been maintained had they banded together early to work for a common purpose. Instead, some collaborated with the enemy for better treatment, and others placed themselves above the common good in other ways.

When I was thirteen years old, my father was assigned as a military attorney to defend an American F-51 pilot who, while a prisoner, falsely confessed on film and radio to North Korean charges of germ warfare. I remember him telling my father that he didn't think anyone would believe his confession, since it was such nonsense. Since it was an obvious lie and he wasn't giving away any military secrets, he didn't think he had betrayed his country.

Years later, as a young flyer myself, the Air Force showed us some of the propaganda films made by the North Koreans. Suddenly, on the screen was my father's client, apologizing for acts he had never committed.

When we compare this with the actions of our men while prisoners in North Vietnam, there is little doubt that focusing on the common purpose would have resulted in teamwork instead of dreadful error during this adversity.

Patton Knew It Was Important to Focus on a Common Purpose

In any organization, there are groups and individuals who are more glorified and recognized than others. Every leader should strive to build distinction into his or her organization, whether responsible for developing high-technology products or for digging ditches. However, as overall leader with responsibility for different groups, you must get the entire organization focused on a common purpose and ensure recognition and some glory for all.

Part of Patton's genius was his ability to get everyone focused on the common purpose by proving the importance of every individual in the organization. Listen to this excerpt from Patton's D-Day speech to the troops just prior to the landings at Normandy. You will see how Patton did it and how you can do it, too.

All the real heroes are not storybook combat fighters either. Every single man in the Army plays a vital part. Every little job is essential to the whole scheme. What if every truck-driver suddenly decided that he didn't like the whine of those shells and turned yellow and jumped headlong into a ditch? He could say to himself, "They won't miss me—just one guy in thousands." What if every man said that? Where in the hell would we be now? No, thank God, Americans don't say that. Every man does his job. Every man serves the whole. Every department, every unit, is important to the vast scheme of things. The Ordnance is needed to supply the guns, the Quartermaster is needed to bring up the food and clothes for us—for where we are going there isn't a hell of a lot to steal! Every last damn man in the mess hall, even the one who heats the water to keep us from getting diarrhea, has a job to do. Even the Chaplain is important, for if we get killed and he is not there to bury us we would all go to hell. Each man must not only think of himself, but think of his buddy fighting alongside him. We don't want yellow cowards in the Army. They should be killed off like flies. If not, they will go back home after the war, goddam cowards, and breed more cowards. The brave men will breed more brave men. One of the bravest men I saw in the African campaign was the fellow I saw on a telegraph pole in the furious fire . . . I stopped and asked him what the hell he was doing up there at that time. He answered, "Fixing the wire, sir." "Isn't it unhealthy up there right now?" I asked. "Yes, sir, but this goddam wire has got to be fixed." There was a real soldier . . . and you should have seen those trucks on the road to Gabes. The drivers were magnificent. All day they crawled along those sonofabitchin' roads, never stopping, never deviating from their course with shells bursting all around them. We got through on good old American guts. Many of the men drove over forty consecutive hours.[14]

Patton's language may have been more profane than many of us would appreciate. Others might say it differently, without the profanity, but with equal effectiveness. But that was Patton. He was speaking to soldiers, and that was his style. What I want you to notice is how he brought every individual in his army in to one big team in his speech, working together for a common purpose.

ANOTHER WAY TO DEVELOP TEAMWORK

There is another way that you can develop teamwork in your organization. That is to encourage your organization to participate in sports together outside work. You should participate yourself. If it is a sport that you are particularly good in, well and good. If not, that's all right too. The important thing is to play these sports with the members of your organization.

These don't need to be contact sports, and maybe they shouldn't be. Try to select a sport that everyone can participate in, male or female, in great shape or not. What sport you select isn't important. Playing together will help your "team" develop the teamwork which will spill over into other areas of your lives—and that's what you are after.

The Man Who Survived Six Days and Six Nights Behind the Lines in Bosnia

It was June 2, 1995. Captain Scott O'Grady was on a mission in his F-16 fighter as part of Operation Deny Flight over Bosnia when he was hit by an SA-6 surface-to-air missile and forced to eject. He survived for six days and nights in a hostile environment before being rescued. His story of heroism and ultimate triumph is told in his book *Return with Honor*. O'Grady credits his rescue in part to activities outside flying and warfare. Listen closely to what he says. "In a combat environment you needed to trust people, to predict their reactions and rely on their snap judgments. But before you

trust people you have to know them. You have to live and work—
and laugh—together."[15] This is as true in a business environment, or
any environment for that matter, as in the environment of battle. So
if you really want to develop teamwork in your organization, get
your "team" to play together outside work.

To Build Your Organization Like a Winning Football Team, Take These Actions:

- Develop pride in group membership.

- Convince your group that they are the best.

- Give recognition whenever possible.

- Encourage organizational mottoes, names, symbols, and slogans.

- Establish your group's worth by examining and promoting its history and values.

- Focus on the common purpose.

- Encourage your organization to participate in activities together outside work.

Now turn to Chapter 9 to look at two important concepts for
building your organization like an athletic team: high morale and
esprit de corps.

NOTES

1. Jon W. Blades, *Rules for Leadership* (Washington, D.C.: National Defense University, 1986), p. 75.

2. Ibid., pp. 76–78.

3. *The Armed Forces Officer* (Washington, D.C.: Department of Defense, 1975), p. 6.

4. S.L.A. Marshall, *Men Against Fire: The Problem of Battle Command in Future War* (New York: William Morrow, 1947), p. 42.

5. Betsy Burton, "Transformations in the Workplace: The Emergence of the Entrepreneurial Manager," in Michael Ray and John Renesch, *The New Entrepreneurs* (San Franciso: Sterling & Stone, 1994), p. 50.

6. Jon W. Blades op. cit., p. 100.

7. Kevin Freiberg and Jackie Freiberg, *Nuts!* (Austin, TX: Bard Press, 1996), p. 152.

8. Ibid., p. 42.

9. H. Norman Schwarzkopf, *It Doesn't Take a Hero* (New York: Bantam, 1992), p. 101.

10. Peter F. Drucker, *The Effective Executive* (New York: Harper & Row, 1967), pp. 68–69.

11. John H. Faris, "Leadership and Enlisted Attitudes," in James H. Buck and Lawrence J. Korb, eds., *Military Leadership* (Beverly Hills, CA: Sage Publications, Inc., 1981), p. 148.

12. *The Armed Forces Officer* (Washington, D.C.: Armed Forces Information Office, 1975), p. 157.

13. Ibid., p. 68.

14. Alan Axelrod, *Patton on Leadership* (Paramus, NJ: Prentice Hall, 1999), p. 241.

15. Scott O'Grady, *Return with Honor* (New York: HarperCollins, 1995), p. 71.

CHAPTER NINE

BUILDING HIGH MORALE AND ESPRIT DE CORPS

Winning athletic teams have two other characteristics that are important. Usually these two qualities go together. They are morale and esprit de corps, and every winning athletic team has them.

Think of high morale as being an individual group member's feeling of well-being or exaltation. Collectively, there is also a group feeling of well-being or exaltation. That is esprit de corps.

You need both to build a winning team. In this chapter, you'll learn how to do exactly that.

How to Develop High Morale

They say that the biggest difference between the American worker and the Japanese worker has nothing to do with Japanese management techniques. Instead, it's that the American worker looks forward to the weekend, and the Japanese worker looks forward to the workweek.

What a difference! When your workers have high morale, they, too, will begin to look forward to the week rather than the weekend. And why not? People with high morale have fun. Naturally, they look forward to having fun and feeling good. That this will happen during the workweek is good for you. That there are five days of fun and feeling good versus only two on the weekend is good for them. So it's a double win.

How can we achieve this? How can you get such high morale that your workers would rather be on the job working than doing other things.

Cut Others in on the Action

If you want your group to have high morale, you must let them in on the action. By this I am saying that your workers must share ownership with you in accomplishing any project or task.

Long before "participation management," the army used to say: "Tell your men what to do, but don't tell them how to do it." You can see that if a worker decides how to do something himself or herself, he or she has a share in ownership.

Admiral Ben Moreell headed the seabees during World War II. The seabees were our naval construction engineers who built important navy bases in combat areas under extremely difficult and hazardous conditions. Moreell said that he had a secret formula that enabled him to get results. "We used artisans to do the work for which they had been trained in civil life. They were well led by officers who 'spoke their language.' We made them feel that they were playing an important part in the great adventure. And thus they achieved a high standard of morale."[1]

One of the greatest management experts of all time was a man by the name of Chester Barnard. Barnard learned his management the hard way. He worked himself up from the bottom at AT&T. Then in the late 1930s, he wrote a book *The Functions of the Executive*, which is still widely read. His conclusions are worth studying.

Said Barnard: "Scarcely a man, I think, who has felt the annihilation of his personality in some organized system, has not also felt that the same system belonged to him because of his own free will he chose to make it so."[2]

When you give your people ownership, they feel much different toward the task than if you set yourself as the only one responsible. The difference is between an important team member and an organizational cog. When you award them ownership, they are under the influence of feelings of an entirely different type.

Colonel John S. Moseby, Confederate States of America was a great guerilla leader during the War Between the States. The Union troops called him "the gray ghost" because whenever they thought they had him trapped, he disappeared. Thousands of Northern troops attempted to catch him, but they were never successful.

His exploits were legendary. Once, raiding far beyond Union lines, he captured a Union general in bed with his mistress; he also captured almost a hundred horses. When told, Abraham Lincoln was said to have commented, "Too bad about the horses. I can replace the general a lot easier."

Why was John S. Moseby so successful? He wasn't trained at West Point, and he hadn't been a soldier before the war. He explained it all in his book *War Reminiscences*, published in 1887. "Men who go into a fight under the influence of such feelings are next to invincible, and are generally victors before it begins."[3]

High Morale and Cheerfulness

Another way you can influence morale is by being cheerful. Cheerfulness has a positive effect on morale.

One of General MacArthur's West Point classmates said that even in the early days, MacArthur imparted his self-confidence to others through his cheerfulness.

A classmate of General Eisenhower's, Brigadier General Carl C. Bank, said: "The one outstanding characteristic notable at all times was his cheerfulness, friendliness and good humor.[4]

It's a fact that many individuals have attributed their success simply to smiling. An official manual on Air Force leadership published after World War II discussed the leadership of five-star General Hap Arnold, who had been commander of the Army Air Force during the war. This manual said that General Arnold's ready smile played a significant part in his being promoted to the command of the Army Air Force. According to this document, "Cheerfulness spells confidence, optimism, fearlessness, and 'I like people,' which everyone recognizes and warms to immediately."[5]

Be Aware of What's Going On . . . Then Act

If you want high morale in your organization, you must constantly monitor what is going on. Keep your eyes and ears open, look for trends, and most important, get around to visit and talk with people in your organization every day. That way you'll not only know how your people feel, but you'll also be aware of everything that is going on.

If the people in your organization become depressed, you should know about it instantly and should immediately take action to do something about it. Sometimes a simple joke can turn things around. Other times you may need to do more. The important principle is to know what's going on in your organization and then to take action immediately to influence it. If you do these two things, you will have a major impact on events rather than the other way around.

Princeton is not only a town where a famous university is located. A major battle was fought there during the Revolutionary War.

This battle was a very near thing. George Washington closely observed his men under fire. He saw that it was becoming too much, that they were in danger of panicking. Once a few men fell back, his entire line could break. Instantly he urged his horse between the American and British lines. He rode up and down between the two lines, ignoring British fire. How could his men be fearful with their commander riding up and back right before their eye? The truth was, they couldn't, and the Continental line held.

Lead by Personal Example Whenever You Can

Do you remember the game "follow the leader"? Followers attempted to do everything the leader did. They rarely hesitated, because they saw the leader do it first. Not only did they know it could be done, but they saw that the leader was willing to do it first.

In 1942, Major General Ira C. Eaker of the U.S. Army Air Forces planned daylight bombing missions against the Germans. Royal Air Force pilots told him that it wasn't possible, that losses would be too great. The RAF had a lot of credibility. They had been fighting the Germans and bombing them since 1939. Still, the Americans had been working on new techniques for daylight bombing. Eaker was undeterred from his plans for daylight bombing. However, his men knew the opinion of the veteran flyers from the RAF. And Eaker knew that this knowledge had caused some of his men to doubt their own abilities. It isn't every day that a major general pilots a plane in combat, but Eaker went on that first daylight bombing mission himself. His force went on to employ daylight bombing with tremendous effect throughout the war.[6]

Yes, frequently leading by personal example will do the trick . . . and you don't necessarily have to put yourself in personal danger.

I mentioned Baron von Steuben in a previous chapter. He was the volunteer who helped George Washington turn an eager, but untrained mob of men into a real army during the Revolutionary War. Among his many contributions, he developed our first drill regulations. Remember in those days, drill was not just for training. It was used in combat to ensure that men fought and maneuvered together on the battlefield. Without drill, only harassment operations were possible.

Said von Steuben, "I dictated my dispositions in the night; in the day I had them performed."

Of course, just writing down what to do isn't leadership. What could von Steuben do to have his drill performed? He formed a model company that he drilled himself in what he had developed the previous night. Than he drilled his company in front of the officers and soldiers of the Continental Army. In this way, he not only showed them exactly what to do, but he demonstrated that what he wanted done would work on the battlefield. No wonder von Steuben became, though a relatively young man, the first Inspector General of the Army.[7]

No less a military figure than Gideon, quoted in the Holy Scriptures of the Bible said, "As I do, so shall you do."

How Long Does It Take to Build High Morale?

You may have heard that it takes months, or even years to build high morale. Let me assure you that this is untrue. General George S. Patton said, "In a week's time, I can spur any outfit into a high state of morale."[8]

Once I saw even the great Patton outdone in building a high state of morale in minimum time. It was in a squadron of attack planes during the Vietnam War. This squadron had low morale because of high losses while flying against heavily defended areas along the Ho Chi Minh trail in North Vietnam and Laos.

The squadron commander hadn't helped morale either. This officer, after having not flown in years, had been plucked from his nonflying role and sent to the war. He was the senior ranking lieutenant colonel, so they made him the commander.

This was a mistake. During his years away from flying and operations, he had lost many of his fighting skills. Worse, in combat he became hesitant. Then, he began to avoid flying the tougher combat missions. Finally, he was relieved of command.

The new squadron commander turned the situation around with only two sentences. He said, "I am your new squadron commander. I am going to flying more missions, and more of the tougher missions than anyone else in the squadron."

ESPRIT DE CORPS

Have you ever wished that you could be a military leader, rather than the leader of some other kind of organization? After all, all a military leader has to do is give a command and it is carried out, right? Wrong.

When I first entered civilian life, I was hired to head a research-and-development organization. The president of the company called me in and said, "Now, Bill, I know that you have led military organizations, but it's not the same thing leading civilians. You can't just give an order and see it carried out."

I assured my new boss that in most instances, military command wasn't that simple. I did, however, promise to go easy at first.

It wouldn't be fair to compare an infantry company or a fighter squadron in combat with an organization that does research and development for a living. However, some kind of comparison can be made between research-and-development organizations in military and civilian life. Do you know what I discovered? I had a lot more power of command in my civilian organization. Here's why. In the military, if an officer performed poorly as a research and development project engineer, the worst I could do was to give him or her a bad assignment and a poor performance report. In civilian life, if someone performed poorly, I had the power to instantly fire him or her.

Therefore, regardless of what kind of organization you lead, you must reserve your command authority for those instances when it is appropriate to use it. Instead, your aim should be to build a desire in the individuals in your organization so that they want to be led by you. This organizational consensus for your leadership and the high feeling of spirit associated with it is called *esprit de corps*.

After World War I, General Harbord, a senior Army leader, commented on his experiences in France. "Discipline and morale influence the inarticulate vote that is constantly taken by masses of men when the order comes to move forward—a variant of the crowd psychology that inclines it to follow a leader," he said. "But the Army does not move forward until the motion has carried. 'Unanimous consent' only follows cooperation between the individual men in ranks."[9]

In other words, there is a group spirit that you must reach in order to motivate groups of people to do things . . . even in the military, and despite the effect of orders.

How do you develop esprit de corps? For my money, esprit de corps is built on three things: your personal integrity, mutual confidence, and a focus on contribution rather personal gain.

You Can't Dodge the Integrity Issue

In Chapter 2, we saw that maintaining absolute integrity is the first of the eight laws of leadership. Actually, integrity is involved with all your actions as a leader. I do not believe you can develop esprit de corps without it. Thomas E. Cronin, a political science writer who was also a White House Fellow, confirmed that integrity "is perhaps the most central of leadership qualities."[10]

Major General Perry M. Smith tells a story about Babe Zaharias in his book *Taking Charge*. Babe Zaharias was a champion sportswoman in the 1932 Olympics. Later, as a professional golfer, she penalized herself two strokes after the round she was playing was over. The penalty strokes cost her first place in a major tournament. Why did she do it? It turns out that she accidentally played the wrong ball. Later, a friend asked her why she penalized herself. "After all, Babe," said the friend, "no one saw you. No one would have known the difference." "I would have known," replied the great Babe.[11]

West Point probably has the strictest honor code in the world. It says: "A cadet will not lie, cheat, or steal, or tolerate anyone else that does."

The code is simple, but it is strictly enforced—by the cadets themselves. An honor violation means that the cadet is expected to resign. Let's say that a cadet copies an answer from another cadet's paper during a test. Later, although he wasn't observed, he turns himself in to the cadet honor committee for an honor violation. He is now expected to resign from the corps of cadets. If someone had observed him copying an answer, he would have reported it to the honor committee. I have seen both happen when I was a cadet.

We saw the code in action in General Schwarzkopf's story in Chapter 2. Here's another true story that may help you to understand how important this code was and is. Once, when I was a cadet and home on leave after my first year at West Point, I went out drinking with some friends from high school. I forgot that the minimum age to drink beer was eighteen, rather than twenty-one, as it was in some states on the East Coast at the time. My friends all had fake identification cards that indicated that they were of age. Being accustomed to ordering beer at eighteen, I didn't even think about it. When asked for identification, I presented my cadet identification card.

The barmaid looked at it closely. It didn't have my age, but did identify me as a Cadet at the United States Military Academy. The barmaid looked at the card with my picture and then looked at me. "You can't get a beer here unless you're twenty-one. This says that you are a West Point cadet. I know that if you tell me you are twenty-one it will be the truth. Are you twenty-one?" I had to admit I was not. My friends couldn't believe it. They told me that like the story of Babe Zaharias, no one would have known I had lied. I am proud to tell you that more than forty years later, I answered, "I would have known."

I have seen men live by this code while cadets, and die by the same code later as officers. The code has saved lives in combat, because what a graduate said could be absolutely depended on as the truth.

The officials at West Point didn't start this code. It came from the cadets themselves, back in the nineteenth century. At first, the honor committee's activities were secret, because the authorities resented this assumption of power by cadets. However, as time went on, the importance of absolute integrity was recognized for its value on the battlefield and in all human relationships. So the honor activities were legalized.

Yes, there have been cheating scandals at West Point, where numbers of cadets have intentionally violated the code. You can count the number of times this has happened on one hand.

I wish I could tell you that all graduates continue to live by the honor code after they graduate. Unfortunately, since we are dealing with human beings, this would be inaccurate. But I can tell you that the ideal is alive and real, and its observance by the vast majority of West Point graduates continues until the day they die. I cannot help but think that much of the West Point reputation for producing leaders of unusual quality has to do with this early development of integrity such that they unfailingly follow it because they would themselves know if they did not.

If you want to build esprit de corps, you must demonstrate integrity like Babe Zaharias's and as contained in the West Point honor code. If you do, it won't be long before everyone in your organization knows that you can be trusted, that you say what you mean and mean what you say. The members of your organization will return the favor. They will demonstrate integrity in dealing with you and each other, and the esprit de corps in your organization will soar.

This Submarine Admiral Says It Must Be "Integrity First"

Rear Admiral Dave Oliver, Jr., was an admiral who practiced and studied leadership at great length, and then wrote a book about it. About integrity, Admiral Oliver has this to say:

"In many large organizations there is a contingent of thought that the contest usually goes to the man willing to sail closest to the fine line drawn between truth and less-than-that. Some self-styled pragmatists regale audiences with stories that might lead a novice to believe that success is the province of only the most gnarled and least scrupulous bureaucratic battlers. That has not been my experience."[12]

Demonstrate Real Concern for Your People

The *Armed Forces Officer* says that esprit is ". . . the product of a thriving mutual confidence between the leader and the led, founded on the faith that together they possess a superior quality and capability."

If you want to build mutual confidence, I have found that you must demonstrate your real concern for the welfare of those for whom you are responsible.

Demonstrating your real concern gets back to the right priorities that you must have as a leader. First comes your mission or organizational goals. Than comes the welfare of your people. If you are a real leader, your own personal interests come dead last.

Those who follow you will accept hardships, put up with your personal mistakes and idiosyncrasies, and even willingly risk their lives. There are, however, certain conditions. First and foremost, the cause must be worthwhile. Then you must demonstrate the priority of interests that I have outlined for you.

When I first started university teaching, I asked my friend and then-chairman, Dr. Marshall E. Reddick how he got such high ratings from his students on his teaching evaluations. "It's easy," he said. "Students will do whatever you ask, even the most difficult assignments, so long as they realize it is to their benefit, and not mine."

Here was a perfect example of applying the priorities of a leader to the classroom. First came the teacher's responsibility to impart knowledge. And then combined with this, Marshall taught in such a way that it was to the students' benefit. Marshall's own interests came last.

Did you think that General Patton was an easy or tough general to work for? He drove his men unmercifully. He was very tough. As I told you in a previous chapter, to improve discipline he required his men to wear not only a helmet, but a tie. And that was in combat!

Patton also made a lot of mistakes. You probably heard about the incident when Patton slapped and berated a soldier suffering from a combat psychosis. Patton also gave a speech in which he used profanity to a group of mothers whose sons had been killed in the war. In a postwar comment, he seemed to equate Nazis with Republicans and Democrats. These mistakes caused Eisenhower to twice fire this four-star warrior despite his abilities.

You may have heard about these mistakes, or seen them depicted by George C. Scott when he played Patton in the award winning movie about this famous general. But did you also know that Patton had one of the lowest combat casualty rates of any commander during World War II?

Even as a twenty-nine-year-old colonel during World War I, Patton demonstrated real concern for the lives of his men. On being given command by General Pershing of the first American tank unit he said, "Sir, I accept my new command with particular enthusiasm because with the eight tanks, I believe I can inflict the greatest number of casualties on the enemy with the smallest expenditure of American life."[13]

You see, Patton repeatedly demonstrated a real concern for his men despite his toughness. Because Patton demonstrated this concern, and had his priorities right, he developed a high mutual confidence that led to an unbeatable esprit de corps. As a result, he was victorious, and his men loved him despite his foibles.

General Fred Franks Takes His Corps from Europe to Combat in Iraq

When General Schwarzkopf commanded Operation Desert Shield prior to Desert Storm, it soon became clear that he had a major problem. He had amassed sufficient ground troops and an Army that could defend Saudi Arabia. However, he lacked the numbers required to go on the offensive to force the Iraqis out of Kuwait. The decision was made to send the VII Corps, commanded by my West Point classmate, Fred Franks.

As you might imagine, Fred had major challenges in moving thousands of troops and tons of equipment where they had been on duty to guard against a Soviet attack in Europe to the deserts of the Middle East to fight a major war. This required a Herculean effort and major restructuring of his command. But even with the immediate challenges of the redeployment and the coming battle, he did not fail to feel and demonstrate real concern for those he led and their families.

"Family support was a big issue since we were already a forward-deployed force with family members, and we would now deploy again, this time without family members. Our army had not done this on such a scale before, so we wanted to ensure we had well-thought-out military community family-support plans, that the Army would help our families take care of themselves."[14]

Get Your Organization to Focus on Contribution

When John F. Kennedy was sworn in as President of the United States, he exhorted his countrymen to "Ask not what your country can do for you. Ask what you can do for your country."

John F. Kennedy knew how to get people to focus on the right objective. He pointed out that we could do great things together if people focused on what they could *do* rather than on what they could *get*. Unfortunately, President Kennedy was assassinated before most of his goals could be reached. But the country's esprit de corps that he began continued on long after him. Through it, we inaugurated civil rights legislation that revolutionized the country, we made the first lunar landing, and we successfully kept Russian missiles out of Cuba.

A switch from gain to contribution is easier than you might think. You see, all of us play one of two games whenever we do anything. One game is "Get All You Can." The other is "Give All You Can." Regardless of which game is played, all players play to win.

You can bet that a group whose members are playing "Get All You Can" has little or no esprit de corps. On the other hand, you can actually feel the positive spirit in a group whose members are playing "Give All You Can."

Which game is your organization playing? If they are playing "Get All You Can," you've got to turn them around—fast. If you don't, your organization will have little esprit de corps and will perform marginally at best. To get your group to play "Give All You Can," you must take positive actions. You must tell them the game, show them the game, and keep score in the game.

To tell them the game is easy. Decide where you want your organization to go. Built a consensus for your goals through discussion and input from your group's members. Decide on a plan of action and make assignments along with milestone dates for accomplishment.

Showing them the game is harder. Everything that can go wrong, will go wrong. You will encounter what Clausewitz called "battle friction." There will be setbacks, discouragement, and defeats. You must positively carry on. You must encourage and demand continued contribution and further sacrifice even in the face of adversity.

Simultaneously, you must keep score in "Give All You Can." That means rewarding the major contributors and sometimes punishing those who are still playing the old game. This is not always easy. Some who contributed something when others contributed nothing during "Get All You Can" continue to play the old game. They have to be brought to understand the new game.

All the time, you must set the example of being the number-one contributor. You need to do this without compromise because you won't fool your organization. Not for a minute. The first time you begin playing "Get All You Can," you can expect your organization to follow your lead the same day.

Once you know that the members of your organization are focused on contributing to its benefit over their own, you won't need to ask if your organization has a high esprit de corps. You will see that esprit de corps with your own eyes, and people will be telling you how happy they are to be in your organization.

Arthur Ochs Sulzberger, Sr., is chairman emeritus of The New York Times Company. He is also a former Marine Corps captain. About his experiences in running *The New York Times*, he said, "I quickly learned that team work—all pulling together toward an identifiable common goal—worked far better than rushing headlong 'over the top' only to discover that no one was behind you."[15]

To Build and Maintain High Morale and Esprit De Corps, Follow These Action Steps:

1. Let others participate in the ownership of your ideas, goals, and objectives.

2. Be cheerful in everything you do.

3. Know what's going on, and take action to fix or capitalize on it.

4. Lead by personal example whenever possible.

5. Maintain high personal integrity.

6. Build mutual confidence by demonstrating real concern for those you are responsible for.

7. Focus on contribution, not personal gain, yourself, and encourage everyone in your organization to do the same.

In the last two chapters we've learned how to build a winning organization, like a winning football team. You know that to do it requires the construction of four building blocks:

- Cohesion
- Teamwork
- High morale
- Esprit de corps

Construct these four elements, and you'll have an organizational team that can play with the "pros" and win, any day.

Colonel LeRoy P. Hunt, United States Marine Corps, had the following message mimeographed and given to his troops just before they landed at Guadalcanal: "We are meeting a tough and wily opponent but he is not sufficiently tough and wily to overcome us because WE ARE MARINES."[16]

Is there any question about why this team won?

Now turn to the next chapter and see how to coach your winning team.

NOTES

1. *The Armed Forces Officer* (Washington, D.C.: Armed Forces Information Service, 1975), p. 132.

2. Ibid., p. 138.

3. Robert Debs Heinl, Jr., *Dictionary of Military and Naval Quotations* (Annapolis, MD: United States Naval Institute, 1966), p. 196.

4. Edgar F. Puryear, *Nineteen Stars* (Presidio, CA: Presidio Press, 1971), p. 19.

5. *Air Force Leadership* (Washington, D.C.: Department of the Air Force, 1948), p. 44.

6. *Air Force Leadership,* op. cit., p. 46.

7. *The Armed Forces Officer,* op. cit., p. 74.

8. Edgar F. Puryear, Jr., op. cit., p. 233.

9. *The Armed Forces Officer,* op. cit., p. 159.

10. Thomas E. Cronin, "Thinking About Leadership," in Robert L. Taylor and William E. Rosenbach, eds., *Military Leadership* (Boulder, CO: Westview Press, 1984), p. 206.

11. Perry M. Smith, *Taking Charge* (Washington, D.C.: National Defense University, 1986), pp. 28–29.

12. Dave Oliver, Jr. *Lead On!* (Novato, CA: Presidio Press, 1992), p. 147.

13. Puryear, op. cit., p. 326.

14. Tom Clancy with Fred Franks, Jr., *Into the Storm* (New York: G. P. Putnam's Sons, 1997), p. 187.

15. Dan Carrison and Rod Walsh, *Semper Fi* (New York: AMACOM, 1999), p. 98.

16. *The Armed Forces Officer,* op. cit., p. 160.

CHAPTER TEN

HOW TO COACH YOUR WINNING TEAM

When I was a young lieutenant learning to be a navigator and bombardier on B-52 aircraft, I had the good fortune to be assigned to a crew on which Lieutenant Colonel John Porter served as the senior navigator.

John Porter had been the "squadron navigator," that is, the senior navigator in the squadron. Then the establishment announced a new policy. Staff officers like John were to serve on crews in addition to their staff assignments.

Someone warned me that with Colonel Porter on my crew, I would have to attend the "Porter School of Navigation." This I understood would be neither voluntary nor easy.

Until he was satisfied that you were a straight-shooter, John stood for absolutely no nonsense. He expected young lieutenant-navigators to absolutely know their stuff. Since it was a foregone conclusion that lieutenants did not know everything they should, John was ready, willing, and able to teach.

The next six months of my flying career were far from easy. John demanded and got my full attention both in the air and on the ground. He insisted that I know everything about navigation and B-52s. If I fluffed off, I was instantly corrected. However, when I did my homework, worked hard, but still screwed up, John was patient.

He went over things for me and showed me where I had gone wrong. He showed me techniques that increased my ability to operate quickly under the dual demands of time and accuracy. Ultimately, I understood what was meant by the "Porter School of Navigation." It was a term of respect.

Thanks to John's training and coaching, I developed into a passable navigator. His coaching built a team of navigators in the squadron who not only knew their stuff, but were motivated to do their best.

Had we had to go to war during the Cuban missile crisis, much of our ability to carry out our mission successfully would have been due to this one lieutenant colonel.

His setting the example for me of how to coach led to my becoming an instructor and later a combat instructor and the squadron training officer in attack aircraft in combat in Vietnam.

Some of the teaching techniques I used later, both in the Air Force Reserve and as a professor, came from John Porter.

So thanks, John. I think your coaching in the Porter School of Navigation paid off.[1]

A LEADER MUST BE A COACH AND TEACHER

There is no question that as a leader you have responsibilities to teach. I mentioned the importance of this concept in earlier chapters. As Major General Perry M. Smith, former Commandant at National War College, says, "Teachership and leadership go hand-in-glove. The leader must be willing to teach skills, to share insights, and experiences, and to work very closely with people to help them mature and be creative. . . . By teaching, leaders can inspire, motivate, and influence subordinates at various levels."[2]

Coaching Must Be a Way of Life

Do you remember the *Kung Fu* series on television, starring David Caradine? The technical adviser on the series, and also

Caradine's double for many of the fight scenes, was a gentleman born in Hong Kong. His name is Kam Yuan. Kam is an engineer as well as a doctor of chiropractry. But he is best known for his Kung Fu skills.

Kam and I became friends when I had occasion to do some business consulting for his "Kwoon." A Kwoon is a Kung Fu gymnasium. I was most impressed by his sincerity and attitude toward his fellow man. Kam is a person who is always willing to give of himself to help others. And he gave of himself even while he ran several businesses, appeared in the *Kung Fu* television series, made a movie, and instructed in his Kwoon.

At the time I was interested in and worked out in another of the martial arts: karate. How, I asked Kam, was he able to maintain his very high standard of Kung Fu, at the same time as he had so many other interests?

"Kung Fu," Kam answered, "is not just a martial art, it is a way of life. I practice it continuously."

If you want to coach a winning team, coaching can't be a one-time or a periodic activity. As Professor of Management Burt K. Scanlon says, "Effective coaching is a day-to-day, not a once-a-year activity. The more time that managers spend in a supportive role with subordinates, rather than doing the work or telling them how to do it, the better the results will be."[3]

So if you want to coach a winning team, the first thing you must do is make coaching your way of life. This means that you should look for opportunities to help those that follow you improve. The greater the improvement among your group's members, the better they will perform their organizational tasks. The better they perform their tasks, the better the organization you will have.

What to Do to Become a Good Coach

If you want to become a good coach, it's not difficult. There are five things you must do.

- Be Accessible
- Counsel
- Give Recognition
- Reprimand
- Discipline

Why You Must Be Accessible

It is a mistake to build a wall between yourself and those you lead. This does not mean that you must become "one of the boys" to the extent that you become overly familiar with them. What it means is that you are completely open with everyone. If there is a problem, or something to be said, you want it to get said.

A wall will prevent all but good news from getting through. That can hurt your leadership and your organization quite a bit.

When I was the director of research and development activities for a company, we were trying to develop a set of earcups for flight helmets that would increase the pilot's ear protection. We'd been working for months without success. Finally, we had what appeared to be a breakthrough. The protective results as measured by an acoustical laboratory indicated success. I waited impatiently for my project engineer to approve a general design of the concept. Instead, he looked at the results and said that something didn't look right. He wanted the tests repeated.

I adamantly refused. "After all these months we are finally successful and you want to repeat the tests? No way!"

"Boss, it will cost very little and will mean only one week's delay."

"We don't need any delay," I countered. "It works now."

"I'm not sure of that," he said.

"Well, I'm sure. Sign the approval."

Fortunately, I had no walls with any of my people. They knew that I expected them to argue their causes as long as they believed in them and until I made a decision. But hadn't I just made my decision?

My engineer looked me in the eye and said, "Boss, if that's the way you want it, I'll sign off. But before I do I want you to remember that if I'm wrong, the cost is very little. However, if I'm right and these tests are wrong, we'll save a bundle. With that in mind and before you make your final decision, I want you to know that if we don't repeat these tests I must state emphatically that you're full of bananas." However, he didn't use the word bananas.

His statement caused me to rethink the problem. He was right. I was too eager to press on after so much previous time invested in trying to solve the problem. Since there was doubt, it made sense to take the time to check it out.

We did, and my project engineer was right. The tests were incorrect for several critical frequencies. We had actually solved the overall problem, and this minor problem was easy to correct.

I shudder to think what would have happened had I been the kind of leader who insisted on instant obedience in every situation. We would have wasted forty thousand dollars or more in tooling costs and some time before the error would have been discovered.

Probably more than half of the screw-ups made in any situation that ultimately cause a major problem are actually spotted by someone in the organization. Either this individual was afraid to go to the responsible leader, couldn't get to the responsible leader, or the responsible leader wouldn't listen. The Watergate and Contra affairs as well as the Space Shuttle *Challenger* disaster all fall into this category.

This doesn't mean that you must always take the advice offered, or that there aren't situations where there is no time for discussion. It does mean that your subordinates shouldn't be afraid to make their feelings known in the strongest terms possible. It also means that there should be a clear channel to ensure that you receive this message.

Part of this has to do with your manner of dealing with those who report to you. If you accept no difference of opinion, you'll get none.

What do you think will happen if only those who agree with you get promoted? Let me tell you that it won't be long before everyone agrees with you. Some of your best people will have long since left your organization.

You must also frequently check on the procedures in force to allow people to see you. You will find that your staff will tend to protect you from those they consider to be time wasters or who would upset you. If you make an unthinking comment that you don't want to see any more time wasters, you won't. The problem is, it will be your staff's decision as to who is, and who is not, a time waster.

COUNSEL THOSE WHO FOLLOW

Counseling means a one-on-one meeting. During this meeting, you can go over what your subordinate has done, good and bad, since the last counseling session. You can also discover what is bothering and what is pleasing the person you are counseling. Sometimes you can find out quite a bit in this way. Along with seeing and being seen, you can keep in touch with the health of your organization this way.

There are two important aspects to counseling that you should not ignore. The first is when to do it. The second is what to do in a counseling session.

When Should You Counsel?

Many organizations require that their managers counsel all employees periodically, usually once a year. A periodic counseling is fine. Both you and the individual being counseled knows that it is coming and can prepare for it. For followers or leaders who are reticent about meeting, a periodic counseling ensures that a meeting will take place. However, periodic counseling, while good, is insufficient.

In one of my early leadership experiences in industry, I hired an older man who was far more experienced than I. In many ways, he did a good job. However, one thing he did angered me. When I assigned a task, I could not depend on him to complete it on my deadline without several reminders. Of course, I reprimanded him. It did no good. He performed well in other ways. He did what I asked. He was not disrespectful. But I had to dun him to get him to complete a project when I wanted it. He could not be depended on to do a job on his own without this nudging. I hadn't the time to let him alone to "learn a lesson" from missing a deadline.

I intended to have a special counseling session with him about this problem, but it seemed that I was always too busy. I knew that after six months his initial salary review with a full counseling session would require me to speak to him in depth. Maybe the fact that he was much older and more experienced than I had something to do with it.

Than one day the date for his salary review arrived. Now I had a problem. He was doing a good job. But to give him a salary increase when he still wasn't completing projects without reminders meant that I accepted the situation as it existed.

I decided that due to this problem, I could not recommend a raise; however, what I would do was to recommend a supplemental review after an additional ninety days.

At the counseling session, I asked if I had been assigning too much work for him to do. He said that I had not. I explained why he would not be getting a raise and about the supplemental review. I suggested some methods he might use to ensure finishing a project without my reminders. He was surprised. He said he expected me to remind him continually. According to him, this was the procedure in his former company.

Whether his explanation was completely accurate or not is beside the point. What is relevant is that this employee effortlessly turned the situation around. After our counseling session, I could depend on his getting his work done on time, every time, without my saying anything. He had no difficulty earning a raise at the supplemental review. In fact, I made his raise retroactive to the time of his initial review. I had no difficulties at all with him afterwards.

Here was a case in which I allowed the situation to fester unnecessarily for six months. I vowed that I would never let it happen again, and it never has.

When to Call a Special Counseling Session

In addition to a special counseling session called for by someone who works for you, you should call for a special counseling session whenever

- Performance is lacking in some way.
- You want to get an opinion about something.
- You think you can help.
- You want to review a past action or project as a learning experience.
- You want to offer advice about the future.
- There is evidence of a problem of some sort.
- Any other reason you may have for communicating privately with someone you work for or who works for you.

How Should You Structure a Counseling Session?

Some leaders think they can easily ad-lib a counseling session. This is a mistake. Depending on its purpose, you should clearly lay out what you want to discuss and what questions you want to ask before the session.

Of course, you should be ready to answer all questions in a straightforward manner. In addition, don't be afraid to ask questions yourself.

Mayor Ed Koch of New York City went everywhere asking, "How am I doing?" He didn't always get a positive answer. But every answer provided him with important information about what he and his administration were doing right and doing wrong in running New York.

Questions You Should Ask During Counseling

Major General Perry recommends that a leader ask these questions during counseling:

- What aspects of this organization do you like the most?

- What areas around here bother you the most?

- What are your ideas for improving this organization?

- What policies, procedures, tactics, subordinate organizations, systems, etc., should we divest ourselves of and on what kind of schedule (now, next year, five years from now, etc.)?

- In your judgment, who are the most innovative, helpful, and cooperative people in this organization?

- What are your personal goals while you are in this organization?

- Where and to what job would you like to go next; why and when?

- What do you consider to be your most significant weaknesses?

- What self-improvement programs do you have underway?

- What do you think your chances are for promotion to the next level, and in what time frame?

- What bothers you the most about my decisions and my leadership style?

- What three things cause you to waste your time the most?

- What are the goals that you have established for your organization?

- Please evaluate the performance of the organization, unit, or group that you led over the past six months. Please outline the high and low points of the period.[4]

General Perry's list of questions may or may not be applicable to your organization. So you should not use his list, or any list of questions for counseling automatically without thinking through the peculiarities of your organization.

One successful leader I know follows the same counseling procedure every time he takes over a new organization. He asks, "What is it exactly that you do? What are your problems? How can I help you? What can I do to make your job easier?"

Why Counseling Sessions Are Important

Counseling sessions provide excellent opportunities for subordinates to talk to you off the record, yet in a meaningful way. Done right, you can find out quite a lot about people that you did not previously know. The biblical quotation, "Ask and you shall receive," is pretty good advice when it comes to counseling.

Your subordinates can talk to you about things that bother them, and you can put rumor and gossip to rest. It is a good opportunity for you and your followers to set goals and work toward performance. Take advantage of this aspect of leadership. Coach your team by good counseling.

GIVE RECOGNITION

Never fail any opportunity to recognize good performance by someone in your organization. For one thing, it is the right thing to do. When someone does something right, he or she has earned your praise. Don't you believe that you should be recognized when you do a good job? Don't you feel that you have earned the recognition of others under these circumstances? Let me assure you that everyone else feels the same way. It is a tenet of human nature. In fact, recognition is one of the most powerful of human motivators.

During World War II, an army air force group commander found that he had as many losses due to accidents and poor maintenance as due to the enemy.

When other techniques failed, he established a system of awards for success in maintenance. The awards in themselves were insignificant. There were certificates of merit, scarce items from the post exchange, and forty-eight-hour passes. He gave these awards for the fewest number of aircraft aborting takeoff due to maintenance, the fewest mechanical failures of equipment on missions, and the most number of days aircraft were available for combat.

This leader used every technique he could think of to give the widest praise and publicity to winners. He held special award ceremonies. He had pictures taken and sent to hometown newspapers. He wrote special letters of commendation and favorable communication.

The awards may not have been very significant. But the recognition and local fame that accompanied them were considered pretty important. So much so that you would have thought that each award was worth no less than a million dollars.

This group commander soon had an outstanding maintenance record.[5]

An old Air Force manual on leadership said, "Make allies of human nature's tendencies. Don't 'buck' them as enemies. This desire for success and recognition is one of your most valuable assets in leading."[6]

Major General "Red" Newman, U.S. Army, retired, author of two books on leadership and generalship says, "In command and leadership many qualities, attributes and techniques are required—including drive, force, judgement, perception and others. But nothing can replace the inspiration and lift that comes from commending a job well done."[7]

The Pink Cadillac Lady on Recognition

Mary Kay Ash, that fabulous woman who built a billion-dollar-a-year cosmetics company using outstanding leadership techniques, says, "Because we recognize the need for people to be praised, we make a concentrated effort to give as much recognition as possible."[8]

And so she does. Yes, Mary Kay gives away pink Cadillacs, expensive fur coats, diamond jewelry, and many other tangible awards for top sales. But she does more. Mary Kay gives out ribbons worth pennies, gets people on stage to receive applause, sends out handwritten notes of commendation, publishes three separate magazines (two monthly, one weekly) to recognize superior performers, and personally recognizes and encourages her people whenever and wherever she can.

Mary Kay feels that one of the strongest forms of recognition costs nothing at all. It is simply praise. Mary Kay believes that your praise will help your people achieve success. She calls this principle "praising people to success." Mary Kay knows that people respond to praise and recognition as to nothing else. And so at every sign of success, even a small one, she heaps on the praise.

"I believe that you should praise people whenever you can; it causes them to respond as a thirsty plant responds to water."[9]

You shouldn't be surprised to learn that her concept is psychologically very sound.

Give Recognition as Soon as Possible

Psychologists tell us that the concept of recognition is on target. But they also tell us something else. Famed behaviorist B. F. Skinner maintained that to get the maximum motivational mileage, you should praise as soon as possible after the praiseworthy behavior occurs.[10]

Unfortunately, even the military sometimes blows this, and I consider it almost criminal its not doing what's right and for effective leadership. I remember in combat that occasionally someone would do something worthy, and a couple of days later he would get the medal. That's the way it should be. Think of MacArthur pinning on the award of the recipient even before he did the deed, as I described in Chapter 2.

All too frequently, however, it's another story. The problem is it becomes very bureaucratic, and too many people get involved with "protecting the integrity of the award." What this really means is that by their thinking, no act is really good enough. So they bounce the recommendation back for lack of a comma, or something equally trivial. Eventually, the person who made the recommendation moves on to another assignment or maybe just gets frustrated after the paperwork gets bounced three or four times, and then he or she gives up. As I said, I consider this criminal! I've personally been involved in helping people get awards that were earned several years previously. And you have probably read of instances where people are just now getting medals earned during World War II. When this happens, this has just the opposite effect on the individual and the organization.

As a leader, making sure people get the medals they earn expeditiously is one of your major responsibilities.

General Grant Shows Us the Way

During the Civil War, we had only one medal, the Medal of Honor. But senior generals were also allowed to give officers under their command promotion to brevet rank for extraordinary accomplishments. This meant a new title and the wearing of the higher rank insignia, but no increase in responsibilities or pay as was normally the case with promotion. It was an honor like a medal.

In May of 1864, Grant battled Confederate forces at Spotsylvania with little luck. Then Colonel Emory Upton led an assault that nearly succeeded by overrunning Confederate defenses at what was called "the bloody angle." Grant wasted no time in bestowing instant recognition.

"I had been authorized to promote officers on the field for special acts of gallantry. By this authority I conferred the rank of brigadier-general upon Upton on the spot."[11]

General Custer's Solution (and Mine)

Everything you thought you knew about General George A. Custer of Little Big fame probably isn't true. I won't go into all the details here. It will have to be the subject of an entirely separate book. Let me just tell you a little. Custer was one of our first combat aviators as a balloon observer in 1862. He became a brigadier general only two years after graduation from West Point. He was the only Union general to beat the famed Confederate cavalry General Jeb Stuart, first at Gettysburg and later again at Yellow Tavern, where Stuart was killed. Custer became the youngest major general while still in his twenties and was considered the best cavalry general of the war. He never lost a battle, either in the Civil War or in the Indian Wars until Little Big Horn. And his opinion of Indians? He said if he were an Indian, he'd fight against the White Man, too. To repeat Peter Drucker's saying once again, "What 'everyone knows' is usually wrong."

Why do I bring up Custer. Because Custer also got frustrated at the approval rate of medals his men earned. His solution? He established his own medal, which he awarded and of which those who earned it were fiercely proud. Coming up against similar problems in 1993, as a general in the Air Force reserve, I read about Custer's solution. It was, of course, unauthorized. But it was effective. So I did the same thing. I established the "Medal of Merit." It was big and impressive and was worn around the neck with a red, white, and blue ribbon. It also came with a wall plaque describing the reason for the award. I awarded it at a ceremony complete with pomp and photographer, just as for official decorations. My comments during the ceremony included the fact that the award was unauthorized and therefore could not be worn as part of the uniform. Moreover, I added, if it were worn during a "Dining Out," the offending individual would be sent to the "grog bowl."

Dining Outs are official full-dress dinners during which there is a considerable amount of wildness and slack given to regulations. Those committing violations of Air Force regulations, real or imagined, at a Dining Out are usually punished by having to drink from the "grog bowl." In the old days, the grog bowl had awful mixtures of alcoholic drinks. As the Air Force has retreated more and more from its hard-drinking image, however, the grog bowls have become filled with the wrong combinations of beverages such as mixtures of chocolates, catsup and mustard that are potent, but nonalcoholic. Of course, all recipients did proudly wear their unauthorized medals at our Dining Outs.

I feel I must render a word of caution to leaders both in and out of uniform here. When you order something contrary to regulations such as the "Custer Medal," you've got to accept responsibility for your actions. I decided that it was the right thing to do, so I did it. But I knew I was violating regulations and was fully prepared to accept my punishment, if that were the result.

Recognition can be one of your most important coaching techniques. Even Emperor Napoleon was shocked at the sheer power of recognition as a motivator. After being told that his soldiers would commit almost any act of bravery for one of the emperor's medals, he exclaimed, "It is amazing what men will do for such baubles."

REPRIMAND WHEN NECESSARY

A leader cannot always be a "good guy." Sometimes you must reprimand and discipline. If you fail to do so, the offense, whatever it is, will likely be repeated. In addition, you will send a message throughout your entire organization that you do not care, that any performance or conduct is acceptable. And, of course, if you do not care you cannot expect others who would follow you to care.

General Patton advised immediate reprimand for every mistake. When one of his men made a mistake, he let that man know it, instantly. Said General Patton, "I cannot kill a man in our combat training, but I can make every man wish to be dead rather than take the wrath of my anger.!"[12]

It is interesting to note that Patton's advice is fully in tune with more modern thinking about reprimands. Kenneth Blanchard and Spencer Johnson advise, in their best-selling book, *The One Minute Manager*, "Reprimand people immediately. Tell people what they did wrong—be specific. Tell people how you feel about what they did wrong—and in no uncertain terms."[13]

When You Must Reprimand, Do So at Once

Remember that a reprimand is criticism. So, as pointed out in an earlier chapter, you should reprimand in private. Sometimes your interview with intent to reprimand brings out causes that justify the actions taken by your subordinate. Then there is no need to reprimand at all, and you will know it immediately. Since you have had the reprimand interview in private, you will embarrass neither yourself nor anyone else.

If you are angry, tell the individual you are reprimanding that you are angry and why. It's okay to be angry. It is not okay to lose your self-control, however. A loss of control means loss of focus on your main objective in performing the reprimand.

When you reprimand, be certain to keep your mind focused on what you are trying to achieve. You do not want to leave him or her hurt, resentful, or frightened. What you do want is for the individual to have the desire to improve on his or her own. Mary Kay's technique of sandwiching the criticism between two compliments as discussed in Chapter 4 is one way to do this. Another way is to follow Blanchard and Johnson's recommendations:

"Shake hands, or touch them in a way that lets them know you are honestly on their side. Remind them how much you value them.

Reaffirm that you think well of them but not of their performance in this situation. Realize that when the reprimand is over, it's over."[14]

ADMINISTERING DISCIPLINE

Occasionally, the offense is more serious. You must administer some form of discipline. When you must administer discipline, do it. Don't delay. The longer you delay, the more difficult it will be for you and for the person who must be punished. In addition, a delay can increase the chances of the disciplining action being perceived as unfair.

Always take some form of corrective action when discipline is needed. If you are disciplining partially as a future deterrent, it is the certainty of the punishment that constitutes the main deterrent component, not the severity of it.

In seventeenth-century England, the punishment for highway robbery was death. Today, the punishment for the same crime is several years' imprisonment. However, there are proportionately far fewer robberies. The reason is that the likelihood of being caught and punished is far more certain today.[15]

In the United States, the incidence of robberies is proportionately far higher than it is in England. There may be many reasons for this. It is not because the punishment has been reduced, however. The penalty for robbery was never death in the United States. One reason for the proportionately higher number of robberies in the United States today is because the likelihood of being caught and punished is less likely than it was once.

One important aspect of discipline is not to administer it, but to achieve and maintain it.

The Latin root of "to discipline" is "to teach." The level of discipline is, as with the level of teaching, what you as a leader make of it. If you want the members of your group to respect their leaders, to respect themselves, and to always perform at the highest standards, they must be taught to do so. This cannot be done instantaneously. You cannot be lax in enforcing performance and then suddenly come on like Attila the Hun.

George Washington said, "To bring men to a proper degree of subordination is not the work of a day, a month, or a year."[16] Washington knew that to achieve high standards of discipline is a rough, tough job that takes time to accomplish.

What he did not say is that once discipline has been allowed to decay, it is ten times as hard for the old leader to rebuild it. This is why leaders who have failed to maintain high standards of discipline are frequently relieved of command in the military or are fired from their civilian positions. It takes a new leader to turn the organization around. A new leader can be a strong disciplinarian and rebuild the organization. The old leader frequently cannot do this.

What Can You Do if Discipline Isn't What It Should Be?

If discipline in your organization has been allowed to wane, what can you do? First, you can set the example for high standards. You can never expect those who follow you to maintain a high standard of discipline if you fail to do this yourself.

Next, pick one area. Focus on that one area alone.

Let's say that your company has a policy that lunch breaks are limited to one hour. Over the years, this policy has become pretty sloppy. Not only are lunch breaks more than one hour, but most are in the neighborhood of one to two hours.

If you are a new leader you can make many changes simultaneously. If you are not, you can't. So you're going to work on this one problem first.

List all the reasons why the current action is unacceptable. It's cheating the company. It's unprofessional. Customers who can't get hold of you when they want to aren't serviced properly. It gives the organization a poor image. It sets a poor example for hourly employees or younger managers, and so on.

Decide on the punishment for failing to adhere to the company's rules. This can be docking of pay or working extra hours, right on up to firing. This is up to you. Just make sure that the punishment is fair and reasonable.

Think through the whole situation. Are there any circumstances that will justify a longer lunch? How will this be handled? Are you being completely reasonable considering everything?

When you're fully prepared, call your group together and tell them the problem and the solution. Be ready to answer any questions. When you know what you are talking about, your group will realize that you are right and will be willing to support you. In fact, you'll probably find that those who have stayed within the rules are very happy about your new policy. They may have felt cheated for years because they pulled more than their share of the load due to others' taking extended lunches.

Once you have this problem under control, move on to the next one. You'll be walking a fine line. Naturally, you want to turn things around as soon as you can. And you should. On the other hand, if you try to move too quickly after you yourself have been too permissive, you'll cause considerable resentment. This resentment will actually slow your progress and may cause other problems.

But you can help to start moving things in the right direction no matter what changes must be made. When Thomas H. Wyman took over the Green Giant Company, a company with annual sales of more than $425 million, he found the culture too relaxed. How do you administer discipline to a culture? According to President Wyman, "It's not very complicated. If you call a couple of meetings at four o'clock (which will obviously last for an hour or two), that begins to communicate a message. Or you leave a note on someone's desk at five o'clock saying you're sorry they couldn't meet with you. You follow up the next day on requests for information. You suggest close-in deadlines. You answer your own mail very promptly."[17]

SIX WAYS TO COACH YOUR WINNING TEAM

1. Make coaching a way of life. Do it day in and day out.

2. Ensure that you are accessible to those you lead.

3. Counsel those you lead periodically and when they need it.

4. Never let an opportunity to recognize someone for good performance go by without taking it.

5. Reprimand whenever you have to.

6. Maintain high standards of discipline.

Finally, for maximum effectiveness, give recognition, reprimand, and discipline as soon as you determine one of these actions should be taken.

NOTES

1. When I wrote these lines more than ten years ago, I had no idea where John Porter was, or even whether he was alive. Back in 1992, however, when I was promoted to brigadier general, I got a call. It was John Porter, and I was able to thank John in person for his ministrations as a leader to a young lieutenant so many years ago.

2. Perry M. Smith, *Taking Charge* (Washington, D.C.: National Defense University Press, 1986), p. 4.

3. Burt K. Scanlon, "Managerial Leadership in Perspective: Getting Back to Basics," in A. Dale Timpe, ed., *Leadership* (New York: Facts on File Publications, 1988), p. 25.

4. Ibid., pp. 39–43.

5. *AFM 35–15 Air Force Leadership* (Washington, D.C.: Department of the Air Force, 1948), p. 23.

6. Ibid.

7. Aubrey Newman, *Follow Me* (Presidio, CA: Presidio Press, 1981), pp. 176–177.

8. Mary Kay Ash, *Mary Kay on People Management* (New York: Warner Books, 1984), p. 25.

9. Ibid., p. 23.

10. William F. Dowling and Leonard Sayles, *How Managers Motivate, 2nd ed.* (New York: McGraw-Hill, 1971, 1978), p. 18.

11. Ulysses S. Grant, quoted in Al Kaltman, *Leadership Lessons from General Ulysses S. Grant* (Paramus, N.J: Prentice Hall Press, 1998), p. 157.

12. Porter B. Williamson, *Patton's Principles* (New York: Simon and Schuster, 1979), p. 35.

13. Kenneth Blanchard and Spencer Johnson, *The One Minute Manager* (New York: William Morrow and Company, 1982), p. 59.

14. Ibid.

15. *AFM 35–15 Air Force Leadership*, op. cit., p. 38.

16. *The Armed Forces Officer* (Washington, D.C.: Department of Defense, 1975), p. 123.

17. Chester Burger, *The Chief Executive* (Boston: CBI Publishing Company, Inc., 1978), p. 88.

CHAPTER ELEVEN

SECRETS OF MOTIVATION

Why are people motivated to do things for you or for your organization? The truth is there is no one single factor that motivates all of your people all of the time. Also, different people are motivated by different things at any one point in time. But the biggest mistake that leaders make with motivation is not even understanding what motivates most of their followers most of the time. And the worst situation is thinking that those who follow you are motivated primarily by one thing, when in fact they are motivated by something entirely different.

WHAT DO EMPLOYEES CONSIDER MOST IMPORTANT ABOUT THEIR JOBS?

Social scientists studied many industries to determine what factors employees consider most important in their jobs. My psychologist-wife tells me that over the years their questionnaires have been given to hundreds of thousands of employees. The results have been known for some time. They are not secret. One study was done by the Public Agenda Foundation and noted by John Naisbitt and Patricia Aburdene in their book, *Re-inventing the Corporation.*[1]

Before I give you these results maybe you would like to take the test yourself. I've given it to thousands of leaders in my seminars. All you need to do is rank the following factors in the order of importance you think your employees would put them, ranking "1" being most important, "2" being second most important, and so on. Take a couple of minutes to do this before going on. You can do this right in the book.

____ Work with people who treat me with respect

____ Interesting work

____ Recognition for good work

____ Chance to develop skills

____ Working for people who listen if I have ideas about how to do things better

____ A chance to think for myself rather than just carry out instructions

____ Seeing the end results of my work

____ Working for efficient managers

____ A job that is not too easy

____ Feeling well informed about what is going on

____ Job security

____ High pay

____ Good benefits

Now, go over your answers. Don't turn the page until you are certain you have these factors in their order of importance to your employees. Then turn the page.

_1_ Work with people who treat me with respect

_2_ Interesting work

_3_ Recognition for good work

_4_ Chance to develop skills

  <u>5</u> Working for people who listen if I have ideas about how to do things better

  <u>6</u> A chance to think for myself rather than just carry out instructions

  <u>7</u> Seeing the end results of my work

  <u>8</u> Working for efficient managers

  <u>9</u> A job that is not too easy

  <u>10</u> Feeling well informed about what is going on

  <u>11</u> Job security

  <u>12</u> High pay

  <u>13</u> Good benefits

WHY JOB SECURITY, HIGH PAY, AND GOOD BENEFITS MAY NOT BE AS IMPORTANT AS YOU THOUGHT

That's right, the factors are exactly in their order as listed. These are the results after interviewing hundreds of thousands of employees. How many did you get right? Ninety percent of those leaders I survey put one or more of these—job security, high pay, and good benefits—in the top five. That is, they thought these factors were the most important to their employees. But these three factors are usually far down the list.

This doesn't mean that job security, high pay, and good benefits aren't important. They are. But these other factors are more important.

I once worked as an executive recruiter. It was my job to find unique top executives for my client companies according to detailed job specifications we prepared together. Usually the candidates for these positions were already employed at high positions in other companies. So a good part of the job was convincing these high-flying executives that it was worth their time to look at a new opportunity.

Yes, compensation, benefits, and security played a part in their decisions. But even though inducements to move in compensation alone could be a 30 percent increase or more, many executives just weren't interested. For those who were interested, the increased salary and benefits were usually more important as signals that the new job was truly more important and a better opportunity. And yes, some executives left for jobs at lower salaries, fewer benefits, and less job security. This was either because the position presented a greater opportunity to them in other ways, or because they were dissatisfied in their current positions despite the higher pay and benefits.

Max DePree is former chairman and CEO of Herman Miller, Inc. That's the furniture maker that *Fortune* magazine named one of the ten "best-managed" and "most innovative" companies. It was also chosen as one of the hundred best companies to work for in America. DePree says, "The best people working for organizations are like volunteers. Since they could probably find good jobs in any number of groups, they choose to work somewhere for reasons less tangible than salary or position. Volunteers do not need contracts, they need covenants."[2]

What Do People Want from Their Jobs?

Go back over the list, looking at items in the upper half. These are

- Working with people who treat me with respect
- Interesting work
- Recognition for good work
- Chance to develop skills
- Working for people who listen if I have ideas about how to do things better
- A chance to think for myself rather than just carry out instructions

What do these all have in common? For one thing, none of them will cost you very much to implement compared with pay, benefits, or providing perfect job security. For another, these are factors that you can improve regardless of restrictions or limitations on salary or benefits placed by your parent organization.

Think about what this means to you as a leader who wants to motivate his or her people to higher performance. Most of these factors considered important by employees can probably be improved by you today, and they will probably cost very little.

Treating People with Respect Wins over People and Wins Battles

Isn't it within your power to treat people with respect and ensure that others who work for you do the same? Certainly every human being deserves to be treated with respect. Many outstanding leaders maintain you should treat those who work for you with even more than respect. Like Mary Kay Ash, you should imagine everyone you see wearing a large sign saying, "MAKE ME FEEL IMPORTANT."

The night before the battle of Austerlitz, Napoleon went from campfire to campfire in his army. At every stop, his men gathered around him. Napoleon joked with his men and thanked them for their loyalty. He assured them of victory and explained how he had arranged for medical aid to come to them as swiftly as possible if they were wounded.[3]

Do you think Napoleon treated his men with respect? You bet he did, and you can bet this respect was returned as well.

" 'Promise us,' shouted a veteran grenadier, 'that you will keep yourself out of the fire.'

" 'I will do so,' Napoleon answered; 'I shall be with the reserve until you need me.' "[4]

James MacGregor Burns, an American political scientist, wrote an outstanding, scholarly book called simply *Leadership*.[5] In fact, the book was so outstanding that it won the Pulitzer Prize. Listen to his succinct advice: "In real life, the most practical advice for leaders is not to treat pawns like pawns, nor princes like princes, but all persons like persons."[6]

If You Want People to Go All Out, Make Their Work Interesting

Can you provide interesting work, or can you make the work that your people must do interesting in some way? There are many opportunities to do this if you think about it. This is why making striving a competitive activity can increase the productivity of your organization.

You would think that a battle is just about as interesting an endeavor as you might imagine. How can a battle be made more interesting? English Field Marshall Bernard Montgomery found a way. Here is Montgomery's famous order to his men before the Battle of Al Alamein in World War II: "The battle which is now about to begin will be one of the decisive battles of history. It will be the turning-point of the war."[7]

Who wouldn't want to do his or her best in one of the decisive battles of history, in one that would be the turning point of the war? Montgomery motivated his army to top performance, and they defeated Rommel and his "unbeatable" Afrika Korps.

The importance of interest in motivation is not a brand-new concept. Almost seventy years ago, Professor Warren Hilton wrote:

> It is not enough to have a mere general passion for success. Mere indefinite wishing for success will never get you anywhere. Besides this general passion, you must have definite interests continually renewed. You must give the mind something specific and tangible and immediate to work upon. You must incessantly add new details. Otherwise interest, attention, and activity will wane.

Your biggest problem is how to keep your efficient output of mental energy at a high level. The solution lies in maintaining interest. . . . You must continually devise new ways of renewing the interest of your men and inspiring them to concentrate their attention upon . . . the mission. You cannot give a young man . . . monotonous and routine duties to perform and expect him to take the interest that you take in your business. You must make his work interesting for him. . . . Keep his and your interest alive by trying to discover new things in old surroundings and new aspects to everyday tasks."[8]

RECOGNITION FOR GOOD WORK IS ONLY FAIR . . . AND IT PAYS DIVIDENDS

How many different ways can you think of to recognize good work? How many different awards and rewards can you give to those who work for you? How many different ways can you think of to publicize your followers' success? How many different personal ways can you say "Congratulations, we're proud of you"?

The President of Israel, Ezer Weizman was commander of the Israeli Air Force in the early 1960s. In those days, the Israeli Air Force was poorly equipped. It was a small air force that had not yet gained the worldwide reputation it established only a few years later.

General Weizman knew every pilot in his air force by first name, and that's how he addressed every pilot. He knew every man's personal problems and interests. He sent flowers to every pilot's wife who gave birth. He coined the air force's recruiting slogan, "The Best for the Air Force." Whenever he picked up the phone, his opening sentence was always, "Well, what's news in the best air force in the Middle East?" Gradually, his men became convinced that despite their small numbers, they were the best.

War came about a year after General Weizman was promoted to Chief of Operations of the Israeli Defense Forces. His pilots didn't let him down in combat. They destroyed 352 enemy aircraft in the first few hours of the Six-Day War.[9]

Everyone Wants Recognition

Believe me, I don't care who it is, everyone wants recognition. Connie Podesta and Jean Gatz, two management consultants, wrote the book *How To Be the Person Successful Companies Fight to Keep*. In it, they report that one CEO confided his frustration and distress: "I have worked so hard to turn this company around. I have managed to keep our profits up without laying off one person. I provide excellent benefits, and I'm willing to pay for my employees to go to school. I spend a great deal of money on picnics, parties, and celebrations because I want them to enjoy their jobs and feel as though this is a family they can count on. Very few of them have ever said thank you or even seem to appreciate how hard I try to make this a great place to work. On the other hand, if one little thing goes wrong or I have to say no to any of their ideas, some of them threaten to quit. And others won't speak to me."[10]

"Tough," you say. "The guy has to learn to be more thick-skinned. If he can't take the heat, he should stay out of the kitchen!" Oh yes, that's all true. But my point is here is someone who has made it to the top of a company. He's making good money and has power and responsibility. And yet, even he craves recognition. If this is true of a person in a position of considerable power, think how true it must be for everyone else . . . including everyone who would follow you.

There are so many ways to recognize your employees. Management expert Bob Nelson actually identified over a thousand. He published them in a book entitled *1001 Ways to Reward Employees*.[11] Better get a copy!

MAKE SURE YOUR PEOPLE HAVE THE OPPORTUNITY TO DEVELOP THEIR SKILLS

Do you create the opportunity for those in your organization to develop their skills? Can you provide special courses in-house? How about a few hours off every week to complete a college degree?

Maybe can you hire a physical-fitness instructor to work with employees during lunch or after work. Sometimes an employee has the ability to do this, or has unique knowledge about which he or she is willing to instruct other employees. All you need to do is ask.

Please don't forget the requirement for you and other leaders in your organization to act as teachers.

Of course by teaching, you also learn. One of the most famous German aces in World War I was a young captain by the name of Oswald Boelcke. Boelcke is especially noteworthy because the tactics he developed more than seventy years ago are still in use by fighter pilots today.

Boelcke went to extraordinary lengths to ensure that new pilots assigned to his squadron were broken in correctly. He would do everything possible to ensure a victory for one of his student-pilots. That included giving up an opportunity to run up his own score of airplanes shot down.

It was Boelcke who developed the idea of "Hunting Squadrons." We would call them fighter squadrons today. He was given command of one such squadron himself. Though he spent much of his time teaching, he managed to down forty aircraft. He died fairly early in the war on October 28, 1916, from an aircraft accident. Had he continued to serve, he might have topped the more famous Manfred von Richthofen who lived two more years and died with eighty victories.

Boelcke's teaching probably helped his country's war efforts more than his personal aerial victories. And his teaching might have helped him gain his victories as well, despite lost opportunities. To quote the New Testament: "Thou therefore which teachest another, teachest thou not thyself?" (Romans 2:21).

LISTENING MOTIVATES

There is little question that listening motivates. It may be far more important in leadership than you ever realized. Some time ago I had the opportunity to talk about top-level military leadership with seven four-star generals and admirals. These were individuals who had reached the top of their profession before retiring. They had been chiefs-of-staff of their services, commanders-in-chief, and one had been Chairman of the Joint Chiefs of Staff.

One of the few factors that set them off from other highly qualified combat leaders who did not reach the top was their ability to listen. In one way or another, every one of them mentioned this as an important, if not critical factor in leadership.

Two Air Force Generals Say: Listen!

General Curtis E. LeMay was one tough cookie. He had seen his share of combat and combat command when he was given command of the Strategic Air Command (SAC), our nuclear retaliatory force. He built it into the most devastating and effective military organization the world had ever seen. He had the image of the tough commander he was, with a constant cigar stuffed into his mouth.

He was known to be absolutely no-nonsense. His modus operandi was to land at a SAC base unannounced and really shake things up when they weren't up to his very high standards. After his impromptu inspection, he would gather the troops around him and speak and answer questions while he stood on a raised platform. And LeMay, tough as he was, would really listen to the comments and concerns of his troops.

On one such occasion he had begun to speak from the platform when a young lieutenant interrupted him. General LeMay listened politely, and he answered the young lieutenant's question. He had barely started to speak when he was interrupted again by the lieutenant. Again he listened politely and answered the question the lieutenant had put to him. Then he began to speak a third time, but for a third time the lieutenant interrupted him before he could get started.

This time, he made a mild comment about the lieutenant's interruptions. But the lieutenant was not to be put off. "You didn't get to be a general by keeping your mouth shut," retorted the young lieutenant.

There was a shocked silence. What would LeMay do? Would he eat the lieutenant alive on the spot? LeMay paused and then commented: "No, that's true. But it is how I got to be a captain."

General Bernard P. Randolph was the commander of Air Force Systems Command. Before the Cold War ended and this command disappeared to be replaced by Air Force Material Command, this organization did all of the Air Force's research-and-development work. This included all of its advanced airplanes, missiles, satellites, and "Star Wars" . . . everything.

In addition to being selected to command an organization that was crucial to the nation's defense, General Randolph was unique in being only the second African American Air Force officer to earn four stars, and he was also the only navigator to achieve this rank. When asked to explain his leadership philosophy in an interview, he answered: "Ask your people what's important to them, and listen."[12]

Listen to Motorola

When Robert W. Galvin was Chairman of the Board and Chief Executive Officer of Motorola, Inc., his company did $1.5 billion in annual sales and employed 50,000 people around the globe. What did the head of a $1.5-billion-dollar company emphasize in his leadership practices? "I emphasize listening," said Chairman Galvin. "We strive to hear what other people want us to hear, even though they don't always come out and say it directly."[13]

Mary Kay Ash Listens

Mary Kay Ash maintains that listening is an art. She says: "If I'm talking to someone in a crowded room, I try to make that person feel as though we're the only ones present. I shut out everything else. I look directly at the person. Even if a gorilla were to walk into the room, I probably wouldn't notice it."[14]

Some Spicy Listening

McCormick & Company, Inc., is a specialty-food company, and as this is written produces almost two billion dollars in annual sales.[15] McCormick & Company has earned an international reputation as a company that knows how to listen to its people and integrate even lower-level employees into decision making. It calls itself "The World's Largest Spice Company." Then-chairman and president Harry K. Harry Wells explained the company's success in these words: "Because of an underlying attitude that the company has developed over the years about how people interact, we have an atmosphere that allows anyone here to sit down and have meaningful dialogues about our policies and our objectives for the future."[16]

The Company that Got the Suggestion Box to Work

Can you create a program to enable you to better listen to new ideas? You say the old suggestion box simply gathers spider webs and chewing-gum wrappers? Well, the Dana Corporation, the auto-parts maker, found a way to make it work. In a recent year, each of Dana's then-45,500 employees submitted an average of 1.22 ideas a month. Really.

Then-CEO, now chairman, Woody Morcott, commented, "It's a core part of our value system." How do they do it? First, they have classes on how to come with and develop new ideas. Then there are awards, luncheons, and much fuss made over those who are prolific at generating good ideas. One plant in Mexico even rewards an employee to the tune of $1.89 for every new idea submitted. By the statistics kept, some 70 percent of all suggestions made are actually adopted. According to leaders at Dana, employee suggestions are making and saving Dana a fortune and keeping the company very competitive.[17]

Last year, sales were $12.5 billion and climbing. And there should be a few more suggestions this year, because now there are 86,000 people working at Dana to make them.[18]

Why not go fifty-fifty on time? Maybe you can donate one hour of company time and your employee can give one hour of time after work to work on his or her idea, using company facilities. Think up some way that the employee will benefit if his or her idea proves out. That's one way to listen to ideas. I'm sure you can think of additional ways.

LET YOUR PEOPLE THINK FOR THEMSELVES

Are you open to letting your people think for themselves? Tell people what to do. Let them decide how to do it for themselves. I don't mean that you shouldn't give help if asked—only that people have their own brains, experiences, and unique backgrounds. That's why they're assigned to the duties they're assigned and not you. That's why they're such valuable commodities.

You can't do all the thinking for everyone in your organization. Try it and you are sure to fail.

Even if you could do all the thinking for all your subordinates, you would be ill-advised to do so. If all of your people thought exactly as you do, your organization would have a pretty limited source of ideas. Perhaps even more important, researchers have discovered that the product of many separate brains working together is greater than the sum of each considered separately. If you try to do all the thinking in your organization yourself, you lose this important synergism.

Let those you lead do their own thinking, and you'll be amazed and surprised at what they come up with and how they use their expertise to solve your problems.

Colonel Motta Gur commanded the Israeli paratrooper brigade that captured Eastern Jerusalem during the Six-Day War of 1967. There was desperate fighting when Gur, in a vehicle called a half track, led his paratroopers into the city. His driver was a huge soldier from the Galilee by the name of Ben-Zur. With Ben-Zur, he passed a column of Israeli tanks and hurried on. At the Lion's Gate to Jerusalem, the entrance was very narrow because of a burning car. Colonel Gur ordered only, "Ben-Zur, drive." His driver continued and without slowing down, managed to avoid the burning vehicle.

As they got closer, they saw that the iron gate had been hit by tank fire and was partially opened. Gur assumed that he would be attacked with grenades as they slowed to open the gate. He said only, "Ben-Zur, drive."

Ben-Zur stepped on the gas, and the door flew off its hinges. Stones flew in every direction, but the vehicle continued down the Via Dolorosa.

They turned left and found the way blocked by a deserted motorcycle in the middle of the road. It could be mined. Gur ordered, "Ben-Zur, drive." Ben-Zur didn't stop and didn't attempt to avoid the motorcycle. Instead, he ran directly over it. If mined, it failed to explode.

Colonel Gur continued in this fashion. At every obstacle, his only order was, "Ben-Zur, drive." The driver made the decision as to how to go over, around, or through the obstacle in order to continue. Eventually Gur, followed by his brigade, arrived at the Temple Mount. For the first time in almost 2,000 years, Jews controlled the Holy Temple.[19]

Colonel Gur eventually became a general and chief of staff of the Israeli Army.

What Does the Combat Model Say?

Let's look at our combat model again. Why does a private soldier making only several hundred dollars a month make a do-or-die assault on a hill, or drive a vehicle into danger as did Colonel Gur's driver, Ben-Zur?

Colonel Mike Malone should know. He has long been known as the army's leading expert on leadership, and he won the army's highest peacetime decoration, the Distinguished Service Medal, for his work in this field. According to Colonel Malone, a soldier goes all out in an attack because

1. His buddies are counting on him.
2. She thinks her buddies will call her a coward if she doesn't.
3. He has learned that his leader knows the right thing to do.
4. She wants to please her leader.
5. He believes he will be court-martialed if he doesn't.
6. She thinks she will be left alone if she doesn't attack.
7. He believes that following orders is the right thing to do.
8. She believes that she will be rewarded for attacking.
9. He believes that attacking is less dangerous than not attacking.
10. She believes that she will feel guilty if she doesn't.
11. He wants to prove his manhood, courage, competence, or worth as a soldier.
12. She enjoys the excitement and thrill of combat.
13. Following orders has become automatic.[20]

Note that job security, high pay, or good benefits play a very small part here. This is consistent with results that Professors Warren Bennis and Burt Nanus from the University of Southern California found in surveying leaders from all kinds of organizations. You can be a terrific leader in most situations despite poor working conditions, low compensation, and few benefits.

WHEN ARE SALARY, JOB SECURITY, AND BENEFITS IMPORTANT?

Salary, job security, and good benefits are important. But they are not of primary importance. You may say, "Listen, in my company people work primarily for the pay and benefits, and that's it." Let's see if that is true.

If you've been in a company for any length of time, you've seen people leave voluntarily. If asked why they are leaving, they will almost invariably respond that they have better offers elsewhere. They may then begin to detail all the advantages of their new positions: higher salaries, bigger jobs, more benefits, bigger offices, and so forth.

If you listen carefully, however, you'll hear a message, even if it isn't verbalized. The message is this: "These people who hired me really appreciate what I have to offer. They recognize my real importance to a much greater extent than here. They are giving me all these benefits because I am especially important."

In other words, although the higher salary and additional benefits were inducements to leave an organization, they may provide only the rationale for the real reason.

Recall again that there are many organizations for which pay, benefits, and job security are nonexistent. Yet those who work in these organizations perform to their maximum. Did you forget the football team we talked about in an earlier chapter? There are also volunteer hospital workers, those who work for low pay on dangerous archeological digs, the Peace Corps, the "Big Brother" programs, the Boy Scouts and Girl Scouts, and hundreds of other organizations.

What part, then, do salary, benefits, and security play in motivation?

What a Scientist Discovered About Motivations Being Interrelated

Back in the 1950s, a social scientist by the name of Abraham Maslow developed a theory of how all motivations fit together. Maslow called his theory the hierarchy of needs. You may have heard of it. But let's see how it might affect motivation from a practical viewpoint.

According to Maslow, we are motivated by various human needs. These needs are at different levels. As one level of needs is satisfied, people are no longer motivated by them. People seek to satisfy the next higher level of needs.

Maslow's first level consists of physiological needs such as eating or breathing. Once these basic physiological needs are satisfied, people seek the next highest level. These are security or safety needs. That's where salary, benefits, and job security come in.

On the next level are social or affiliation needs. After this comes the esteem level. Respect and recognition are motivational at this level. Maslow's highest level is self-actualization, that is, to be everything you are capable of.

Maslow also identified two categories of needs not on his hierarchy. These were the desire to know and understand and aesthetic needs.

What Maslow's theory tells us is this: Once your people are above a certain level, they are no longer motivated by the levels below. Do you stop and worry about breathing? Not unless you have health problems affecting your ability to breathe. It is the same with salary, benefits, and job security. If an employee has salary, benefits, and job security in amounts he or she finds acceptable, of itself these may no longer motivate.

Of course, if there is a threat of losing these three factors, they may become motivational once again.

Maslow's hierarchy of needs is important to us because it helps to explain why high salary, good benefits, and job security may not be as important as other motivational factors, except as symbols of these other factors.

Let me show you what I mean. Some years ago, a company I worked with gave a salary review every year. The amount of annual salary raise was keyed to performance. A top performer could get as much as a 10 percent increase plus an adjustment for cost of living. An average performer received a lower percentage increase for the year. Someone performing below par didn't receive an increase.

One year the company had a very bad year. The company could have frozen all wages. Instead, what it did was to freeze salaries for management only. A pot was created and a formula developed for dividing the pot based on the previous year's performance. As a result, a top performer making, say, $50,000 a year received an increase of less than $700 a year. Still, the increase was a motivator because it was a symbol of high achievement and was not awarded to everyone.

The Man Who Found Two Categories of Motivators that Accomplish Different Things

Another scientist by the name of Frederick Herzberg came along a few years later to build on Maslow's work. Herzberg collected data on job attitude among employees in hundreds of companies. From studying these data, he concluded that people have two categories of needs that affect satisfaction or dissatisfaction with a job.

The first category he called hygiene needs. He gave them this name because these needs serve the function of preventative medicine in the workplace. They prevent job dissatisfaction. They are also distinguished by the fact that these needs are never completely satisfied. You have to keep maintaining them, or you lose performance. You can't increase performance with them. But if your organization is already performing well, you can maintain these high standards with the hygiene factors. Hygiene factors include money, status, treatment, and security.

According to Herzberg, motivators are satisfying factors that relate to the job itself. They involve feelings of achievement, recognition for accomplishment, challenging work, increased responsibility, growth, and development. These are the factors that produce job satisfaction as contrasted with the hygiene needs that prevent only job dissatisfaction.

How can we use Herzberg's theory to help us motivate people to be satisfied with their jobs? We know if we reduce the hygiene factors, we're going to get job dissatisfaction. How would you feel if someone reduced your salary? So to avoid job dissatisfaction, we maintain the hygiene factors at their present levels.

Can we increase job satisfaction by, say, increasing salary? No, not according to Herzberg. Remember, salary is a hygiene factor. If we want those we lead to be more satisfied with their jobs, we must use the motivators. That is, we must look for ways that we can increase

- Feelings of achievement.
- Recognition.
- Challenge in the work.
- Responsibility.
- Growth and development.

Every successful military leader has done this, and you can do it too. If there is adversity, so much the better.

Have you ever heard of Lewis B. "Chesty" Puller?

Puller is the only Marine in history to win five Navy Crosses. The Navy Cross is second only to the Congressional Medal of Honor. Very few men win one Navy Cross. It is extremely rare for someone to win two. Chesty Puller won five. He quit Virginia Military Institute in 1918 to enlist in the Marine Corps and fought over a hundred combats in the Banana Wars of the 1920s, in China in the 1930s, the Pacific during World War II, and then came out of retirement to fight through the Korean War.

So admired was Puller that marine recruits would sing this little ditty to the tune of *Good Night, Ladies.*

Good night, Chesty! Good night, Chesty!
Good night, Chesty—wherever you may be!
After you the Corps will roll, Corps will roll, Corps will
rooooll,
After you the Corps will roll—on to victoree!"[21]

In December 1950, Colonel Chesty Puller led a regiment in retreat to the port of Hungnam, Korea. Overwhelming numbers of attacking Chinese had cut off the entire First Marine Division. The Korean winter was bitter cold and there had been a snowstorm in the morning. There were many wounded. Conditions were grim. Puller stomped up and down the lines. He stopped often to herd men together.

"You're the First Marine Division—and don't you forget it. We're the greatest military outfit that ever walked on this earth. Not all the Communists in hell can stop you. We'll go down to the sea at our own pace and nothing is going to get in our way. If it does, we'll blow the hell out of it."

To others of his own regiment he exhorted, "You're the finest regiment in the finest division in history. We're not retreating! We've about-faced to get at more of those bastards. Be proud you're First Marines."[22]

When Chesty Puller finally retired from the Marines permanently, he retired as a lieutenant general.

ACTION STEPS TO MOTIVATE THOSE YOU LEAD

1. Work on the most important factors first. High salary, good benefits, or job security are of lesser importance.

2. Treat those you lead with respect . . . always.

3. Make the work interesting.

4. Always give recognition for good work.

5. Give those you lead a chance to develop their skills.

NOTES

1. John Naisbitt and Patricia Aburdene, *Re-inventing the Corporation* (New York: Warner Books, 1985), pp. 85–86.

2. Max DePree, *Leadership Is an Art* (New York: Dell Publishing, 1989), p. 28.

3. John Laffin, *Links of Leadership* (New York: Abelard-Schuman, 1970), p. 189.

4. Ibid.

5. James MacGregor Burns, *Leadership* (New York: Harper & Row, 1978).

6. James MacGregor Burns, quoted in William Safire and Leonard Safir, *Leadership* (New York: Simon & Schuster, 1990), p. 202.

7. John Laffin, op. cit., p. 265.

8. Warren Hilton, *Applied Psychology: Processes and Personality* (San Francisco: The Applied Psychology Press, 1920), p. 97.

9. Eli Landau, "Ezer Weizman," in Moshe Ben Shaul, ed., *Generals of Israel* (Tel Aviv, Israel: Hadar Publishing Co., Ltd., 1969), p. 72.

10. Connie Podesta and Jean Gatz, *How To Be the Person Successful Companies Fight to Keep* (New York: Simon & Schuster, 1997), p. 184.

11. Bob Nelson, *1001 Ways to Reward Employees* (New York: Workman Press, 1994).

12. "AFSC's New Boss, Gen. Randolph," *Airman* (December 1987), p. 9.

13. Chester Burger, *The Chief Executive* (Boston: CBI Publishing Company, Inc., 1978), p. 48.

14. Mary Kay Ash, *Mary Kay on People Management* (New York: Warner Books, 1984), pp. 30–31.

15. McCormick & Company web site: http://www.mccormick.com, July 22, 1999.

16. Chester Burger, *op. cit.*, p. 24.

17. Richard Teitelbaum, "How to Harness Gray Matter," *Fortune* (June 9, 1997), p. 168.

18. *Dana Corporate Data Fact Sheet*, web site: www.dana.com, July 22, 1999.

19. Arieh Hashavia, *A History of the Six-Day War* (Tel Aviv: Ledory House, undated), pp. 226–229.

20. Dandridge M. Malone, *Small Unit Leadership* (Presidio, CA: Presidio Press, 1983), pp. 3–4.

21. Burke Davis, *Marine!: The Life of Chesty Puller* (New York: Bantam Books, 1964), p. 6.

22. Ibid., p. 3.

CHAPTER TWELVE

SEVEN STEPS TO TAKING CHARGE IN CRISIS SITUATIONS

A friend of mine worked as a project manager in his father's $10 million engineering company. He was his father's only son and had been well educated at one of the country's most prestigious private colleges. His father didn't believe in sharing power with a progeny, however. He felt that there would be plenty of time to train his son to run the company in the future.

Nine years later, when my friend was only thirty years old, his father suddenly died of a heart attack. In one day, he went from middle manager to the top job in the company.

I met this man only five years later. In five years, his company had quadrupled in size. His leadership was heralded by experts, and he and his company were written up in several important business magazines.

How had this unique individual taken charge and asserted his leadership under crisis conditions? How had he managed to do so well?

If you want to know something, there is frequently only one way to find out. That is to ask. So I asked.

"It wasn't easy," my friend said. "First there was the shock over my father's death. Than there was finding out the company's situation. My father hadn't confided in anyone. Everyone had a little piece of the puzzle. No one had the full story.

223

"The most difficult thing, however, was to assert my leadership. I was now leading people who had been very senior to me in the company. Some had been with the company since before I was born. Not all of them were able to adjust to my style, my goals, or even just me. They refused to accept my leadership.

"I tried to make it as easy as possible for them, and to give them every chance. But when you got right down to it, I was in charge. I had no choice but to fire more than a few.

"Gradually, things got better. People could see that my policies and strategies were working to improve the position of the company. They got behind me completely.

"When I think back to those first few months, I don't know how I did it. It was the toughest thing I had to do in my life. But I had to do it. I had no alternative."

How would you like to take charge of an organization under those circumstances? As a leader, sometimes you don't have any choice.

A LEADER MUST TAKE CHARGE IN CRISES

When Lieutenant General Bernard L. Montgomery took charge of the British Eighth Army in Africa during World War II, he faced major problems. The Eighth Army had been defeated repeatedly by German General Rommel and his Afrika Korps. After finally winning a victory, Montgomery's predecessor, General Claude John Auchinleck, had been persuaded to attack again prematurely. He had been defeated. There was the possibility of an immediate counterattack by Rommel. The Eighth Army had made withdrawal after withdrawal over the months. Orders were out to prepare for yet another withdrawal. Morale in the Eighth Army was at an all-time low. Then Montgomery arrived.

Here's what Montgomery did immediately:

- He canceled all previous orders about withdrawal.
- He issued orders that in the event of enemy attack, there

would be no withdrawal. The Eighth Army would fight on the ground they held. Or in Montgomery's words, ". . . if we couldn't stay there alive, we would stay there dead."

- He appointed a new chief of staff.
- He formed a new armored corps from "various bits and pieces."
- He changed the basic fighting units from brigade groups and ad hoc columns to full divisions.
- He initiated plans for an offensive, saying, "Our mandate is to destroy Rommel and his Army, and it will be done as soon as we are ready."

Speaking later of the events of his first day in charge he said, "By the time I went to bed that night, I was tired. But I knew that we were on the way to success."[1]

Only a few months later, Montgomery's Eighth Army attacked at El Alamein and won a major victory. It was the turning point of the war in the North African theater of operations. It helped to eventually gain for Montgomery a promotion to field marshal. That's the British equivalent to the rank of full general in the United States. It also won for him the title of Montgomery of Alamein.

What You Need to Do to Take Charge

If you are a leader, there will come a time when you must take charge of a group under difficult circumstances. It may be an old organization that is in trouble. It may be a new organization that you must build from the ground up. It may be an emergency situation. I call these crisis problems, "take-charge" situations. When a take-charge situation occurs, will you be prepared to take charge? In a take-charge situation, you must take these steps immediately:

1. Establish your objective.
2. Communicate with those you lead.

3. Act boldly.

4. Be decisive.

5. Dominate the situation.

6. Lead by example.

7. Hire and fire.

KNOW WHERE YOU ARE GOING: ESTABLISH YOUR OBJECTIVE

In Chapter 2, we talked about the need for vision. Vision is necessary for leadership under all circumstances. Remember, you can't get where you are going until you know where "there" is. Without vision, you have no "there," no objective.

When Montgomery was given command of the British Eighth Army, he wasn't just told, "Here's your Army, see what you can do with it." He was given a definite objective by his boss, Field Marshal Alexander: "My orders from Alexander were quite simple; they were to destroy Rommel and his Army."[2]

And Montgomery believed that having a clear objective was critical. "I hold the view that the leader must know what he himself wants. He must see his objective clearly and then strive to attain it; he must let everyone else know what he wants and what are the basic fundamentals of his policy. He must, in fact, give firm guidance and a clear lead."[3]

Leaders In Emergency Situations Must Have Objectives Too

Some time ago I watched a videotape that was made of my eldest son's plebe class as it went through New Cadet Basic Training at West Point. For probably more than a hundred years, this training has been known as "Beast Barracks." During Beast Barracks, new cadets are taught the basic skills they must have in order to function as cadets. Among the many skills my son was taught during his field training was pulmonary resuscitation.

One scene on the videotape showed cadets being evaluated in their ability to do this. I was impressed not only in the way they had been taught to perform the resuscitation, but in the positive manner they were taught to give direction in support of the objective of saving life.

As each cadet performed the resuscitation maneuver, he or she would point to an imaginary onlooker and command, "You. Go for an ambulance and return here."

The instructions left no doubt as to which onlooker was being sent and exactly what the onlooker was to do.

What the new cadets were taught is an excellent example of the leader knowing what he or she wants and striving to attain it. West Point is well aware that their cadets may be called upon to lead on other than the battlefield.

So the first rule for taking charge is to have a clear objective of where you want to go or what you want to do.

Now that You Know Your Objective, You Must Communicate It to Others

General Patton was a real believer in communicating. So much so that in training, he kept a microphone constantly nearby. Porter B. Williamson, one his officers during this period, reported:

"Our desert radio broadcasting station had one unusual feature. There was a microphone in Gen. Patton's office and a second microphone was by his bed in his tent. Day and night Gen. Patton could cut off all broadcasting and announce a special message or order from his personal mike. When the music would click off we knew we would hear, 'This is Gen. Patton.'

"Often Gen. Patton would say, 'I want every man to be alert tomorrow because we are doing the maneuvers for a lot of brass from Washington who don't know the first form thing about tanks or desert warfare. We must show them how wars can be won with speed. I am counting on every man.'"[4]

General Patton also believed in answering his own phone. In his book, *War as I Knew It*, he says: "In my opinion, generals—or at least the Commanding General—should answer their own telephones in daytime. This is not particularly wearisome because few people call a general, except in emergencies, and then they like to get him at once."[5]

Yes, General Patton knew the importance of communication in taking charge, and he spared nothing to ensure that he could communicate with those he led. And he wasn't the only one to use this technique.

Admiral Kirk commanded the amphibious landing of the Seventh Army in southern France. He used the ships' public-address systems to broadcast the results of each day's operation. Loudspeakers on every ship under his command heard his words. And as the landing progressed, he gave his sailors and those soldiers who had not yet disembarked a running commentary of the action. You know that a commander who keeps his or her people that well informed is in charge.[6]

Norm Lieberman was the project manager working for North American Aviation in charge of the development of the F-100 in the late 1950s. He used the same technique. A public address system was set up in the factory. From his office, he communicated with his engineers and other workers instantly and effectively. I'm told that the F-100 was completed without cost overruns and in minimum time. The Air Force thought quite a bit of the airplane as well. Maybe our aerospace company leaders should use this technique today.

Colonel "Jumping Jim" Gavin, commander of the 505th Parachute Regimental Combat Team and later a lieutenant general, couldn't communicate with his men so easily. Due to security, he couldn't communicate with his men at all prior to takeoff of his historic combat drop in Sicily during World War II.

How do you communicate with several thousand paratroopers flying in different airplanes without breaking radio silence? Gavin used a different but equally effective technique. After takeoff, every man was given a small slip of paper that read:

Soldiers of the 505th Combat Team

Tonight you embark upon a combat mission for which our people and the free people of the world have been waiting for two years.

You will spearhead the landing of an American Force upon the island of SICILY. Every preparation has been made to eliminate the element of chance. You have been given the means to do the job and you are backed by the largest assemblage of air power in the world's history.

The eyes of the world are upon you. The hopes and prayers of every American go with you . . .

James M. Gavin"[7]

How You Say It Is Important Too

Sometimes how you say something is as important as the message itself. Phrase your remarks in as colorful and interesting fashion as you can. If you do, your words will spread like wildfire throughout your organizations.

General Patton was certainly an expert at this. If you haven't seen the movie *Patton*, it's worth your time and the price of a ticket just to see George C. Scott faithfully reproducing Patton's dramatic messages.

Few can beat his message to his Third Army on the eve of battle: "Why by God, I actually pity those SOBs we're going up against. By God, I do."[8]

You don't need to be profane to be colorful or dramatic. Some messages are so powerful that they come down to us through the years, long after they were originally uttered. During the Civil War, it was Confederate General Nathan Bedford Forest who said that to win in war you only had to "Git thar fustest with the mostest."

On another day, a subordinate informed General Forest that Federal troops were stretched from his front and were now in his rear. His reply was, "Wall, then we're in their'n."[9]

It was a Marine general who commented on his unit's withdrawal from North Korea after his outnumbered division was surrounded and cut off by Chinese troops in these famous words: "Retreat, hell. We're just attacking in another direction."

You may also be familiar with "I have not yet begun to fight," "Don't fire until you see the whites of their eyes," "Damn the torpedoes, full speed ahead," or "I shall return." All were uttered by leaders in battle in communicating with their men. They had a tremendous impact on the leader's taking charge.

If you want your words to get out fast . . to be repeated again and again . . and maybe to go down in history: Communicate in a colorful and interesting way.

Starbuck's Worst Crisis

According to Chairman and CEO Howard Schultz, the worst crisis Starbucks every faced began in June 1994, when a severe frost in Brazil caused coffee prices to rise dramatically. Schultz got a call from a subordinate. "With that call, my whole life changed—not only for the summer but for the year that followed. In fact, it took two full years to finally work through the problems that hit us that day."

The crisis for Starbucks was complex. It not only involved customers and their willingness to pay higher prices, but Wall Street. Explained Schultz: "I don't think most Starbucks people really understood the gravity of the situation and how fearful we were. Earnings had been growing more than 50 percent a year for four years, and Wall Street investors were counting on a continuing stream of profits in coming years. If we failed to meet their expectations, our stock price might drop so low we would have trouble raising funds for future expansion."[10]

The big-three coffee roasters increased their prices immediately. As the crisis deepened, they raised their prices again. The price of Folgers went up twice in a single week.

Schultz took the lead in communication. He explained the situation to his partners and got their support on price increases. He communicated with his investors and his customers. Schultz communicated in a way likely to get the attention of those he led, and he did so continuously.

"We made frequent conference calls and left voice-mail updates nationwide, as well as posting signs in our stores, trying to keep people abreast of the situation. What we tried to do with our customers was to honestly and directly explain that our costs had risen and we had no choice but to pass on a certain amount to them in order to continue to do business."[11]

If you want to take charge, you must communicate what you want done.

Be Bold

There is an old saying among pilots: "There are old pilots, and there are bold pilots. However, there are no old, bold pilots."

This adage is intended to discourage younger pilots from foolish, reckless, flying . . except when necessary. There are most certainly times when bold flying and boldness in general is necessary. If there is an objective you are trying to reach, that's what you are getting paid for as a leader. In some situations, if you fail to be bold, you will not be able to take charge.

Patton was known as "Old Blood And Guts." He was a take-charge, bold, decisive leader. But he was not reckless. His boldness was for a definite purpose. He said: "In planning any operation, it is vital to remember, and constantly repeat to oneself, two things: 'In war nothing is impossible, provided you use audacity.' If these two principles are adhered to, with American troops victory is certain."[12]

Let's look at Patton's two principles again. They form one concept in two parts. Patton refers only to war. But you will find his concept true in all leadership situations. Nothing is impossible if you use audacity. Audacity is no more than a synonym for boldness.

It means that as long as your contemplated actions are not illegal, unethical, or dishonest, you should not be afraid to proceed simply because risk is involved. If you believe you are right, go ahead!

BE A DECISIVE LEADER

People do not like to follow leaders who cannot make up their minds or have trouble coming to a decision. To take charge means coming to a decision and communicating it.

In July of 1863, General Meade defeated Robert E. Lee at the Battle of Gettysburg. But because he was indecisive about pursuing Lee, Lee's Army of Northern Virginia was able to retreat across the Potomac River without further harm. If General Meade had pursued Lee immediately, he could have cut off the Army of Northern Virginia before it crossed the Potomac. Lee's army could have been defeated and the war ended that year. Instead, because Lee was allowed to escape, the Civil War went on for another two years with ten of thousands of casualties.

During World War II, a bomber group suffered excessive losses over several difficult missions. Morale was so bad that higher headquarters actually considered disbanding the unit. If that weren't enough, the group sent eighteen bombers on a mission. They ran into such incredible opposition that only six aircraft returned. Now they were really in trouble.

If you saw the old movie *Twelve O'Clock High*, with Gregory Peck, you saw a fictionalized account that incorporated this true story.

The group commander had to take decisive action, or he knew it was all over. He received permission for a "stand-down" of two days.

The first day he ordered the bar opened and allowed his crews to cope with their depression as best they could. Meanwhile, he and his staff went to work and planned a program of intense activity for the next day for every man in the group. It began at reveille and lasted until evening. There were inspections, drills, target study, and practice missions. Every man worked hard the entire day. By night they were exhausted and had no difficulty sleeping.

On the following day, more relaxed, they flew a successful combat mission without excessive losses. Over the following weeks, replacements came and were trained, and the group was effective until the end of the war.[13]

Maybe you think you have trouble coming to a decision because you don't have all the facts. Let me assure you that you will never have all the facts. That's just the nature of leadership. This means that almost all the time, you must make decisions without knowing everything that would help you to make a decision.

It is true that the longer you wait, the more facts you will have, and sometimes it is necessary to wait for these important facts before making a decision. But you must weigh the delay against the negative impact. Elements of the situation can change. An opportunity may be lost. Your competition may "git thar furstest with the mostest." Those who follow you will at best be uncomfortable at not having a decision. If you make indecisiveness a habit, they will not want to follow you.

Some leaders I have seen tell themselves that they are putting off a decision in order to get more facts. But the real reason is that for one reason or another they are afraid to make a decision. Failing to make a decision is also a decision. It is a decision to leave everything to chance or to the initiative of others. It is not a sign of a take-charge leader. And it ultimately results in a failure.

To be a take-charge leader, follow the recommendation of W. Clement Stone, the self-made multimillionaire. Stone says that when you feel yourself putting off anything without reason say these three words out loud: "Do it now!"

DOMINATE THE SITUATION

As a leader in circumstances where you must take charge, you must dominate the situation, or it will dominate you. By this, I mean that you must take positive actions to gain control. You must continue to initiate actions to maintain control.

If you fail to do this, you will spend your time and energy continually responding to the actions of others, or to crises of your environment. We call this "firefighting." And firefighting will steal all your time, leaving no time for you to take charge with new initiatives.

There are two reasons for this, and they aren't complicated. In any take-charge situation, there is a desperate need for leadership. If you do not take the initiative, someone must fill the leadership vacuum. Someone else will attempt to take charge. You may be the assigned leader. This other person may not be as experienced, as qualified, or as trained as you. It makes no difference. If you fail to act at once and take the initiative, someone else will attempt to fill the leadership role and you will have to fight to regain it.

The second reason why you must immediately dominate the situation has to do with the environment. If you fail to take the initiative, the environment tends to build up on you. First, you have one problem. Now you have two problems. Now you have yet another. Pretty soon the situation becomes unmanageable.

To Dominate the Situation, Take the Initiative

To dominate any take-charge situation, all that is required is that you take the initiative. In other words, you let others or your environment play catch-up to your actions rather than vise versa.

When Montgomery took charge of the Eighth Army, his predecessor anticipated a further withdrawal in response to Rommel's actions. Montgomery turned the situation around by refusing to withdraw and immediately planning for an attack. Imagine, after one day he went to bed satisfied that he was on the "way to success"! Other historical commanders and leaders also went to bed happily knowing that they had taken the initiative.

Hannibal, the great Carthagenian general, was attacked by a force more than three times his size in 216 B.C. The Roman general Varro had more than 72,000 men under his command. Hannibal had only 22,000. Hannibal's generals advised an immediate retreat. Instead, Hannibal took the initiative. He designed a plan that encouraged Varro to attack Hannibal's weak center while ignoring his two strong wings.

After Hannibal's center had been pushed back, the Romans were so bunched together because of the strong Carthegenian wings that they could not wield their swords fully. At this moment Hannibal ordered his two wings to close behind the Romans like gates. His cavalry completed the destruction. It developed into the most decisive battle in the history of warfare. More than 60,000 Romans were left dead on the field of battle.

Note that you can take the initiative and dominate the situation even if you initially don't have it and the odds are against you. Much of taking the initiative has to do with your own perception of the situation.

Winston Churchill reported the following incident about Montgomery in his book *The Hinge of Fate*. Montgomery was on his way to the airport to leave England to take command of the Eighth Army. He was accompanied by General Ismay, who was head of the Chiefs of Staff Committee. Remember that until Montgomery came on the scene, Rommel was unbeaten.

> Montgomery spoke of the trials and hazards of a soldier's career. He gave his whole life to his profession, and lived long years of study and self-restraint. Presently fortune smiled, there came a gleam of success, he gained advancement, opportunity presented itself, he had a great command. He won a victory, he became world famous, his name was on every lip. Then the luck changed. At one stroke all his life's work flashed away, perhaps through no fault of his own, and he was flung into the endless catalogue of military failures.

"But," expostulated Ismay, "you ought not to take it so badly as all that. A very fine Army is gathering in the Middle East. It may well be that you are not going to disaster."

"What!" cried Montgomery, sitting up in the car. "What do you mean? I was talking about Rommel!"

In his book, Montgomery said, "The good military leader will dominate the events which surround him; once he lets events get the better of him he will lose the confidence of his men, and when that happens he ceases to be of value as a leader."[14]

Matsushita Takes Charge

Maybe you never heard of Konosuke Matsushita. If not, it's time you did. After World War II, Matsushita was one of the central figures in the Japanese economic miracle. The year Matsushita died, the revenues of his company, Matsushita Electric, were $42 billion. That exceeded the sales of Bethlehem Steel, Colgate-Pamolive, Gillette, Goodrich, Kellogg, Olivetti, Scott Paper, and Whirlpool combined!

On one occasion, one of Matsushita's divisions was losing money. Matsushita was immediately on the scene. As reported by Harvard Professor John Kotter, this is how the conversation went:

"I could understand if sales were zero and the deficit was in personnel costs," Matsushita yelled, "but you've got sales of one hundred
billion yen and are nine billion in the red. Responsibility for running
this mess lies with you and the executives under you. The head office
must also take responsibility because they recently lent you that
twenty billion yen. Tomorrow, I'm going to talk to them about getting it back."

"But Mr. Matsushita, that would mean disaster for us! It's five days to
payday. At the end of the month we will owe money for materials and
parts. If you take that twenty billion yen back now, we won't be able
to pay for them."

"That's right, but I'm not going to lend you any money if you and your colleagues are going to run an operation like this. I'm pulling your loan tomorrow."

"But then we'll go bankrupt!"

"You've got four thousand superb employees working here. Talk it over with them, get their ideas, and come up with a reconstruction plan that will work. If you can get a plan like that together, I'll write a letter of recommendation to Sumitomo Bank for you. With that letter, they're sure to give you a twenty billion yen loan using the land, buildings, and equipment here as collateral. Now, get to work!"[15]

Sometimes a leader must dispense strong medicine in a take-charge situation. To be successful, you must dominate the situation.

LEAD BY EXAMPLE

A very old leadership maxim states that you should be willing to do everything you ask those you lead to do. However, in a take-charge situation, it goes above a willingness. At times, you must actually do everything you ask those who follow you to do.

Colonel Jack Broughton was the chief of operations of an F-105 wing during the Vietnam War. The F-105s, had a difficult mission. They attacked North Vietnam and downtown Hanoi. It was the most heavily defended target area in the world, protected not only by thousands of ZPU, 23mm, 37mm, 57mm, 85mm, and 100mm antiaircraft artillery, but also by numerous batteries of surface to air missiles (SAMs). Of course, there were also MIG fighters.

For political reasons, there were more restraints placed on American flyers in the Vietnam conflict than any war in which air forces were involved. Certain military and political targets were strictly off limits. In some cases, the enemy was warned prior to an attack. When our forces fired on, there were restrictions on returning the fire if it was coming from civilian structures. If an aircraft was battle damaged and had to jettison its load of bombs in order to get back, the "rules of engagement" limited the site of those jettisoned to nonpopulated areas. Aircrew had been lost trying to obey these rules, and loss rates were high.

A senior air commander normally doesn't fly all the combat missions that his crews fly. He has additional responsibilities that put demands on his time. But Jack Broughton flew all the tough ones.

"It is important that you know the people you fly with and that you know what they are doing. This does not come from sitting in an air-conditioned office and clucking sternly over unimportant details. It comes from getting hot and sweaty and from getting your fanny shot at. There is no way to shake out people and procedures except by being a part of them. You only learn part of the game when you fly the easy ones; you have to take at least your share of the tough ones. The troops watched that schedule pretty closely. They knew who was leading for effect and who was for real, and they responded accordingly."[16]

Another air commander who led by personal example in a take-charge situation was Jimmy Doolittle. As a lieutenant colonel, Doolittle led the first bombing raid of Japan early in World War II. Then they promoted him to general and sent him to Europe.

One of the airplanes his airmen was given to fly was the B-26 "Marauder." There had been many problems with the B-26. So many were lost while in training in Florida that the airmen had a saying: "One a day in Tampa Bay." The airplane was known as a "killer" . . . of our own aircrew.

In combat, there was a reluctance to use the aircraft to its full potential. General Doolittle was faced with a take-charge situation. He visited one his B-26 groups and listened sympathetically to his pilots' complaints about the airplane. He then asked if he could fly one.

He put it through all the normal maneuvers. Suddenly, he "feathered" one of the props. Since the B-26 only had two engines, this means that he was now flying the airplane on only one engine. He landed the airplane on one engine and then took off again. Still flying with only one engine he repeated all the maneuvers he had done previously. Finally he landed.

"Well," he told his pilots, "it isn't the best airplane that America can build, but I think it can do the job."

The B-26 went on to rack up a tremendous operational record in combat during World War II.[17] General Doolittle went on to become the first reserve officer promoted to four-star general.

This Coast Guardsman Led by Example

Let me tell you about a leader and hero by the name of Douglas Munro. Douglas Munro was Signalman First Class in the Coast Guard. On September 27, 1942, Signalman Munro was a petty officer in charge of 24 Higgins boats, a type of craft used for landing vehicles and personnel. Munro's boats were engaged in evacuating a battalion of Marines trapped by a superior number of enemy forces at Point Cruz, Guadalcanal.

Under constant fire from enemy machine guns, Signalman Munro led five of his landing craft toward the shore. The fire was so intense that he knew they would be unable to evacuate the Marines. So he positioned his small craft, with its two guns, as a shield between the beachhead and the enemy. Naturally, he drew most of the fire in this position. His boat was hit repeatedly. But through his actions, they got the trapped Marines off the island, saving the lives of many who would otherwise have perished. With the task nearly completed, this brave hero was killed by enemy fire. He was posthumously awarded the Congressional Medal of Honor.[18]

Few leaders in business or civilian life need to put their lives at risk or to sacrifice themselves for others as did Douglas Munro. But we can be inspired by his act and recognize that leaders in all fields, if they really are leaders, must lead by example, especially when taking charge in crisis situations.

Parachute General James Gavin jumped with his division on the "D-Day" invasion of Normandy. Young Colonel George S. Patton led his tanks on foot against the enemy during World War I. As a brigadier general in the same war, MacArthur went forward with the first line of his men in the attack. Major General Moshe Dayan of the Israeli Army came under direct fire while up front in an attack during the Sinai Campaign of 1956, and his jeep driver was killed. Dayan was Chief of Staff of the Israeli Army at the time.

All these men were in take-charge situations. It was time to lead by personal example, and they did.

HIRE AND FIRE

In a take-charge situation, you don't have time to fool around. You must get rid of those individuals who are performing poorly, and you have to replace these people with people who can do the job.

For most people, firing is not an easy thing to do. Those you must discharge may have worked at a job for some time. They may or may not have done their best. Either way, firing can mean they have loss of money, prestige, security, and sense of self-worth. Still, if you are going to be true to yourself and to your organization as a leader, you have no choice.

Remember, we're not talking about ordinary day-to-day management. We're speaking about take-charge situations. If your organization has a worthwhile purpose and mission, that must come first under these circumstances.

This is easier to see in warfare, where the acts of people spell the difference between life and death, victory and defeat. It is more difficult to understand in peacetime situations.

What harm it is if you keep people on board who are not performing up to standard? First, these individuals are probably incapable of doing any better than they already have. Otherwise, the take-charge situation wouldn't exist. Also, it is essential to get people in important positions who can do the job as you want it done.

You can't do this with incumbents occupying the key positions. Finally, you can't motivate others to go all out in a crisis when you demonstrate that you are willing to expect less than the best from others.

I want to make certain that you understand fully what I am saying. Just because you are a leader doesn't mean that you fire everyone in sight that you think you can replace with someone better. That's not ethical. It demonstrates poor leadership. There may well be situations that are not crises when for various reasons you should tolerate people in your organization who are not performing to your standards. An individual who is no longer capable of turning in top performance, but who has done a good job in the past may be one example. Also, if possible, you should first attempt to save a person from being fired. You do this through counseling and the coaching techniques we've discussed earlier.

But in a take-charge situation, don't waste time.

Guidelines for Firing

If firing needs to be done, do it at once. Here are some guidelines:

- Don't mess around with halfway measures or second chances. Make the decision to fire, and do so at once.

- Don't delegate a firing. Do it yourself.

- Don't fire in public. Call the person into your office and do it privately.

- Be forthright and tell the person why he or she is being fired.

- Let the person know that you're not saying a person is no good at any job, only that he or she hasn't met your standards at this job.

- Depending on who is being fired, and at what level, get additional help before you act, if required. That is, you may want to talk to your legal people, public relations, the human-resources department, an outplacement firm, a psychologist. Or no one. Only you can decide if you need additional help.

HIRING IS JUST AS IMPORTANT IN A TAKE-CHARGE SITUATION

When Lee Iacocca turned the Chrysler Corporation around, it was the most amazing turnaround situation in this century. Everyone said it couldn't be done. But Iacocca went ahead anyway. The U.S. government guaranteed a needed loan. That helped—a lot. If you think it was just the government guarantee on a loan that made things come out, however, you would be dead wrong. Iacocca did it primarily with people. Like General George C. Marshall, he tracked the careers of several hundred executives in his field. These were kept in a special notebook. So important was this notebook that he obtained special permission from William Ford, president of the Ford Motor Company, where he had been an executive, to take the notebook with him.

Many of the new executives he brought to Chrysler came from this notebook. According to Iacocca, "In the end, all business operations can be reduced to three words: people, product, and profits. People come first. Unless you've got a good team, you can't do much with the other two."[19]

This should tell you clearly that you should be directly involved with hiring executives who will work with you. If you have a notebook of executives yourself, congratulations. Most leaders aren't so well prepared. But don't worry if you do not. You can learn a lot through the interview process if you do it right.

The problem with most leaders in putting their team together in a take-charge situation is that they don't prepare for the interview at all. They ask one or two questions, and if everything seems okay they offer the job. I mean, after all, this is a take-charge situation, right?

It may be a take-charge situation, but this is the wrong approach to take. You see, in a take-charge situation you want to get rid of the deadwood instantly. But it is possible to replace poor performers with worse performers, or with individuals just not suited to the job you want them to do.

General Perry M. Smith put together a wonderful checklist to help you hire the right person for the right job—to get a feel for the individual and for the chemistry between you and your prospective subordinate. Here are the questions that he recommends you ask:

- Do you want the job? Why?
- What talents, qualities and strengths would you bring to this job?
- What are your weaknesses?
- How long would you like to hold this job?
- What is your leadership/management style?
- If I asked a subordinate of yours to describe you and your leadership style, what would be the response?
- If you are not selected, whom would you recommend for this job?
- What are your long-term personal goals?
- Do you expect to be promoted soon?
- Are there any "skeletons in your closet"?
- Whom in your present organization do you admire the most and why?
- What is the standard of integrity in your present organization?
- Are you considering any other positions?
- If I select you for this job, would you take it as your first choice over other positions you are considering?

- Are you approaching a retirement decision soon?
- How many people have you led or supervised in your career?
- Have you ever fired anyone? Have you ever been fired?
- What experience do you have with
  — operations?
  — planning?
  — finance?
  — marketing?
  — engineering?
  — research and development?
  — manpower and personnel?
  — computer systems?
- Have you had any setbacks in your career?
  — If so, what were the most significant lessons learned from the setbacks?
  — What organizational setbacks have you observed at first-hand?
- What is the toughest problem you have ever faced in your professional career? How have you handled it?
- What questions have I failed to ask you?
- What questions do you have for me?[20]

I'm not saying that you must ask all these questions during the hiring interview. You should ask only those that you consider relevant to the situation. And, of course, you should feel free to add some of your own questions that you consider appropriate.

The point is, take the time when hiring in a take-charge situation to put together the best possible team you can.

SEVEN STEPS TO TAKING CHARGE IN A CRISIS SITUATION

1. Establish your objective at once. You can't lead anyone anywhere until you know where you want to go.

2. Communicate what you want done in a way likely to get the attention of those you lead.

3. Act boldly. This is not the time to be cautious. This is the time to take risks.

4. Be decisive. Don't put off making decisions.

5. Dominate the situation by taking the initiative. If you don't, the situation will dominate you.

6. Lead by example. Make your motto "follow me," and live by it.

7. Get rid of people who can't do the job and hire people who can. Do a thorough job of interviewing to minimize the risk of a bad choice.

NOTES

1. Bernard L. Montgomery, *The Memoirs of Field-Marshall Montgomery* (New York: The World Publishing Company, 1958), p. 94.

2. Ibid., p. 93.

3. Ibid., p. 75.

4. Porter B. Williamson, *Patton's Principles* (New York: Simon & Schuster, 1979), p. 31.

5. George S. Patton, *War as I Knew It* (New York: Pyramid Books, 1966), p. 309.

6. *AFM 35–15, Air Force Leadership* (Washington, D.C.: Department of the Air Force, 1948), p. 33.

7. James M. Gavin, *On to Berlin* (New York: The Viking Press, 1978), p. 18.

8. Ibid., p. 32.

9. Ibid.

10. Howard Schultz and Dori Jones Yang, *Pour Your Heart in to It* (New York: Hyperion, 1997), p. 235.

11. Ibid., pp. 230–237.

12. Op. cit., George S. Patton, p. 308.

13. *AFM 35–15 Air Force Leadership*, op. cit., p. 30.

14. Bernard L. Montgomery, op. cit., p. 75.

15. John P. Kotter, *Matsushita on Leadership* (New York: The Free Press, 1997), p. 10.

16. Jack Broughton, *Thud Ridge* (New York: J. B. Lippincott Company, 1969), p. 30.

17. *AFM 35–15, Air Force Leadership*, op. cit., p. 33.

18. U.S. Army Center of Military History, *Full-text Listings of Medal of Honor Citations*, web site www.army.mil/cmh-pg/moh1.htm, July 23, 1999.

19. Lee Iacocca, *Iacocca* (New York: Bantam Books, 1984), p. 167.

20. Perry M. Smith, *Taking Charge* (Garden City Park, NY: Avery Publishing Group, Inc., 1993), pp. 177–178.

CHAPTER THIRTEEN

SEVEN ACTIONS TO DEVELOP YOUR CHARISMA

Charisma comes from a Greek word meaning a divine gift. This implies that it is something you are given. The further implication is that this is done at birth.

Napoleon Bonaparte didn't see it that way. He said: "My power is dependent upon my glory, and my glory on my victories. My power would fall if I did not base it on still more glory and still more victories. Conquest made me what I am; conquest alone can keep me there."[1]

What Napoleon was saying is that his being perceived as a charismatic leader was based on his success. To maintain his charisma, he had to keep being successful. There is some truth in this. Warren Bennis and Burt Nanus, the two researchers from the University of Southern California we spoke about in earlier chapters, found that successful leaders tend to be viewed as charismatic.

Again, this says that if you want to be a charismatic leader, you must first become a successful one. I don't know about you, but I have a problem with this, even if it does contains an element of truth. What if you don't want to wait until after you are successful to be a charismatic leader? Won't being charismatic help you to be a successful leader? Are there any actions you can take to become charismatic before you become successful? Yes, there are.

THE CHARISMATIC LEADER

Some years ago, I was fortunate in being selected to attend the Industrial College of the Armed Forces at the National Defense University in Washington, D.C. The Industrial College of the Armed Forces trains selected senior military and civilian officials destined for positions of high trust and leadership in the federal government.

Prior to a student beginning his or her studies at the National Defense University, detailed leadership evaluation surveys are sent to a number of the student's subordinates, superiors, and colleagues. All three categories of respondents complete these surveys anonymously. Each survey contains 125 questions in twenty-one major areas having to do with the student's leadership abilities, attributes, and characteristics.

Those selected as students for National Defense University are already proven leaders. As you might expect, these leadership evaluations are generally pretty favorable.

In the year I was at National Defense University, the scores for 995 questionnaires for 115 students at the university averaged above 4.00 out of 5.00 for all characteristics measured.

The expected average for a population of leaders is 3.0. Thus, above 4.00 means that those surveyed thought these leaders demonstrated every single one of twenty-one major areas of leadership fairly often. This is much better than the average leader.

The average in the "charisma" area for the 115 students was 4.32. That's an amazingly high score. But one individual's score was off the chart. Every one of his subordinates had scored him in this leadership area as a perfect 5.00! Translated, it said that every subordinate felt that this leader demonstrated charisma frequently, if not always.

Eagerly, I sought out this individual to discover the secrets of his unusual evaluation in this mysterious quality. I found an average-looking man of average height. If you had met him and did not know of his charisma score, you would not have suspected him of anything special. Yet, as famed social scientist Max Weber wrote, "Men do not obey him by virtue of tradition or statute, but because they believe in him."[2]

What was his secret? He maintained that a great deal of his success as a leader was due to his being perceived as charismatic. In other words, it wasn't that he was successful as a leader first. He did agree that once he was successful, being perceived as charismatic was a lot easier. According to this man, however, he became successful as a leader partially because he was charismatic. More important, his charisma was not accidental. He intentionally set out to develop it. Further, he took definite actions to develop his charisma again in every new group he led.

Dr. Ronald Riaggo, a social psychologist who is director of the Kraviss Leadership Institute at Claremont McKenna College, has developed his own methodology for creating charisma. Dr. Riaggio says, "But charisma is not something that is given to a person. It is not an inherited or inborn quality. Charisma is something that develops over time. More importantly, each and every one of us has the capacity to develop our own charisma.[3]

To develop his charisma, the proven charismatic at National Defense University took seven different actions. Over the years, I observed that other leaders with charisma take similar actions. If you want to develop your charisma, here are the seven actions that they took and that you can take to develop your charisma too:

1. Show your commitment.

2. Look the part.

3. Dream big.

4. Keep moving toward your goals.

5. Do your homework.

6. Build a mystique.

7. Use the indirect approach.

Let's see what each action entails.

SHOW YOUR COMMITMENT

If you want to be perceived as charismatic, it's not enough to be committed to whatever it is you are trying to accomplish. You must show your commitment to those you lead.

Several historic military leaders have burned their boats after landing for an assault from the sea. Usually their biographers indicate this is done to give their followers "no alternative." The apparent message is that they must win, since they can no longer return to the sea.

I don't think this is the main reason for this action. The attacking troops could still surrender if they wished. I think the real reason these leaders burned their boats is that it was an extremely effective method of demonstrating the leader's own commitment to the goal or objective.

There are many ways to demonstrate commitment. These include being persistent in the pursuit of a goal, going to extraordinary lengths, self-sacrifice, risk taking, and the expenditure of personal resources.

Do you perceive the founding fathers of our country to be charismatic? They demonstrated commitment in all these areas. They committed their "lives, fortunes, and sacred honor" to the goals of the group.

How Demonstrated Commitment Helped Make a Man a Millionaire

Joe Cossman is a multimillionaire. Today, he lives in Palm Springs, California, and by his own choice travels around the world helping people start their own businesses. But he was born poor.

After service during World War II, Joe got a job in Pittsburgh, Pennsylvania, working for an export company. Not being a college graduate or having any special skills, he earned the princely sum of $35 a week. After supper every night, he wrote letters from his kitchen table to contacts he had made around the world. He wanted desperately to export products on his own.

He spent more than a year writing hundreds of letters, following false leads that went nowhere, and giving up all his free time to this activity. Remember, this kind of persistence demonstrates commitment.

One day he saw a small ad in *The New York Times* advertising cases of laundry soap, which at that time was scarce. He confirmed the availability of the soap by telephone and sent letters to his contacts abroad.

Several weeks later, he was notified that his bank had received a letter of credit for $180,000. This meant that he would receive the $180,000 when he produced bills of lading that the soap had been loaded on board the ship. The letter of credit gave him thirty days to do this. If he failed to supply bills of lading within thirty days, the letter of credit would be worthless.

Joe's soap wholesaler informed him that he had the soap in New York City. All Joe had to do was to get to New York to make the financial and shipping arrangements. Joe approached his boss and asked for several weeks' leave of absence from the job. His boss refused. Joe then went around Pittsburgh and offered friends 50 percent of the deal to anyone who would go to New York City to put the deal together. No one was willing to accept Joe's offer.

In desperation, Joe approached his boss again. If he couldn't get the time off, he would quit. His boss saw Joe's commitment and gave in. Joe and his wife had a total of $300 savings in the bank. But Joe's wife knew his commitment also. She had faith in him. They took the $300 out of the bank, and Joe headed for New York City.

After checking into his hotel, Joe again called his soap wholesaler. The number had been disconnected, and the wholesaler was nowhere to be found. But Joe was still fully committed.

He went to the library and found lists of soap companies in the *Thomas Register of Manufacturers*. Returning to his hotel room, he began calling soap companies all over the United States. But there was a telephone strike! It took him a long time just to get an operator. Through the strength of his commitment, he convinced her to stay on the line while he made all of his calls. After running up a phone bill of more than $800, he located a company in Alabama that had the soap. But he would have to come to Alabama to pick it up.

Joe searched all over New York for a trucking company that would go with him to get 3,000 cases of soap, and do so on credit. At this point, he began to have another problem. Much of the thirty days had gone by. Could Joe bring the soap to New York in time? Joe continued to demonstrate strong commitment to his goals. Those who lent him money would have said that there was just something about him that led them to believe that he was going to succeed.

He got the soap to New York City with less than a day to load the soap on the ship. The unions weren't as strict in those days, and Joe himself helped load the soap. They worked all night. By noon the following day, it was clear that they weren't going to make it by the time the bank closed. With less than an hour before closing time, Joe abandoned the loading dock to look for the office of the president of the steamship line.

As Joe told me, "I hadn't bathed in more than a week. I hadn't slept all night because of helping to load the soap. I was unshaven and had been borrowing small change from the truck drivers for lunch. The soap company was after me for the money for the soap, the trucking company for the money I owed them. The hotel didn't know where I was, and they wanted their money too. Even my wife didn't know my whereabouts. I looked and felt like I could use a case of that soap, myself."

In this condition he barged into the office of the president of the steamship line and told him the whole story. The president looked Joe straight in the eye: Joe's commitment came through. "Cossman," he said, "if you've gone this far, you're not going to lose the deal now."

So saying, he gave Joe bills of lading, even though the soap was not fully loaded. This meant that his company assumed the risk of loss for the soap until the loading was complete. He also had his personal limousine take Joe to the bank.

On this first successful business deal, Joe made a profit of $30,000. That's not bad for a man who had been making $35 a week.

How was Joe able to lead and successfully influence everyone he came in contact with on this business deal? Joe was committed. His commitment was compelling. To others, his commitment was seen as that certain something we call charisma.

You Can't Show Commitment If It Isn't for Real

It's hard to show commitment if you aren't really committed. In fact, it's impossible, because those you want to lead will see right through you. Commitment is something that can't be faked. Dr. Tony Alessandra, a business expert who has made presentations before some of America's top corporations, asks, "What do you feel passionately about? What do you care *really* deeply about? Whatever your objective—whether it's ending world hunger or ensuring better care for stray animals—you'll never influence anyone to change their ideas or take action if you don't feel strongly about it yourself."[4]

But if your commitment is real, listen to Roger Ailes. A media consultant who has consulted for a number of CEOs and political campaigns, he says: "The essence of charisma is showing your commitment to an idea or goal."[5] If you want to be perceived as charismatic, think of ways to show your commitment.

LOOK THE PART

Some years ago, a man did serious research on the effect of what you wear on success on the job. The results were so astounding, that his book, *Dress for Success*[6] became a nationwide best-seller. John T. Molloy's research demonstrated conclusively that what you wear is important in becoming successful in what you do. If you are in business, you might want to pick up a copy of this book. For most jobs in the United States, Molloy's advice can be extremely valuable.

You should know that what kind of leader you are and whom you are leading can call for different types of dress for maximum effectiveness, however. You wouldn't be perceived as much of a charismatic leader if you tried to lead ranch hands in a business suit. In some countries even businessmen or women do not dress in the way businesspeople dress in the United States. Also, the way you dress should be carefully built around the particular image of the kind of leader you represent.

The military has recognized this for a long time. Generals frequently design their own uniforms for the image of themselves they wish to portray.

Field Marshal Montgomery was known for his special beret on which he had fixed the emblems of the major units that he commanded. He also made a pullover sweater a part of his uniform. He effected a casual image, even in the heat of battle. When soldiers saw someone wearing a multiemblemed beret and casual sweater they instantly knew it was their commander.

Patton also strongly believed in "looking the part." His special uniform consisted of a shiny helmet, pistols on both hips, and a knotted tie, even in combat. Few of his soldiers could mistake him either.

Eisenhower invented the special short military jacket that he wore. Eventually, the entire United States Army adopted it. They called it the "Ike Jacket."

MacArthur effected a different image. He started wearing a special uniform even as a young colonel in combat during World War I. He refused to wear a helmet or carry a sidearm. He stated his reasoning as: "A helmet hurts my head, and decreases my effectiveness as a leader. I don't carry a sidearm because it is not my business to fight, but to direct others in fighting."[7]

During World War II his tieless khaki uniform, gold-braided hat, corncob pipe, and sunglasses became famous and a symbol of the MacArthur mystique.

Many other military leaders have looked the part by their dress. Some have worn standard uniforms, but had them tailored and made of better material than the standard. Some commanders carry a "swagger stick." This is a sort of short canelike affair that could be described as the American version of a marshal's baton. General Matthew Ridgway, commander in Korea after MacArthur, always wore grenades over his winter greatcoat. Brigadier General Robin Olds, F-4 commander and ace in Vietnam, wore a nonregulation oversized mustache. His pilots loved him for it. General H. Norman Schwarzkopf wore the desert battle dress he wore in the Middle East even after his return to the States after the war. That uniform was part of his charm and his charisma..

When my classmate Colonel "Tex" Turner was director of military instruction at West Point, he wore camouflaged battle dress even in the classroom environment. Tex, who formerly commanded the U.S. Army's Ranger School is a tiger leader, and he makes sure that he looks the part. The cadets feel that Tex can walk on water.

When General Alfred M. Gray was commandant of the Marine Corps, he also wore camouflaged battle dress . . . even in the Pentagon. To my knowledge, he is the only one of the Chiefs of Staff ever to have done so. But you couldn't miss him when you saw that uniform. It said, "I am a warrior, and my service is a fighting outfit."

You don't need to wear battle dress. But if you want to appear charismatic, you must take the time to define the image of your type of leader and then dress that way.

Two hundred years ago, French General Barthelemy-Catherine Joubert said: "A well-dressed soldier has more respect for himself. He also appears more redoubtable to the enemy and dominates him; for a good appearance is itself a force."[8]

When I was promoted to become a general officer and attended the orientation course, called "charm school" by all, one senior general told us: "Remember, even when you are wearing civilian clothes—dress like a general."

That's good advice for all of us, regardless of what profession or occupation we may be in. Dressing like a general means dressing like a professional of our profession, whatever it may be.

DREAM BIG

In an earlier chapter, I showed you why you must have high expectations. I hope I demonstrated to you that you can achieve no higher than you expect to achieve. It is the same in setting goals for others or for a group. There is one additional important thing you should know. No one wants to work hard or make sacrifices for small goals. And why should they? They can reach small goals any day by themselves. They don't need you. Accomplishing them means nothing. They aren't exciting. They give no great feeling of accomplishment when achieved. But if you show those you lead difficult goals, big tasks, and truly worthwhile missions, people will sacrifice everything in order to help you achieve them.

Dr. Charles Garfield observed an extraordinary leap in performance among engineers, workers, and production people in a major aerospace corporation that was building the Lunar Excursion Module for Apollo 11. "Every week, I heard stories about people who were lifting their performance to levels that none of them would have predicted a few months before," he said.[9] This continued during the entire period of preparing for the moon mission. Then, on July 20, 1969, Neil Armstrong and Buzz Aldrin walked on the moon. It was over. People's performance returned to their normal average level. "They had risen to a peak; then they had fallen back to earth," said Garfield.[10]

To maintain performance, the leaders of this organization should have immediately gone on to the next big dream. For, as long as you ask for really big things, nothing is impossible.

How Dr. Robert Schuller Built the $20 Million Crystal Cathedral When All He Had Was $500

Have you heard of Dr. Robert H. Schuller? Dr. Schuller is a minister. He is also the author of more than twenty books, many cassette tapes, and has his own television show. He came to California with no congregation and only $500. Twenty-five years later he built the $20 million Crystal Cathedral, which seats 4,000. Millions listen to his sermons every week.

How did he build a $20 million cathedral when all he had was $25? Dr. Schuller preaches what he calls "possibility thinking." He says emphatically that you can accomplish the impossible. According to Dr. Schuller, it's only a matter of finding the right person to help you.

People will help you to reach goals that are impossible. In fact, they will give you their blood, sweat, and tears, as Winston Churchill demanded, if your goal is big enough.

What Kinds of Goals Are Possible?

What kind of goal? It can be anything, so long as it is big and worthwhile. In his book *Battle Cry*, Leon Uris wrote a fictionalized account of Uris's own experiences in the Marines during World War II. His hero, Lt. Colonel "High Pockets" Huxley, marches his battalion on a grueling twelve-hour march to set a divisional training record. With difficulty, bruises, and bleeding feet, they make it and set the record. Then, instead of taking trucks back to camp, Huxley orders a few hours' rest and a return march back. His men come near to collapse. But as they rest at the side of the road, they see the other marine units returning to camp by truck after their treks. That they are being made to do something big and difficult inspires Huxley's battalion for one final effort. They make it back to camp and beat their own record at the same time.

At the Battle of the Bulge, the 101st Airborne Division was cut off and surrounded by superior numbers of attacking German units. Who would come to the rescue? Patton announced that he would disengage from the enemy on one front, march a hundred miles, and be in action with three divisions within forty-eight hours. Patton knew that if he demanded the just barely possible, if it was a really important, tough job, his men would come through.

If you want to have big dreams, you need only recall the words from the song *High Hopes* sung by Frank Sinatra. They go something like this: "You may not think that an ant can't do much with a rubber tree plant, but if he has high hopes then: Whoops! There goes another rubber tree plant!"

Tony Robbins has spoken to and changed the lives of millions of people. He has worked with many heads of state, including the President of the United States. Michael Jeffreys, who wrote the bible on the subject of motivational speakers, says, "Many people in the United States feel that Anthony Robbins is the most dynamic, most charismatic speaker on the platform today."[11] Yet, Robbins, only a high-school graduate, has never been to college. What's his secret? I'll let Tony Robbins tell you himself. "For most of my life I've had a sense of destiny. I can remember at seven years old having images in my mind of reaching mass numbers of people and making a huge difference."[12]

Have big dreams and foster high hopes among those you lead and your charisma will never be in doubt.

KEEP MOVING TOWARD YOUR GOALS

Having big dreams and goals is important. But you can't let it rest at that. You must actually keep moving toward the tough goals you have set. Remember, you are the leader. People don't move until you move first. But when you do move toward a big dream, it will have a marvelous effect on those you lead. Your backers will be pleased.

"What did we tell you?" they'll say to others. Then there will be those who were on the fence. They supported you, but they could have gone either way. "We knew he could do it all the time," they'll say. And there are those who were against whatever it was your big dream is. They said that it couldn't be done. They won't say much. They'll only mutter, "Well, I'll be damned." And your charisma will increase among all concerned.

Moving toward your goals is tougher than just setting the goal, but it isn't all that hard. First, it means that you have to have a plan. Then you set a number of intermediate goals. Dr. Schuller didn't start out right away building the Crystal Cathedral. He set his overall goal. Then he accomplished a number of intermediate objectives. Every big goal has a number of smaller intermediate objectives that are accomplished first. And every objective has a number of tasks.

To show movement toward the big goal, know what the intermediate objectives and the tasks are and make certain those you lead know as well. Assign each task to a specific individual along with a time when you expect that task to be accomplished. Then, check periodically to see what's happening. Publicize every success, every movement toward your big goal. When those you lead run into problems, give them the help they need in order to proceed. But never stop. Whatever your goal is, maintain progress toward it. Then, like Joe Cossman, few can resist your charm. And those you lead will be commenting on your charisma.

DO YOUR HOMEWORK

Have you ever watched gymnastics on television during an Olympic competition? Incredible, wasn't it? Many of the performances seem flawless. Even more amazing, in many cases it appears to take no effort at all to do something you or I couldn't have done in "a million years." The fact is, however, that those we watched turn in such marvelous performances are made up of the same stuff as you and I.

When they first started out, they couldn't do any of those things either. It would have been beyond their wildest dreams. Yet, there they were doing incredible things and winning well-earned medals for their accomplishments.

How do I know this? Because it happened to me, and I know the secret firsthand.

When I was a boy, I had recurrent rheumatic fever. As a result, as I grew up I couldn't participate in sports. I was generally weak. At age fifteen, I knew that I had to get strong if I were ever to get to West Point. West Point required a minimum of six pull-ups. I couldn't do a single one. Over the next two years, I worked hard to prepare myself. The result was that I overcompensated. When I took the test at age seventeen, I did fifteen pull-ups.

When I got to West Point, all new cadets who had demonstrated more-than-average upper-body strength were screened for the gymnastics team. The reason was that very few Army gymnasts had previous experience with the sport before coming to West Point. The gym team needed whoever it could get.

I managed to make the team as a rope climber. Rope was a very simplistic event. You sat on the floor with your arms stretched above your head and your hands clenching the rope. When you felt ready, you exploded off the floor and climbed hand over hand, without the use of your legs. At the top of the rope, twenty feet off the ground, was a circular pan coated with charcoal. You reached out with one hand and made a swoop at the pan. You were timed by three timers from the time you left the ground until you touched the pan.

An acceptable time for completing the climb I described was something under four seconds. The best time I could manage my first year was about six seconds. That was not very good, but it was the best I could do. But every day I did my homework. This consisted of climbing the ropes again and again while wearing weight belts weighing about twenty pounds. I have never seen such a direct relationship between work and progress. So week by week, I could see my time getting just a little bit better.

At the end of my first year, someone jokingly asked me if I was going to set a record. By then, I knew that the secret of improvement was all in the practice. I answered that I would, but not until my last year.

Three years later, I did this, climbing 3.4 seconds. Climbing during my first year and my last was a world of difference: By my last year, I could climb twenty feet on a rope repeatedly in less than four seconds and not even get winded. It felt like no muscular effort at all. The feeling was that of a balloon carrying me upward. People who watched me said I climbed "effortlessly." What made the difference between a record-setting climb and just a good climb was only how fast I could move my arms without a hand missing its grasp for the rope. It was always exactly eight strides and a lunge with my free hand for the charcoal-coated pan. The secret between my early poor performance and my later outstanding performance was simply one thing: homework.

It is the same thing with charismatic leadership. Those who see you perform see only the effort you make on the spot. They don't see the hours and hours of homework that you put in. Yet, if you do something difficult apparently without effort, you will be perceived as charismatic.

Doing your homework can make your reputation for a lifetime as a charismatic leader. At the Battle of Chippewa during the War of 1812, British General Phineas Riall attacked with 1,700 regulars and about 700 Indians and Canadian militia. He headed for Winfield Scott's brigade. Riall identified them as militia by their gray uniforms. He had beaten this militia and had seen them break and run in previous engagements.

Winfield Scott commanded this militia. He was still a young man in his twenties. What Riall didn't know was that Scott had done his homework the previous winter. He had drilled his militia until they were ready to drop. But they knew their stuff.

Under fire from Riall, they formed their line effortlessly. With parade-ground precision they moved to meet Riall with bayonets.

Riall stared at the advancing Americans in amazement and uttered a tribute to Scott's abilities that has come down through the years: "Those are regulars, by God!" Scott drove Riall back with heavy losses. He became a general before the age of thirty, and eventually general-in-chief of the U.S. Army. But the homework Scott did prior to the Battle of Chippewa was the original source of his charisma.

BUILD A MYSTIQUE

Have you ever seen a magic show? The magician does all sorts of wonderful tricks. These tricks may be grand and involve the disappearance of elephants or the freeing of the magician after being chained in a locked trunk and lowered under tons of water. Or the trick could involve simple cards or coins. The size of the trick doesn't matter. That we are fooled does. Most magicians seem to have charisma. This is because we don't understand how the magician is able to do his or her tricks. This gives the magician a certain indefinable mystique. And this why magicians never tell you how they do their tricks. They know that to do so means the loss of some of their mystique.

Sure, we know we are being fooled. It doesn't matter. The magician knows how to do something that we don't. He or she has an aura of mystery and charisma.

When someone seems to know how to do something that we cannot comprehend, we follow them eagerly. Somehow, the person seems to possess this special quality that arouses both loyalty and enthusiasm. Somehow the person has enthusiasm.

The interesting thing is if we think a person has a secret of how to do something, that person can attain a certain measure of something very close to charisma even after he or she is long dead. Let me prove this to you. You probably have heard of Karl von Clausewitz. He was a general during the Napoleonic Wars. His book *On War* was published after his death. Today, it is read and studied by military personnel and politicians the world over. But did you know that a hundred years ago, Clausewitz was not so well thought of by those who study strategy. As twentieth-century strategist Liddell Hart said, "Clausewitz invited misinterpretation more than most."[13]

Clausewitz was German, but even Germans did not think much of Clausewitz. Whom did military men favor a hundred years ago? They studied the works of another Napoleonic general by the name of Henri de Jomini.

Major General George B. McClellan, writing in 1869, said, "Jomini was the ablest of military writers, and the first author in any age who gathered from the campaigns of the greatest generals, the true principles of war, and expressed them in clear intelligible language."[14]

Although Clausewitz was available, the great generals of the U.S. Civil War read Jomini.

Why did things change? In 1870, Germany won some remarkable victories over the French in the Franco-Prussian War. Clausewitz was a German. Everyone assumed that the reason for the German victories was some secret found in Clausewitz. Clausewitz began to acquire a popularity that has continued with German prowess on the battlefield. The irony is that the German victories were based primarily on Jomini's concepts.

The same principle was demonstrated again in the early 1980s. At the height of the interest in worldwide Japanese business success, it was reported that Japanese managers studied Miyamoto Mushashi. Mushashi was a seventeenth-century Japanese Samurai who was reputed to have killed more than sixty men in personal combat before the age of thirty. Mushashi had published a small book on strategy in dueling. This obscure work had been found and translated into English. It was published as a curio, accompanied by scenes of Japanese art. In one year, this "tabletop" book became a management best-seller and sold more than 100,000 copies. You can still occasionally find a copy at a bookstore.

If men who have been dead one or two hundred years can suddenly acquire a mystique after their deaths, surely you and I can acquire the full dose with a little effort.

The basic way to do this is never to explain how you did something. People are amazed that you accomplished so much in so little time? Fine, let them stay amazed. Don't explain that you were up every night for a week. Just smile. If everyone wonders how you lost twenty pounds, don't tell them you were on a diet or have been exercising. Smile. You developed a major marketing strategy in three days? So what if it was due to updating a strategy you worked out five years ago? Don't explain yourself, just smile your mysterious smile.

Now please don't confuse this with another issue. You want to keep those you lead informed and give them the maximum information that you can. As explained in an earlier chapter, do explain to your people why you want them to do thus and so, if there is time. And you can also explain why you did a certain thing that worked out. That way, you train those that work for you. But never explain how you did something unless you are instructing, teaching, or coaching, or unless a subordinate is asking for help. For the routine "Wow! How did you do that?" just smile and you'll build your mystique.

USE THE INDIRECT APPROACH

One of Aesop's fables is a story about an argument that the sun and the wind had as to which was the strongest. The wind noticed a man walking along wearing a coat. He challenged the sun. "I am the stronger, and to prove it, I'll bet I can get the man to remove his coat before you can." The sun accepted the bet. The wind blew and blew. But the more he blew, the tighter the man held on to his coat. The wind increased its power to hurricane force, but still the man held on to his coat. Finally, the wind gave up. The sun went on an entirely different tack. He merely shone down warmly on the man. After a little while, the man removed the coat on his own.

Aesop's fable is a perfect example of the indirect approach. The idea is to get people to do things because they, and not you, want it so.

The indirect approach in strategy was developed more than two thousand years ago by a Chinese general by the name of Sun Tzu. In this century, B. H. Liddell Hart was one of the first to realize that it applied not only to war strategy but also to a wide range of human activities, including leadership.

In his book *Strategy*, Liddell Hart said: "In all such cases, the direct assault of new ideas provokes a stubborn resistance, thus intensifying the difficulty of producing a change of outlook . . . The indirect approach is as fundamental to the realm of politics as to the realm of sex. In commerce, the suggestion that there is a bargain to be secured is far more potent than any direct appeal to buy."[15]

The indirect presentation of your ideas to others has a major advantage. It implies that you and those you make your suggestions to agree and that there is no coercion.[16]

Dealmaker Donald Trump tells the story of how the manager of the Grand Hyatt hotel was successful with him by using the indirect approach. Trump built the Grand Hyatt and still owned a 50 percent interest. The former manager couldn't stand the interference of Trump and his wife. So, he complained to the head of the Hyatt Hotels. This got the manager himself replaced.

The new manager was a lot smarter. According to Trump, "The new manager did something brilliant. He began to bombard us with trivia. He'd call up several times a week, and he'd say, 'Donald, we want your approval to change the wallpaper on the fourteenth floor' or 'We want to introduce a new menu in one of the restaurants' or 'We are thinking of switching to a new laundry service.' They'd also invite us to all of their management meetings. The guy went so far out of his way to solicit our opinions and involve us in the hotel that finally I said, 'Leave me alone, do whatever you want, just don't bother me.' What he did was the perfect ploy, because he got what he wanted not by fighting but by being positive and friendly and solicitous."[17]

Many military posts and bases require inspection of the family housing areas weekly to ensure that the lawns are being cut and the grounds cared for. But General George Marshall, Chief of Staff of the Army during World War II and later Secretary of State, had a better way. According to Mrs. Marshall, the then Colonel Marshall took command of a shabby and uncared-for post and got it fixed up without a single word of criticism. Colonel Marshall industriously cleaned and trimmed his own grounds, cut the lawn, and planted flowers. Before long, everyone on the post was out working on his or her own grounds, and the whole post flourished. That's the indirect approach![18]

When I was a high-school student, I met the grandfather of my boyhood friend, Ted Wells. Ted Wells's grandfather was a retired major general. One evening I was sitting next to the general and watching a basketball game. Having just finished eating a hot dog, I let my used paper napkin fall on the bleachers. For a minute, the general didn't say anything. Then, very gently, he said, "You know, Bill, I hate to leave any trash on the bleachers. It sets such a poor example for others."

Needless to say, I fell over myself picking up that napkin. The general well understood the indirect approach.

There is an old line that goes, "You can tell a fighter pilot, but you can't tell him much." You've probably heard the same with "Marines" substituted for "fighter pilots." In fact, this saying is accurate when applied to any group. Fighter pilots aren't the only ones who don't like to be told what to do. The truth, is no one does. This tells us that we should use the indirect approach whenever possible.

To use the indirect approach, look for opportunities to get people to do things without telling them to do it directly. Look for a way that doesn't hurt the pride or self-respect of those you lead.

One way to do this is simply to present the facts of the situation and let those you lead come to the obvious conclusion. When they do, give them the credit for the idea.

Another way is to be courteous in giving orders. "Betty, we're going to have a division meeting at eleven o'clock. Would you please notify the department managers?" That's usually better than, "Get the department managers to my office at eleven o'clock!"

Sometimes, you can give an order by turning it into a request. "George, don't you think you can get the move made by Monday?"

The indirect approach is based on suggestion. When using suggestion, keep these facts in mind:

- You must have the attention of the individual you are trying to influence. There must be an absence of conflicting ideas and distractions. If you don't have this attention, you may not be able to use the indirect approach.

- The more personal prestige you have due to position, birth, money, accomplishment, etc., the greater the strength of your suggestion. However, even the fact that you are a leader gives your suggestion some strength.

- The closer you are socially to the person you are trying to influence, the stronger the strength of your suggestion. But social closeness isn't essential for using the indirect approach. It just means that it could make it easier to use the indirect approach in a specific instance.

- Repetition of a suggestion increases its strength. Once you get someone to do something through the indirect approach, it will be more and more difficult for them to stop. For example, once others emulated then Colonel Marshall taking care of their grounds, it would be increasingly difficult for them to stop.

- Positive suggestions are more effective than negative suggestions. You can use the indirect approach to get people to do things, or to get people to stop doing things. But it is easier to use the indirect approach to get them to do things.[19]

Seven Actions to Build Your Charisma

1. Show your commitment.

2. Look the part.

3. Dream big.

4. Keep moving toward your goals.

5. Do your homework.

6. Build a mystique.

7. Use the indirect approach.

NOTES

1. John Wareham, *Secrets of a Corporate Headhunter* (New York: Atheneum, 1980), p. 35.

2. Max Weber, in Hans Gerth and C. Wright Mills, *From Max Weber: Essays in Sociology* (New York: Oxford, 1958), p. 79.

3. Ronald E. Riaggio, *The Charisma Quotient* (New York: Dodd, Mead, & Company, 1987), p. 4.

4. Tony Alessandra, *Charisma* (New York: Warner Books, 1998), p. 235.

5. Roger Ailes, "The Secret of Charisma," *Success* (July/August, 1988), p. 14.

6. John T. Molloy, *Dress for Success* (New York: Warner Books, 1980).

7. Douglas MacArthur, *Reminiscences* (New York: McGraw Hill Book Co., 1964), p. 70.

8. Barthelemy Catherine Joubent, quoted in Peter G. Tsouras, *Warriors Words* (London: Arms and Armour Press, 1992), p. 448.

9. Charles Garfield, *Peak Performers* (New York: Avon, 1986), p.23.

10. Ibid., p. 26.

11. Michael Jeffreys, *Success Secrets of the Motivational Superstars* (Rocklin, CA: Prima Publishing, 1996), p. 2.

12. Ibid., p. 1.

13. B. H. Liddell Hart, *Strategy, Rev. ed.* (New York: Frederick A. Praeger, 1962), p. 352.

14. *Jomini, Clausewitz, and Schlieffen* (West Point, NY: Department of Military Art and Engineering, USMA, 1954), p. 1.

15. Ibid., p. 18.

16. *Air Force Leadership, AFM 35–15* (Washington, D.C.: Department of the Air Force, 1948), p. 44.

17. Donald J. Trump and Tony Schwartz, *Trump: The Art of the Deal* (New York: Warner Books, 1987), p. 140.

18. Ibid., p. 45.

19. Ibid., p. 76.

CHAPTER FOURTEEN

LEADER PROBLEM SOLVING AND DECISION MAKING

A leader is a decision maker and a problem solver. You can't get away from it, the two go hand-in-hand. Rodger D. Collons, Professor of Creative Leadership at The American College, found in his research that the ability to solve problems or contribute to problem solving is a prime characteristic of many effective leaders.[1]

Further, the problems you must solve are frequently difficult. Sometimes a lot is riding on your decision. Your decision making is done under conditions of great risk and uncertainty. That makes making the decision in itself a difficult task.

DECISION MAKING IS AN IMPORTANT FUNCTION OF ALL LEADERS

Ellmore C. Patterson was formerly Chairman and Chief Executive Officer of J. P. Morgan & Co., Inc. This is one of the largest banking enterprises in the world, with assets exceeding $25 billion. When chairman, Patterson emphasized the critical importance of decision making: "We make it clear to new employees from the start that there'll always be uncertain or unknowable factors in a situation. We want them to collect and consider all relevant information. But over-study can't substitute for decision-making."[2]

Peter Drucker says, "Executives spend more time on managing people and making people decisions than on anything else—and they should."[3]

As Chairman of the Joint Chiefs of Staff, Admiral William Crowe was the highest ranking military officer in the United States Armed Forces. In an interview in *Time* magazine, Admiral Crowe stated: "I have known individuals who made a big decision and never gave it another thought. I don't. When it's a big issue, I don't sleep soundly."[4]

And military leaders sometimes do have major decisions with which they must cope. The Bible states that Gideon had to attack against vastly superior numbers about 1100 B.C. He faced a host of well-trained, battle-experienced Midianites in a fortified encampment. His troops consisted of a ragged assortment of untrained soldiers. All Gideon had to do was say that anyone who wanted could leave and twenty-two thousand of his soldiers departed for home without looking back. That was two-thirds of his army!

Gideon had to come up with something fast. He decided there was no point in trying to fight his enemy conventionally. So his decision (and it had to be a tough one to make) was to further reduce his force to 300 hard-core fighters of superior courage. He gave each of the 300 a trumpet, a torch, and an empty pitcher and divided them into three companies.

That night the three companies surrounded the Midianite camp. The empty pitchers covered their torches. On Gideon's signal, they broke the pitchers and blew their trumpets. Than they shouted: "The sword of the Lord, and of Gideon."

You can imagine what went on in the Midianite camp. Usually each torch represented at least a company of men. The Midianites thought they were under attacked by thousands of Hebrews. The Bible (Judges 7) tells us that ". . . the Lord set every man's sword against his fellow, even throughout all the host: and the host fled to Beth-shittah in Zererath, and to the border of Abelmeholah, unto Tabbath." Not surprising that today Gideon is taken as the model for commando operations in the Israeli Army.

A Flying Gideon Makes the Right Decisions to Begin a War

Decision making under the press of combat is not something unusual for commandos of any army. During the Gulf War, Colonel George Gray was commander of the 1st Special Operations Wing of the U.S. Air Force, part of the Air Commandos. Gray had a major problem.

Baghdad, facing an imminent air assault, was ringed with radar stations that would give ample warning of attack. Consequently, losses in the first wave of allied aircraft were likely to be very high. The obvious solution to Gray was to have his Pace Low helicopters fly right on the desert deck and land teams of Army Green Berets on the ground to blow up the radar sites.

However, like Gideon, Colonel Gray had a problem. The politics of the situation and the risk of blowing the whole war plan were such that General Schwarzkopf wouldn't approve anybody on the ground "across the line" before H-hour.

Larger aircraft had the right weapons, but the precise accuracy needed wouldn't be available. Pave Low helicopters had the electronics to find the precise targets in the darkness, but were armed only with machine guns for defense. Army Apache helicopters were heavily armed, but didn't have the navigation equipment needed to find the target in the dark.

Colonel Gray came up with a solution that he presented to General Schwarzkopf. Gray's Pave Lows would act as pathfinders for the Army Apaches, which would destroy the radar sites. General Schwarzkopf liked and authorized the training and preparation for the mission. At last they were ready, and General Schwarzkopf watched the rehearsal and then turned to Gray. "Can you guarantee me 100 percent?" he asked. After a long pause, Colonel Gray responded: "Yes, Sir, I will."

"Okay, Colonel, you can start the war," Schwarzkopf told him.[5]

The rest, as they say, is history. Allied losses, even in the first wave, were minimal. The successful air campaign translated into minimal losses on the ground as well, and General Schwarzkopf's total losses were only a few hundred, despite the large number of troops engaged and his resounding victory.

YOU MUST PREVENT PROBLEMS FROM OVERCOMING YOUR VISION

On the way to reaching your goal, you are bound to come up against obstacles. Everything that can go wrong, will sometimes go wrong. That's the nature of the process in reaching any worthwhile goal. It's normal to have problems. Expect them. But as a leader, be ready to solve these problems when they occur.

How can you be assured of solving these problems? First, you have to understand that there are two types of problems you will encounter. One type you usually shouldn't attempt to solve personally. The other type, only you can solve. Let's look at both.

The Type of Problems You Shouldn't Attempt to Solve Personally

Many problems you encounter you should leave to others in your organization to solve. There are several reasons for this. If you become your organization's routine problem solver, you will soon find that the members of your organization will bring more and more problems to your doorstep. Soon, you will be spending all of your time problem solving and will have very little time for strategic planning or even general thinking. You will spend all of your time "fire fighting," and mostly it won't even be your own fires!

Another reason that you don't want to try to solve all problems yourself is that you will rob your subordinates of valuable training in problem solving that they need. More than one leader has failed because he or she became the indispensable man or woman in his or her own organization. Then came the one time when this leader wasn't available to solve an important problem. Subordinates either procrastinated until no solution could save the situation, or they came up with a poor solution because of their lack of training.

Finally, when those who follow you are successful in solving a problem, there is a feeling of accomplishment and an increase in self-confidence. This can enhance the overall performance of your organization in the future. When you solve all problems yourself, you deprive members of your organization of these benefits.

This doesn't mean that when there is a problem you do nothing but smile. Of course you should help those who follow you solve their problems with ideas or suggestions if asked. Make it as easy as you can for them to solve their problems. But they should be their problems, not yours.

As General Perry M. Smith says: "By being the problem solver of last resort, the leader can help the organization grow and thrive."[6]

Situations in Which You Must Be the Problem Solver

There are some situations in which you must be the problem solver. And it doesn't make any difference at what level you are operating.

E. M. Lee, president and CEO of Information Handling Services of Englewood, Colorado, says: "The CEO has to be the problem-solver. He has to be able to crack open problems, as I call it, then call on others for expertise, reduce the problem to manageable pieces," and finally develop, "a framework for judgement."[7]

Here are some situations in which you must be the problem solver:

1. The problem pertains to leadership of your organization.

2. You have unique expertise, knowledge, or experience required in the problem's solution.

3. It is an emergency situation.

4. Those who follow you are stuck.

How the Chief of Naval Operations Solved an Unsolvable Problem

One of the problems faced by the United States Navy in the 1970s was a stubborn form of racism that even the best efforts of top leadership in the Navy had been unable to eradicate. The problem resulted from the fact that the Navy had a largely all-white history. Thousands of African Americans had served in the U.S. Army for more than a hundred years. Not so, the Navy.

One result was that there were African Americans who were general officers in both the Army and the Air Force. There were no black admirals in the Navy. Then Admiral Elmo Zumwalt became Chief of Naval Operations.

In the past, African Americans hadn't reached senior positions in the Navy mainly because they had not been assigned to the important command and staff positions earlier in their careers. These experiences were usually general requirements for reaching higher command. The Navy was making some progress. But the rate of progress was so slow that it constituted a serious injustice against a significant number of naval officers.

The problem was further complicated by the fact that a tour of duty as the Chief of Naval Operations is for only a fixed number of years. This meant that the actions or inactions of a successor could reverse changes made by any Chief of Naval Operations.

This was a situation in which only Admiral Zumwalt could solve the problem. With great moral courage and against considerable opposition, Zumwalt made significant changes in the promotion-and-assignment system in the Navy. He set out not only to ensure equal opportunities for promotion of minorities to top leadership positions, but to correct the imbalance of the past. He also realized that the changes must be made in such a way that they could not be reversed.

That these changes were not universally popular is a vast understatement. But they succeeded. Although some procedures were reversed after Admiral Zumwalt's retirement, his basic system of fair treatment remains to this day. As Admiral Zumwalt told me in a conversation in 1999, "Others wanted to make these changes, but thought they weren't possible. A leader has to be willing to try."

KNOW HOW TO SOLVE PROBLEMS

Effective leaders know how to solve problems. They don't just muddle about worrying what they're going to do, hoping that the answer will come. They have certain structured methods they employ as tools. Depending on the problem and the situation, they select the right tool for the right job. Then they proceed. Here are three tools to help you solve your problems as a leader:

1. Brainstorming

2. Psychological techniques

3. Analysis of alternatives

WHAT IS BRAINSTORMING?

Brainstorming is a group problem solving methodology. The basic idea is simple. Two or more individuals get together and bounce ideas off one another. No idea, no matter how outlandish, is excluded. Ideas are built on each other, and eventually a preferred solution emerges. Two decision-making researchers, my friends Dr. Alan Rowe from the University of Southern California and Dr. Jim Boulgarides from California State University, Los Angeles, have found that brainstorming forces people to think freely by removing the barriers of inhibition, self-criticism, and criticism of others.

"The technique tends to generate more ideas and increases the chances of success," they say.[8]

Use brainstorming under the following conditions:

- Your group contains a lot of expertise, and you want to make use of as much of this expertise as possible.

- You want maximum commitment to the problem solution. You are more likely to get this with brainstorming because everyone you invite will participate in the problem solving and the solution. Thus, they will have ownership in the solution.

- You want a creative solution. You're going to really let your hair down in a brainstorming session. You'll listen to all sorts of ideas. Some will be pretty strange and unworkable. Still, the fact that you're willing to listen will dredge up some ideas that are very creative. In fact, I'm willing to bet that whatever solution comes out of a brainstorming session, you wouldn't have thought of it on your own.

How to Conduct a Brainstorming Session

It is a real challenge to conduct a brainstorming session. The challenge is to get the maximum ideas that you can and not to kill any ideas prematurely. You must also maintain some control without dimming the enthusiasm. And believe me, in an effective brainstorming session, the ideas will be coming thick and fast. Usually it works best to have something to write on like a blackboard with someone who can write fast and legibly recording the group's ideas.

First, introduce the problem. State any limitations or conditions to the problem, but keep even these open to closer examination. Answer any questions about the problem that you can. Then ask for ideas for solving the problem.

Write every idea someone suggests on the blackboard so that everyone can see it. Encourage new ideas and the building on ideas that have already been suggested. This means that you should constantly give recognition for suggestions as they are made. Don't allow any member of the group to criticize any ideas that are suggested, no matter how ridiculous or bizarre. Focus on how to make "stupid" ideas work rather than on why an idea won't work.

Wait until the group runs out of ideas before examining the ideas suggested for their practicability. Be ready to entertain new ideas at any time. Keep recording the main points made by the group on the blackboard or where they can be seen. Continue to answer questions that group members may have about the problem.

Eventually, you'll have a few solutions that appear to be the most promising. Focus your discussion on these until eventually there is a group consensus regarding the preferred solution.

Make sure that each member of your brainstorming session is aware of your appreciation for his or her contribution. You are still the group leader. Even though the group came to a consensus solution to the problem, it is still your decision as to whether you should adopt this consensus decision or not, or whether or not to adopt it in some modified form. This doesn't in any way detract from the fact that the members of the group made important contributions to your understanding of the problem.

General Courtney Whitney was with General MacArthur for more than twenty years. When asked what made MacArthur great, he replied, "He made his men feel that their contribution was an important one—that they were somebody."[9]

So when you complete your brainstorming session, don't forget this important final step.

Brainstorming Can Work Wonders

The brainstorming methodology can work wonders for any organization. I have witnessed this many times myself.

Major General William Rowley retired as a general in the Air Force Reserve. Today, he is an international businessman. As a brigadier general, he took over an Air Force Reserve research-and-development organization in California that had serious problems. This organization had been without an assigned general officer for six months. Other reassignments and retirements had left the organization without many of its old leaders. By the time of General Rowley's assumption of command, morale was low and productivity was down.

Here again was a problem that only the leader could solve. General Rowley called together his staff of senior reservists for a brainstorming session. In eight hours of productive work, this meeting resulted in a new organizational structure, new organizational goals, and a renewed purpose in life. Rowley demonstrated once again the truism of General Patton's claim that any organization could be spurred into a state of high morale "in a week's time."[10]

A month later this organization conducted one of the largest training conferences of its type ever held. Its peacetime contributions to the active-duty force that it supported were so great and its readiness for mobilization at such a high standard that it earned numerous letters of commendation. Later, General Rowley was deservedly promoted to major general.

Psychological Techniques

Psychological techniques have to do with using the mind. It is easy to understand why some leaders avoid using psychological techniques. Leaders tend to be hardheaded men and women of action. The psychological tends to smell of the soft and uncertain, the "touchie-feelie" stuff with which we are uncomfortable. Yet, many of these same leaders would be surprised to learn that they may already have used psychological techniques in their problem solving without realizing it.

Have you? Maybe you have. Have you ever experienced a case where you had a problem that bothered you and finally fell asleep without a solution? Frequently, with no prompting, you awoke in the morning, and there was the solution. It just popped into your mind. You didn't even need to think about it. If you thought about this at all, you probably thought that this was your intuition at work.

In reality, whether you planned it that way or not, you used a psychological technique in arriving at this solution. What really happened? Your conscious mind was unsuccessful at coming up with a solution. The conscious mind eventually gets tired. It has to sleep, and eventually it did. But you also have a subconscious mind. It never sleeps. It is awake twenty-four hours a day, but it is in control only when your conscious mind is asleep. What happened was this: Your conscious mind went to sleep without the solution. It turned the problem over to your subconscious mind. Like a changing of the guard, your subconscious mind went to work on the problem, and it found the solution. At the right time after you woke up, it gave this solution to your conscious mind.

How Donald Trump Found the Importance of Psychological Decision Making

Famous builder, entrepreneur, and dealmaker Donald Trump can attest to the importance of this phenomenon. In his book *Trump: The Art of the Deal*, he relates how a friend wanted him to invest fifty million dollars in a "no-lose" proposition. At first Trump agreed. As Trump tells it: "The papers were being drawn up, and then one morning I woke up and it just didn't feel right." Trump decided not to invest. Several months later, the company went bankrupt, and the investors lost all the money they put up.[11]

Dr. Zelma Barinov has been investigating decision making for more than twenty-five years, first finishing her doctorate in Information Science and Cybernetics in Moscow and then heading a department at a research center. According to Dr. Barinov, 98 percent, and in some cases 100 percent of crucial decision-making information is nonverbal. She says, "Your unconscious is the most influential player on your decision team."[12]

WHY THE SUBCONSCIOUS MIND CAN SOMETIMES DO A BETTER JOB THAN THE CONSCIOUS MIND

Once you have all the facts, it is not unusual for your subconscious mind to do a better job of problem solving than your conscious mind does. Why is this so?

One reason is that your subconscious mind has no distractions. Your conscious mind is distracted by other problems, worry, fear, the pressure of time, and other elements.

Also, your subconscious mind has more time to work on the problem. Most people can't stay still long enough to really get to work on a problem without being disturbed or having to do something else. Not so with your subconscious mind. It keeps working as long as you are asleep.

Finally, your subconscious mind may not be limited by false assumptions that your conscious mind may make. For example, you may remember a certain "fact" incorrectly. But your subconscious mind knows better. It remembers perfectly. Thus it can come to a solution that your conscious mind would reject simply because of a faulty premise.

The Thomas Edison Exception

There are exceptions for those who can sit still long enough for their conscious minds to work. Thomas Edison is one well-known example. Edison's favorite technique for problem solving was to go to a darkened room in which he could not be disturbed and simply sit and think. He would sit and think for hours, confident that eventually the answer would come to him. He was confident that it would, because it always did. Edison was therefore willing to spend hours in his "thinking room" waiting for a solution.

Encouraging Your Subconscious Mind to Come Up with the Solution

Now there's no question that your subconscious mind can come up with the solution to a particular problem. But if you want to use this phenomenon as a problem-solving technique, you've got to use a definite approach. I recommend the following procedure:

1. Get as much information as you can about the problem. Read everything you can. Talk to people who have a bearing on the solution. Investigate similar problems and how they were resolved.

2. Before you go to sleep, set aside a period of a half hour to an hour in which you do nothing but think about the problem and analyze the data you have obtained.

3. Go to sleep naturally. Do not try to force the issue. Relax and do not worry. Keep a pencil and paper by your bed. Although the solution usually comes the following morning when you are awake, it can come in the middle of the night. If it does, and you are suddenly awake, write the solution down immediately. It is possible to be in a semiawake state and have the solution in the middle of the night only to forget it so that you don't know it in the morning.

Analysis of Alternatives

The U.S. military establishment developed the analysis of alternatives or staff study technique in the 1890s. It is an effective method for considering the major factors involved and comparing alternative solutions. It is also useful as a means of documenting your analysis and thinking and presenting it to others. It is so popular today that many different professions use it. It is taught in the Harvard Business School. Attorneys and some medical practitioners also use it. And, of course, the military still uses it. A method that has such flexibility to be of use in entirely different professions must be pretty powerful, and it is.

There are six steps to the analysis of alternatives method.

1. Define the problem's center of gravity, and write the problem statement.

2. Determine the relevant factors.

3. Develop alternative solutions, and think through the advantages and disadvantages of each.

4. Analyze and compare the relative merits of each alternative.

5. Draw conclusions from your analysis.

6. Choose the alternative that best solves your problem.

Let's look at each step in this process.

DEFINING THE PROBLEM'S CENTER OF GRAVITY AND WRITING A PROBLEM STATEMENT

Defining the problem's center of gravity and writing a problem statement is probably the most important part of this problem-solving method. If a doctor doesn't diagnose the correct illness, the medicine prescribed may not cure. In fact, it can cause harm. The same principle holds with problems.

J. Edward Russo and Paul J.H. Schoemaker are two professors who have studied the decision-making process extensively; Dr. Russo at Cornell University, and Dr. Schoemaker at my MBA alma mater, the Graduate School of Business at the University of Chicago. They state that decision-trap number one that gets in the way of good decision making is "Beginning to gather information and reach conclusions without taking a few minutes to think about the crux of the issue you are facing or to think through how you believe decisions like this one should be made."[13] They call this "plunging in." It's very important to identify the center of gravity of the problem situation before you "plunge in." Otherwise, the solution you implement may not work; it could actually worsen the situation.

What is the center of gravity of a problem? This is a concept borrowed from Karl von Clausewitz. Clausewitz lived during the time of Napoleon and served as a general in the Napoleonic Wars. His book *On War* is the most famous book about the nature of war ever written.

Clausewitz said that in any war situation, the enemy has one or more centers of gravity. A center of gravity is "the hub of all power and movement, on which everything depends." According to Clausewitz, "That is the point against which all our energies should be directed."[14]

The same is true with a leadership problem. We must identify the center of gravity of the problem situation so that we can direct all our energies against this point.

Let me give you an example. Let's say that you have a superior engineer in your organization.[15] He's been a reliable employee as well as a skillful and inventive engineer for the last seven years. Some months ago, this engineer's immediate supervisor found out that the engineer had started a part-time business on which he worked evenings and weekends. The products he made and sold were similar to your company's.

For several months, the supervisor took no action. He thought that the business wouldn't amount to much and that the engineer would eventually lose interest. One afternoon, however, the supervisor saw the engineer using a company telephone to order materials for his business on company time.

The supervisor reprimanded him immediately. He told him that he would report the incident to you, the boss, which he did. You sent the engineer written notice that he must either drop the business or resign from your company. You gave him thirty days to wind down the business or leave.

Thirty days later, the supervisor asked the engineer directly whether he still had the business. The engineer answered that he talked to friends and officers of the engineer's union, to which he belonged. He stated that he wouldn't give up his business or resign. His argument was that he was a good employee and that his outside business did not interfere with his work for your organization. The small amount of business that he did could not hurt your company. Also, he was not using company resources, nor soliciting company accounts. Therefore, what he did with his own time was of no concern of the company's.

The supervisor reported the conversation to you.

Clearly, you have a problem. Now maybe you would have handled the problem differently when you first heard from this engineer's supervisor. But let's assume you acted exactly as I stated. What do you do now? First look for the center of gravity in the problem.

Is it how to avoid firing this engineer? Not really. You may have to fire him if this is the best solution from your analysis. The same could be said about focusing on how to keep this engineer in your organization.

Is the center of gravity what policy should your company establish regarding employees establishing outside businesses? This may be a problem that needs to be worked on for the future. However, it doesn't let you off the hook with this engineer.

How about focusing on your warning to get rid of the business or leave the company? Well, that may be an important relevant factor. But it can't be the center of gravity. Wouldn't the problem still exist even if you hadn't given the engineer a warning?

If you look at the situation closely, you'll see that the center of gravity is this engineer's outside business activities. What action to take about them is a fair problem statement based on the problem's center of gravity.

Here are some hints for identifying any problem's center of gravity and wording the problem statement:

- Be careful of issues that are not the center of gravity of the problem.

- Don't mistake a symptom of a problem for a problem. "Profits are down" is a symptom. Dig deeper to find the center of gravity by asking yourself why profits are down.

- Try to avoid problem statements of an either/or nature. These are problem statements that permit only two alternatives. Whether to fire this engineer or not is such a statement.

- As you proceed through the analysis, don't be afraid to rework your problem statement, or even to focus on a different center of gravity if you see something you missed earlier.

DETERMINING THE RELEVANT FACTORS

Both the words "relevant" and "factor" are important. If the factor isn't relevant to the center of gravity of your problem, ignore it. Combining it with factors that are relevant will simply confuse the issue.

The word is "factor" not "fact," because you should also include assumptions, calculations, and estimates as well as facts. Be sure to differentiate assumptions from facts when you write down your relevant factors. That way you are more likely to question the accuracy of your assumptions. And you know that you're assuming some risk should your assumptions prove to be wrong.

What relevant factors did you find regarding this engineer's outside business activities? Here are the relevant factors I found:

Facts

1. This engineer had been a superior engineer and a reliable employee for seven years prior to this problem.

2. The products he makes for his business are similar to those made by your company.

3. The engineer's supervisor knew about the business, but took no action for several months.

4. The engineer was observed conducting his business on company time and using a company telephone.

5. You ordered him in writing to divest his business or resign.

6. He stated that he would neither resign nor give up his business.

Assumptions

1. His friends and union officers support his position as stated. He will complain to the union if fired.

2. As stated, he is not soliciting company accounts.

3. His current level of business won't hurt the company's business.

4. His outside work is no longer done on company time, or he would agree to this if it were demanded.

5. Current company policies do not specifically forbid outside businesses. However there are conflict-of-interest issues involved. These include ownership of ideas resulting from company work, secrecy clauses, and so forth.

6. This engineer is not a key employee. That is, his leaving the company will not have a direct negative impact. It could, however, impact on morale if he is perceived to have been treated unfairly.

Now we are in a position to look at alternative solutions.

Developing Alternative Solutions with Their Advantages and Disadvantages

After the important preliminary work that we just completed, we are in a position to look at alternative courses of action that can solve the problem. As we do this, we also want to make certain that we list both advantages and disadvantages for each potential solution that we consider.

Is there ever a potential solution that has all advantages and no disadvantages? Probably not. In such a situation, the solution is usually obvious, and no problem solving methodology is necessary. It could be that the potential solution has all advantages and no disadvantages, but the advantages are very slight. Marginal advantages in themselves would be a disadvantage.

If your problem concerns changing a way of doing something, one "solution" should be to continue your current way of operating. This is because even if bad, your current action may be the best thing you can do. This won't solve your problem as you originally conceived it. But you will at least know that you are doing the best you can, unless you change other conditions defined in your problem.

Once you have your alternative solutions listed, check each against your problem statement. Does your solution solve the problem as you have stated it? If not, you must rework your problem statement.

Let's look at some same alternative solutions to solve the problem of our engineer's outside business.

1. Fire him

   Advantages

   A. Will enforce discipline

   B. Will discourage employees from starting outside businesses in the future

   C. Will solve conflict of interest problems between the company and engineer's businesses

   Disadvantages

   A. May lead to union problems

   B. Could lead to problems with other employees if they believe the action is unfair

   C. Will lose an experienced and otherwise superior engineer and reliable employee

2. Retain him

   Advantages

   A. Will avoid union problems

   B. Will maintain services of experienced and otherwise

superior engineer and reliable employee

C. Will avoid problems with other employees due to a perception of unfair treatment

Disadvantages

A. May cause discipline problems with others

B. Could lead to a direct conflict of interest between company and engineer's business

C. Will establish a precedent of tolerating outside businesses

D. May encourage other employees to start outside businesses

3. Ask this engineer to resign, but retain him as a consultant

Advantages

A. May avoid union problems

B. Will maintain discipline

C. Will remove the possibility of conflict of interest

D. Will be fair considering the engineer's past service and performance

E. May discourage other outside businesses

Disadvantages

A. May encourage other employees to aspire to become consultants rather than company employees

B. May not solve the problem if the engineer chooses not to resign or not to work as a consultant

Analyzing and Comparing the Relative Merits of Each Alternative

In this step, you analyze the relative importance of the advantages and disadvantages of each potential solution. A particular solution may have only one disadvantage. But if that disadvantage is particularly important, that may be an indication that this solution has little merit. A review of your problem statement and the relevant factors will keep you focused on what you are trying to do.

Here are some thoughts in analyzing the relative merits of the engineer problem.

Several important issues bear on this problem. First, there is the disciplinary issue. The engineer was told to resign or get rid of his business. He did neither. Fair treatment is most important. This engineer has performed in a superior manner in the past. There is no current conflict of interest or use of company resources. Whatever action you take, you must consider its effect on other company employees, potential union involvement, and even a legal suit. There is also a policy issue. Your current solution will set precedent and policy for the future. Formal policy also needs to be established. Otherwise, you're going to be plagued with similar problems in the future.

These issues argue against firing the engineer. Starting his own business was the first mistake of a superior and reliable employee. The action would probably be perceived to be unfair by other employees. The union would most likely become involved. None of these results are desirable.

Unfortunately, it will be difficult to retain this engineer under the circumstances. Even if you decide to accept the potential conflict of interest, the possibility of encouraging other employees to start their own part-time businesses is too serious to permit.

Getting the engineer to resign in exchange for employment as a consultant is the only potential solution that isn't negatively affected by the main issues.

What if he won't resign? Than you'll have to fire him. Having made the offer of a consultancy, however, you have been fair, and there is a good chance that this will be perceived accordingly. You will maintain discipline and not encourage outside businesses. There are also reduced chances for a lawsuit and reduced chances for a loss should such a suit occur.

Before going on to the next step, review everything you have done. Make certain that you have said exactly what you intended to say. Ensure that you haven't left anything out. If you need to make changes or modifications, do it before proceeding to the next step.

Drawing Conclusions from Your Analysis

When you draw your conclusions from your analysis, state them without explanation. Introduce no new material. Keep them short. This will make your conclusions stand out, which will aid you in reworking faulty ones. By faulty, I mean those that have insufficient support in your analysis or don't result logically from your analysis.

This is so important, I want to say it again. Your conclusions must come from the reasoning process in your analysis. Each conclusion should be obvious from the work you have done in the preceding section. If not, there is an error in your logic, or you have insufficient support for your conclusion from the previous section.

What are some logical conclusions from the engineer problem? Here are a few:

1. All the solutions have some negative aspects.

2. Asking this engineer to resign, but retaining him as a consultant will retain the engineer's services with minimum negative effect on your operations.

3. If the engineer fails to resign, he should be fired.

4. This solution should be presented to the engineer for what it is . . . fair to both sides.

5. A formal policy on outside employment should be established as soon as possible.

Choosing the Alternative that Best Solves Your Problem

We are now ready for the last step. If we've done our work correctly, the best solution is obvious. In this case, it is to ask the engineer to resign, but retain him as a consultant.

Under other conditions, one or another of the other solutions may have been better. What if your company has a policy of no consultants, which you can't change? If the engineer were critical to your operations, you might want to retain him at all costs. What if the engineer is doing business with a competitor? You may have to fire him with no possibility of consulting. There are endless variables and many additional potential solutions depending on the situation.

The important thing is that you understand and be able to apply the process.

IF YOU WANT TO SOLVE LEADER PROBLEMS FAST, START DOING THIS TODAY

1. If you have problems that can best be solved by your group acting together, use brainstorming.

2. For problems that you must solve by yourself, use a psychological technique or the analysis of alternatives.

One final bit of advice. Many leaders have discovered that within their problems lies the key to even greater success. To repeat again the words of that successful Confederate General, Nathaniel Bedford Forest: "If the enemy is in our rear, then we're in his."

Earl Nightingale, the famous motivational speaker and philosopher and then president of the largest motivational audiotape company in the world, once related a couple of stories that confirm General Forest's philosophy.

Mr. Nightingale said that a vendor at the Chicago World's Fair couldn't get paper cups from his supplier to sell his ice cream. So he dreamed up the idea of using waffle mix. His wife ironed the waffle mix into conical shapes and let them dry. Now the container that held the ice cream was also edible! This invention made this vendor a millionaire. He called it an ice cream cone.

Nightingale also told the story of a successful businessman. Whenever his staff would come to him with a serious problem, this businessman would always answer enthusiastically, "Good, excellent." He knew that the other side of any problem was a potential fortune. In solving these problems, he frequently came up with ideas that made him lots of money. His problems were the key to his success. No wonder he was enthusiastic about them.

Do worry about your problems or the decisions you must make as a leader. Get started on turning your leadership problems into successes by using the techniques in this chapter.

NOTES

1. Rodger D. Collons, "Spotlight on Leadership Traits," in A. Dale Timpe, ed., *Leadership* (New York: Facts on File Publications, Inc., 1987), p. 30.

2. Chester Burger, *The Chief Executive* (Boston: CBI Publishing Co., 1978), p. 37.

3. Peter Drucker, *On the Profession of Management* (Boston: Harvard Business School Press, 1998), p. 33.

4. Bruce van Voorst, "Of War and Politics," *Time* (December 26, 1988), p. 74.

5. Orr Kelly, *From a Dark Sky: The Story of U.S. Air Force Special Operations* (New York: Pocket Books, 1996), pp. 294–296.

6. Perry M. Smith, *Taking Charge* (Washington, D.C.: National Defense University Press, 1986), p. 5.

7. Charles R. Day, Jr., "What It Takes to Be a CEO," in A. Dale Timpe, ed., *Leadership* (New York: Facts on File Publications, Inc., 1987), p. 9.

8. Alan J. Rowe and James D. Boulgarides, *Managerial Decision Making* (New York: Macmillan Publishing Co., 1992), p. 123.

9. Edgar F. Puryear, Jr., *Nineteen Stars* (Presidio, CA: Presidio Press, 1971), p. 149.

10. Ibid., p. 233.

11. Donald J. Trump and Tony Schwartz, *The Art of the Deal* (New York: Warner Books, 1987), pp. 27–28.

12. Zelma Barinov, *Instant Decisions* (Bala Cynwyd, PA: Access Press, 1998), pp. 17, 154.

13. J. Edward Russo and Paul J.H. Schoemaker, *Decision Traps* (New York: Fireside, 1990), p. 4.

14. Michael Howard and Peter Paret, eds. and translators, *Carl von Clausewitz: On War* (Princeton, NJ: Princeton University Press, 1976), pp. 595–596.

15. Adapted from "Theodore Thorburn Turner," a case in *Principles of Management, 4th ed.*, by George R. Terry (Homewood, IL: Richard D. Irwin, Inc., 1964), p. 222.

CHAPTER FIFTEEN

TAKE ACTION!

In this book, you have the collective experience of hundreds of leaders of all backgrounds from over the millenia. From their collective wisdom, victories, defeats, triumphs, and tragedies were forged the techniques and concepts from which you and I benefit today. These leaders paid in blood, sweat, tears, treasure, and toil for these lessons, as did those who followed them. This body of knowledge is invaluable. It cannot be the product of work in a laboratory by any scientist, no matter how brilliant. And no individual could have paid to have it discovered, no matter how wealthy. Although being an American, I used mainly American examples, no country is the sole owner of them.

The eight universal laws of leadership discussed in Chapter 2 are the foundation for everything else we do as leaders. The techniques, and when and when not to apply them, are different. For those who are just starting their journeys as leaders, many of these ideas will be new. To other more experienced and senior leaders, much will be familiar. Here, seeing the concepts presented will help you to make distinctions and further develop the applications of these techniques to your style.

But simply possessing this information is insufficient. This knowledge is wasted if it is not put to use. Moreover, you cannot simply read about these concepts to master them. To do this, you must apply them in your daily environment. The leader is the one who gets things done. And he or she gets things done by taking action. I hope you will not be only the reader of this book. Rather, jump in and use what you have learned. Make mistakes and adjust your procedures. Take your lumps and improve, for the art of the leader is action oriented. And so I conclude by admonishing you. If you want to lead . . . take action!

INDEX